Emma Marshall

In the city of flowers

Adelaide's awakening

Emma Marshall

In the city of flowers
Adelaide's awakening

ISBN/EAN: 9783337112912

Printed in Europe, USA, Canada, Australia, Japan

Cover: Foto ©Andreas Hilbeck / pixelio.de

More available books at **www.hansebooks.com**

IN THE
CITY OF FLOWERS

OR, *ADELAIDE'S AWAKENING*

BY
EMMA MARSHALL
Author of "UNDER THE MENDIPS," "IN COLSTON'S DAYS"
"ON THE BANKS OF THE OUSE," &c.

LONDON
SEELEY & CO., 48, ESSEX STREET, STRAND
1889

CONTENTS.

CHAPTER	PAGE
I. DRYBOROUGH	1
II. LADY ANNA	25
III. AN ENCLOSURE	49
IV. THE TIDE TURNS	73
V. EN ROUTE	99
VI. COMPLICATIONS	128
VII. SAN MINIATO	155
VIII. AWAKENING	181
IX. "LE PREMIER PAS"	209
X. ONLY A NAME	231
XI. PROBLEMS HARD TO SOLVE	266
XII. DISCLOSED	303
XIII. IN CRUTTWELL COURT AGAIN	327
XIV. "VAIN IS THE HELP OF MAN"	351
XV. UNDER A NEW MASTER	373
XVI. AFTER ONE YEAR	391

IN THE CITY OF FLOWERS.

CHAPTER I.

DRYBOROUGH.

CRUTTWELL COURT stood within a mile of the old county-town of Dryborough; a town which had defied the march of modern improvement, and held almost fiercely to its ancient traditions. When the railway came within an easy distance of the town, and a board was put up at the little roadside station, on which was painted in large letters " Dryborough Junction," a step was made in the direction of progress. The landlord of the Crown Inn started a smart omnibus, which travelled the four miles of straight sandy road three times a day, to meet the trains.

But very often the omnibus rumbled back empty, and the people who turned to look at it as it passed were disappointed if they had hoped to see a passenger inside. A dusty pedestrian might perchance have been picked up, or a basket and a hamper for the Court, but of paying passengers there were few

Naturally a town thus self-contained and self-supporting did not, as a rule, desire incursions from the outer world. Of course there were exceptions to this rule, as to every rule—the landlord of the Crown Inn was one. He had set his hopes high when the branch line was opened from Tillingham, on an access of customers: strangers who wished to see the fine old church, the ruins of the castle, and the old gateway leading to the Court. But apparently these antiquities of Dryborough did not attract the general public, and the spirits of the landlord of the Crown sank, and he began to think seriously of stopping the omnibus.

People held their own at Dryborough. No one attempted to question the fact that Dr. Townley was the cleverest surgeon to be found in the United Kingdom. Had not his father—yes, and his grandfather—held the whole practice of the neighbourhood in his hands, including the family at the Court? Once or twice a smart young doctor had come to try his fortune in Dryborough, but he had been promptly "snuffed out," as the doctor expressed it. Was not his own qualified assistant and pupil worth fifty such whipper-snappers? Then there was Miss Castigan, who had educated the young ladies of Dryborough for forty years, first as her mother's assistant, then as sole principal, with resident governesses at her command. Could any new-fangled High School mistress touch the hem of Miss Castigan's garment? Dryborough answered that question by a hearty negative, and a succession of girls, from the children of the vicar and his curate, and the lawyer and land-agent, were finished by Miss Castigan, and finished well.

Miss Castigan was decidedly aristocratic in her notions, and she drew her line of demarcation at the children of shopkeepers and farmers. "A distant connection" of hers—whom some people believed to be her first cousin—met the wants of the "lower class" in a smaller house in the High Street. Miss Castigan held strictly to the "upper class," as in duty bound, when entrusted with the education of Hester Ponsonby and Adelaide Millington.

It is true that both girls had now finished their education, but there was still some connection kept up, as Adelaide continued her drawing and painting lessons under the care of a niece of Miss Castigan; and Hester still received lessons in music from the organist of the church, who acted as music and singing master at Miss Castigan's school. Miss Castigan, by-the-bye, disliked the word "school," and never spoke of anything but her "establishment."

Cruttwell Court, surrounded by its fir-trees, which flourish in that sandy soil and clothe the slopes which the Dryborough people count for hills, was a solemn sombre house. In the burning heat of a July noontide, the shadow of the firs might be welcome, perhaps; but in the dark days of winter their plumy branches seemed to shut out light, and life, and brightness, from Cruttwell.

The Squire who reigned there was a gouty, irascible invalid, dependent on his wife for attention within doors, and on his agent, Mr. Smithers, for the management of his estate out of doors. His wife, Lady Mary Beauchamp, always seemed like a plant which gets neither sun nor air. She was tall and stately. Her face was pale, and she never wore any bright colours to relieve the monotony of her appearance. The Squire had no children by his second marriage, but there was a tradition in the town that his first wife had left him a son. Mystery shrouded the Squire's past. He had left Cruttwell Court for many years; when he returned to it, he brought the daughter of an Irish peer to be mistress of the house, and to minister to his whims, which seemed to increase in number every year.

Lady Mary was a good and gentle woman, who probably had told out some story of romance in her youth, and in later times had accepted the offer of a home and a husband, when Irish affairs were getting more and more hopeless, and her brother, the Earl of Fernclyffe, had candidly confessed he was unable to pay her the small yearly income to which she was entitled by her father's will from the estate. If the estate paid one shilling where it once had paid twenty, what was the Earl to do? It was plain Lady Mary must find some means of support. There was nothing left for her but to marry—the only thing a woman of her position, it seems, can do in such circumstances: *noblesse oblige!* For Lady Mary could scarcely have been a nursery governess or lady-help, and she was not educated even up to the standard of Miss Castigan's establishment, for a higher position. Thus, falling in with the Squire at a German bath—whither he had gone for the cure of his gout—Lady Mary accepted his offer, and found herself, to her own and Lord Fernclyffe's supreme satisfaction, provided for for life. The quiet of Cruttwell Court, and the absence of society in Dryborough, was congenial rather than otherwise, and when her cousin, Mrs. Ponsonby, came as a widow to live in a small house between the Court and the town, Lady Mary was quite content.

Mrs. Ponsonby had one child, a girl, who was, as we know, one of the most desirable of Miss Castigan's pupils, and Adelaide Millington was her chief friend. Adelaide's stepfather had married her mother long before she could remember, and her step-sisters were only reminded by the difference in name that they were the children of another father. Mr. Wardlaw, indeed, was perhaps more inclined to spoil Adelaide than his own girls, and she had the reputation of being very clever, and altogether of a superior type, reaching a standard of excellence to which her two dull little sisters might, by Miss Castigan's showing, never hope to attain. They were rather proud of having Adelaide for a sister; jealousy did not enter their heads; and what with

Hester Ponsonby's warm affection, which blinded her to any faults in Adelaide, it was not to be wondered at that she valued herself pretty highly, and was quite satisfied to be told that she was the coming artist, whose pictures might one day be hung at the Royal Academy, fetch a large price, and raise her family to affluence.

Mr. Wardlaw was one of those men who make shipwreck in life from a certain want of persistence in any one direction. He had a small fortune, which made absolute work for his living unnecessary. He dabbled in literature, and edited certain books of old classics. He had taken Holy Orders early in life, had been a master at a public school, then retired to a country living, where he hoped, he said, to end his days. But after a few years he tired of "the common round and daily task." His enforced duties became irksome to him, and he resigned his living, which was not twenty miles from Dryborough, to which he was attracted by seeing a house advertised to let, near the church and with a fine view of the castle and the ancient Norman gateway of Cruttwell Court.

Mrs. Wardlaw always acquiesced in what her husband wished; and though leaving the home where she had been so happy, and her children had been born, was pain and grief to her, she bravely accepted the inevitable, and about ten years from this time had made her home in the house at Dryborough, which Mr. Wardlaw had really taken without consulting her.

He had a large room at the back of the house for his study, which held his books, and the two little rooms, one on either side of the small passage, were enough for his wife and the children. Mr. Wardlaw sank down into contented appreciation of the retirement of Dryborough, and supplemented Miss Castigan's education with a little Latin and Italian, which Adelaide caught up readily enough; while Nina and Susie shed bitter tears over the old grammars, which represented to them nothing but hard words they could neither learn nor understand.

I said the fir-trees which shadowed Cruttwell Court were a welcome shade in summer, and it was on a hot August afternoon that Adelaide Millington and her friend Hester were slowly walking up the avenue from the old gateway.

Nothing could be more picturesque than the far-stretching avenue, as the sun pierced the dark plumes of the firs, and shot bright beams of golden light across the drive, at the farther end of which the house was seen—a solid block of gray stone, which, even in the surrounding brightness, looked grave and solemn. One of Adelaide's arms was linked in Hester's, and under the other she carried a portfolio.

"Do you really think Lady Mary will care to see the picture?" Adelaide asked.

"Of course she will; it is so lovely. You know that, Adelaide!"

Adelaide untied the string of the portfolio, and

took out a water-colour drawing of a boy fishing by a stream.

"Sit down a minute, Hester," she said, making a rest of her knees, against which the folio leaned, and looking half fondly, half sadly at her latest production. "It wants something," she said with a sigh; "I see that; but I don't know what it wants."

"I don't think it wants anything. Miss Castigan says it is the best picture you have ever done; and so did Mrs. Birley; and mother says she would give anything if I could do *one* thing well, instead of being a Jack-of-all-trades and master of none. I can't think what is the matter with you, Adelaide, to-day. You are so dreadfully in the dumps. It is so strange, when you ought to be pleased."

"Pleased!" Adelaide exclaimed, starting up; "of course I am pleased. But you know, Hester, sometimes I should be glad of a little real criticism. I never can get that here, because no one knows how to give it. Of course I can paint—and no one can paint as well in Dryborough. But since I went to London and saw the Academy and the National Gallery, I *have* felt an immense longing to see more, to know more. Dryborough is not the world, and yet we all think it is."

"It is a very pleasant world to me," said Hester. "I am very well contented. I have you for a friend, to begin with; and I like Mary Birley very much, and some of the girls at Miss Castigan's are nice enough."

CRUTTWELL COURT.

"And some of the boys at the Vicarage, too," Adelaide said, laughing; "this one, for instance."

As she spoke the figure of a young man was seen coming from under the old Norman gateway, and after a quick look right and left he advanced to the stump of a tree, where the two girls were sitting.

"Oh!" said Hester, with a heightened colour, "do come and look at Adelaide's picture. Is it not lovely?"

"I am not a great judge of pictures," Hugh Birley said; "that is, not pictures on cardboard. I prefer living ones, like that I saw just now through the gateway—a study in pink and white!" he added, with an admiring glance at Hester's pretty pink cotton dress, which contrasted with Adelaide's white canvas.

Hugh Birley was at Oxford, and flattered himself he knew a little more of the world than the generality of people living in Dryborough. He was neither particularly clever, nor particularly good-looking, but a little self-confidence goes a long way, and there were some people who looked upon the Vicar's son as a person of distinction, and he accepted the position as if it were his right. It was not likely that two people who each set a high value on themselves should agree very well together. Adelaide thought Hugh conceited, and he thought her very ignorant of the ways of the world.

"She ought to know that ridiculous baggy gown is out of fashion now. What a guy she makes of herself in that big hat, too! But she does very well as a foil, and makes the study in pink and white complete," he thought, as he watched Adelaide replacing the picture in the portfolio, and preparing to walk towards the house.

"We are going up to see Cousin Mary," Hester said. "*She* always admires Adelaide's painting, as everyone does."

Adelaide was a little in advance—perhaps purposely—and Hugh Birley lingered at a slower pace by Hester's side, also purposely. As they drew near the house, Hester looked rather anxiously onward, to see if Mr. Beauchamp were on the terrace. She knew that the presence of Hugh Birley, or, indeed, any young man, was an irritation to the Squire. It was said of Lady Mary that she was the only person in the world who did not lose patience with the invalid. She was never heard to answer him sharply, or even shortly.

"Cousin Mary is never snappish," Hester would say. "She has the most provokingly good temper. I do like people to fire up sometimes. It is dull to be always the same, and never to contradict anyone. Cousin Mary provokes me."

Perhaps she provoked the Squire, too. There is such a thing as being angry when you fail to make someone else angry. It is not too much to say that Mr. Beauchamp would have been better pleased to see his wife lose her self-control, and, as he said, "pay him back in his own coin." But in all the twelve years of their married life he had never succeeded in this not very amiable desire.

Hester saw that no one was on the terrace, and that Adelaide had gone round to the lawn on the other side of the house. On this lawn a large French window opened from Lady Mary's morning-room.

Adelaide found her there, as she expected, enjoying the quiet hour which the Squire's nap after his luncheon afforded her. She was sitting to-day in her arm-chair, her head thrown back, and her long white hands folded in her lap; when she saw Adelaide she started up.

"Hester is here—we came up together; and as you were not on the terrace I came round. I hope I did not frighten you, Lady Mary. Perhaps I ought to have gone round to the hall-door."

"No, my dear; you are always welcome here. But where is Hester?"

"Hugh Birley overtook us, and he is with her, I suppose."

Lady Mary was on the alert at once.

"Oh, my dear, I must go and tell Hester that I cannot invite Mr. Birley to come in. Mr. Beauchamp's chair may be wheeled on the terrace at any moment, and—and—as you know, he does not care for the society of young men. It rather bores him, and perhaps——'

Lady Mary broke off suddenly in her speech. She had that habit, and on this account her conversation was often disjointed and rather difficult to follow.

Lady Mary now hastily put up a sunshade and stepped out on the lawn, Hester's rippling laugh falling on her ear, as she stood at the corner of the house with Hugh Birley.

"Come and sit in the shade under these trees," Lady Mary said, answering Hester's greeting with a kiss. "Will you come, too, Mr. Birley?"

"I did not know whether I might set my foot on this enchanted ground. It is, I know, a forbidden territory, like the garden of Princess Ida," Hugh Birley said with a bow and a smile.

But Lady Mary did not smile. She merely said :

"There is a nice seat under that tulip-tree; shall we go there? How is your mother to-day, Hester?"

"Mother has one of her bad headaches," was the reply. "She sent her love to you, Cousin Mary, and I was to thank you for the flowers and the strawberries."

"The roses have been very fine this year. Now they are nearly over, and we must look forward to the autumn blossoming," Lady Mary replied.

"Adelaide has brought you her last picture to see, Cousin Mary; I am sure you will like it. Do show it, Adelaide."

But Adelaide, who had seated herself on the bench, had put the portfolio on the ground, and did not seem inclined to open it.

"I shall show it, if you do not," Hester said, springing towards the portfolio.

But Adelaide was too quick for her, and had got possession of it before Hester could unfasten the strings.

"It does not answer to throw pearls before—— perhaps that is what Miss Millington is thinking. Now with Lady Mary's permission," Hugh said, "I will stroll up to the summer-house at the top of the plantation, and when I am gone the pearl may be disclosed." He looked at Hester, and said: "Will you come?"

"May we, Cousin Mary?" Hester asked.

Lady Mary, who had been thinking over the easiest way of getting rid of Hugh Birley, said:

"Yes, certainly. And, Hester, do you mind going out at the gate at the top of the plantation, and then coming back here for Adelaide? Mr. Birley will excuse seeing the Squire, for——"

"I had never dreamed of that honour," said Hugh, with a bow which was half sarcastic and half deferential. "I will not intrude further upon you, and, having seen Miss Ponsonby safely to the farther side of the grounds, I will take my leave."

"Yes—thanks—that will be best, because—I don't know——"

The speech was unfinished; but Hester had turned away, so that if it had been finished it would not have been heard.

"Does Hester's mother approve of that friendship?" Lady Mary said. "You see so much more of the Ponsonbys than I do, perhaps you can tell me, Adelaide."

"Indeed I don't know what Mrs. Ponsonby thinks about Hugh Birley. *I* think him very conceited and disagreeable, and I only wonder at Hester's taste."

Adelaide's eyes flashed, and her lips curled. Then gentle Lady Mary laid her hand on the portfolio.

"Let me see this picture, my dear. I am sure I shall admire it."

Instead of the pride and delight with which Adelaide generally showed her performances, she said, with a sudden ring of sadness in her voice:

"I don't think it *is* worthy to be admired. There is something wrong in the figure—it looks so stiff—and I could not get the leaves right. The sky may be pretty, but not the trees; they ought to look as if they were waving, not as if they were as straight as pokers. Oh, Lady Mary, I *do* so wish I could go and copy *good* pictures; not stupid things like the copies Miss Smart gives me! I read in a book the other day that there was nothing so useful as the study of the Old Masters."

"Would you like to try and copy some of the old portraits here?" Lady Mary asked. "There are two or three rather pretty pictures. I do not know much about art, but, still, I believe they are thought to be good pictures. And, you know——"

"I know you are very kind," Adelaide said. "I wish very much to begin oil-painting; it is so much easier. If you make a mistake in water-colours, it is made for ever; in oils, you can paint over and over again, and it does not matter. I will try and save up and buy a box of oil-paints and an easel, and then perhaps you will really let me try?"

"Indeed I will. Would you like to sell this picture?"

Adelaide's face flushed crimson.

"Of course I should like to sell it, only I should not like anyone to feel obliged to buy it."

"Well, leave it with me, my dear, and I will send it to Tillingham and get it nicely framed, and then find a purchaser. My sister, who thinks of wintering in Florence, is very fond of pictures; she may like this—at least—well, there is no harm in trying. And if not——"

"Imagine living in Florence!" Adelaide exclaimed; "how delightful! I really do not think anyone in Dryborough ever thought of Florence or the picture-galleries there. I was reading about the Pitti Palace in a book of father's the other day, and of the wonderful pictures at the Uffizi. Here is the Squire!" Adelaide said, starting up. "Perhaps I had better go now?"

Lady Mary waited to give an answer till she saw in what mood her lord and master might be. If fractious and contradictious, Adelaide had better go; if, as was sometimes the case, he was inclined to be friendly to Adelaide, she might stay to tea, and wait for Hester's return.

The Squire was hobbling along with the help of his servant's arm and a stick.

"Mary," he called—"Mary, what are you doing in the sun? *I* can't sit out of doors. Come and read the paper to me in your room; it is too hot—too hot for anything! Take care, you rascal! you'll throw me over!"

These words were addressed to a frolicsome young Dachshund, who had just been let out from a long imprisonment, and was in a state of rapture only to be expressed by leaping frantically upon everyone, and wriggling at Mr. Beauchamp's gouty feet, encased in black cloth slippers edged with fur. How Blitz yearned to get hold of that fur and worry it! But his mistress called him off: "Blitz, Blitz! here!" Then she went down the grassy slope to her husband's side, and said:

"It is very cool here under the tulip-tree. Won't you try it?"

"No; I won't. I don't want to be eaten up by midges. And how am I to get up to that seat? Who is that?" he asked in a rasping voice.

"Only Adelaide Millington."

"Oh!" said the Squire, with a grim laugh, "the young artist. The future Madame le Brun or Angelica Kauffman who wants to take my portrait —eh, Miss Addy?"

Of all things Adelaide hated to have her name shortened. Her name altogether was rather a grievance to her. She would have preferred something more suggestive. She only associated the name of Adelaide with the portrait of the Queen of William IV., with her stiff sausage curls and, in her eyes, ugly cap, with large bows. And, indeed, the name had come to Adelaide direct from that good Queen. An aunt of her father's had been lady-in-waiting to the Queen Dowager. She was godmother to her little grand-niece, and stipulated that she should be named Adelaide. Sometimes when Mr. Wardlaw called her with the soft Italian pronunciation of every vowel—Adeláídé—she was more reconciled; but Addy! She detested the Squire on many accounts, but I think the chief cause of offence was that habit of calling her "Miss Addy."

The Squire was to-day in a good-temper—for him—as his man-servant, Preston, had told Mrs. Veal, the housekeeper. "For him" implied a great deal, and only meant, I am afraid, that Mr. Beauchamp had not thrown a book or his stick at Preston, or poured out a torrent of words which cannot well be written here, when his leg was bathed!

"I think I had better say good-bye, Lady Mary," Adelaide said. "I shall meet Hester at the east gate, and I can take her home to tea. Good-bye, Mr. Beauchamp," she said, with a little dignified bow.

"Where are you off to? Nonsense; stay and amuse me a little. When are they going to bring tea? Everyone seems half-asleep. Yes, I'll sit out of doors; who said I wouldn't? What are you about, Mary?"

"I was bringing your easy-chair near the window," Lady Mary said. "I thought you preferred being in the house."

"Nonsense! I said I didn't wish to sit under that tree; I didn't say I wished to be broiled indoors. Look sharp now, my lady, and order tea, and spread the rug on the ground and pull the chair out. It ought to have been ready, Preston, you blockhead!"

At last all the preparations were made, and the Squire sank heavily, with a growling sigh, into his chair. Almost at the same moment a footman appeared with a basket tea-table, and Hester came round from the front of the house.

Hester, with her round, good-tempered face, her bright smile and pretty lithe figure, was by no means a favourite with the Squire, while "Addy," with her quaint dress and artistic aspirations, interested him. He loved to tease her, and to see her flush with annoyance. Especially he liked to joke about her pictures, and laugh at the calm manner in which she would take any amount of praise from his gentle wife and Mrs. Ponsonby, and, as he was pleased to say, her "baby-faced daughter."

The Squire had a strange, and to some people, unaccountable dislike to young men. He had never a civil word for any who by chance came to the Court— and by chance or design there were very few. Hugh Birley was not easily discomposed, but even he rather shrank from exposing himself to a battery from Mr. Beauchamp. Some people said that the reason of the Squire's dislike to young men was to be found in the fact of his own childless condition. There was no son to inherit Cruttwell Court, and it would devolve on a distant cousin, whom the Squire had never seen or wished to see. As the estate was entailed on male heirs, Godfrey Lysaght inherited it as the son of the son of a younger brother. He had married a Lysaght, and had taken the name with his wife. The Squire never made Godfrey Lysaght any sign of kinship, and, secure as to his claim, Godfrey had left his irascible kinsman to himself. There had been some flutter in the Lysaght family when the Squire married Lady Mary, and Godfrey Lysaght's father, who was then living, had waited anxiously lest there should be any children born of the marriage. All fears had, however, been set to rest before his death, and Godfrey felt secure as the heir of a fine property and an old house, where Beauchamps had lived for many generations. It was believed that Godfrey had not even seen Cruttwell Court—certainly he had not made himself known there; and he was, in fact, a mythical personage, about whom no one ever thought or wished to think.

"Well, where do you come from?" was the Squire's greeting to Hester. "Have you been gallivanting with that young jackanapes? I caught a glimpse of him from the window. He knows better than to come here—the wisdom of a wise dog, eh, Miss Addy?"

Hester had no quick repartee ready, but Adelaide

came to the rescue for her friend: "I should think you might wait till Mr. Birley showed the folly of the foolish dog, Mr. Beauchamp, before you talk of taking strong measures."

"Well said—well said, Addy. What! another picture? Hand it here." The Squire fitted his gold glasses on his very strongly-developed nose, and held out his hand for the picture. "Humph! very pretty—very pretty! Copied?"

"Yes; from one of Prout's——"

"Ah! you should study originals. Make a study of me, for instance. Mary, call this brute off, will you, or I'll have him hung up on the nearest tree."

Blitz obeyed his gentle mistress's call, and settled himself on her gown, as she sat at the tea-table, though he kept his eyes well open and fixed on the fur of the gouty slipper, for which his soul longed. Blitz was a very dear friend and companion of Lady Mary's; and there were times when into Blitz's ear were poured some plaintive utterances which no other ear but his ever heard. For, in spite of Lady Mary's calm exterior and unruffled demeanour, she had her moments of something nearly akin to despair. She had felt that she had before her two paths: miserable dependence on her brother, and poverty, or marriage and affluence — miserable affluence she sometimes told herself, and she could find it in her heart to envy those who gained their living by honourable exertion.

Pitiable indeed is the condition of the woman

who finds herself thrown on the world with no power of earning her living. In these times of upheaval, when there is so much uncertainty in the future of every family, whether noble or simple, it is surely wisdom to put tools, at least, into our daughters' hands with which, if left alone in the world, they may carve their own way to competence, if not to riches. When Lady Mary was young, such an idea was never entertained, and thus, when absolutely penniless she was absolutely helpless— and, taken by the charity of a relative to Wiesbaden, was glad to solve the difficult problem of how to live, by marriage with Mr. Beauchamp. He was then less irascible, less entirely forgetful of consideration for those about him. Nothing touched him so much as the loss of fortune and personal comforts, and he had felt real sympathy with the gentle high-bred lady, whose position he soon found out, and whose musical cultivated voice in reading the papers, was a pleasant change from Preston's dull provincial monotone, or the chance service of some casual acquaintance.

Why should he not have that voice always at command, the touch of those slender fingers when she moved his cushions? Then there was the agreeable sensation of hearing his wife called by her title, and the pleasure of receiving the warm congratulations of her friends when at last the affair was completed. Lord Fernclyffe was really charmed. Both his sisters were now married to rich men, and he need have no further concern about them. Thus, it will be seen, selfishness was a very prominent factor in the marriage of Lady Mary Clyffe with Mr. Beauchamp of Cruttwell Court.

Lady Mary certainly suited her husband admirably, except, as I have said, in the serenity of her temper. It takes two to make a quarrel, and Lady Mary would never give the Squire the chance of engaging in one. Then she was quite content to ask no questions about his past, her predecessor, or the son, whom he shortly told her he had lost, and wished to forget. "He is dead to me," was all the information he had ever vouchsafed, and Lady Mary was satisfied.

Naturally, there were various opinions of Lady Mary in the little world of Dryborough. Some thought she was proud, some that she was unsociable, some that she was a colourless person, who was very uninteresting.

Mrs. Birley, at the Vicarage, in all the bustle of her active life, resented what she called her "stand off" manner, while Mrs. Wardlaw was quite contented to leave what intercourse there was between her family and the Court to Adelaide.

Adelaide's friendship with Hester Ponsonby had in some measure brought about the intimacy at the Court; and Mrs. Wardlaw never aspired to do more than pay a formal visit two or three times a year, which Lady Mary returned, when the principal topic of conversation was always Adelaide.

Mr. Wardlaw led the life of a scholarly recluse, and concerned himself very little about his neighbours. He had a conversation sometimes with Mr. Birley about the old Oxford days, and with the good doctor about chemistry and botany; in both subjects, by reading and keen observation, Dr. Townley was very much in advance of the ordinary country practitioner. Beyond these Dryborough did not offer any social temptations to Mr. Wardlaw, what society there was being on old-fashioned lines. A heavy dinner in the higher circles at seven o'clock, and a tea-party in the lower at the same hour, when tea and thin bread and butter were handed round on trays; and punctually at nine the same trays were again handed round with wine in glasses, sponge-cakes and biscuits, with now and then, on grand occasions, jellies in cups, interspersed with pink-topped creams.

If the Court had taken its proper place and been the sun round which the lesser orbs had revolved, the social atmosphere of Dryborough might have changed. As it was, it was decidedly behind the times. Mrs. Ponsonby's newly-made tennis-court, played on this summer for the first time, was a wonder in the eyes of the old-fashioned Dryborough folks.

The antiquated game of croquet had been patronized by the two maiden sisters of the doctor, and the daughters of the Squire's agent, Mr. Smithers. But tennis was denounced as a wild game; and the first tennis-party at Mrs. Ponsonby's was attended from motives of curiosity, which were satisfied by watching Hugh Birley and Hester Ponsonby playing "a single," and afterwards a set played by the two Wardlaws and Adelaide, with the younger brother of Hugh Birley, all four being quite below the mark to enter the lists with the two champions, Hester and the Vicar's eldest son.

Mrs. Ponsonby's relationship to Lady Mary gave her a certain prestige at Dryborough; and the comments which were whispered by the half-dozen spectators gathered round the little tennis-court at Home Cottage, would have been more severe had it not been supposed that the hostess and her deeds were above criticism. For had not her mother been a sister of the old Earl of Fernclyffe? and was she not therefore entitled to respectful toleration, even though she encouraged a game which the Miss Townleys, in their secret hearts, considered "wild" and Miss Castigan unladylike?

CHAPTER II.

LADY ANNA.

"HAVE you any intention of taking Dryborough in our summer round of visits, my dearest?" The speaker was Lady Anna Cowper-Smith, and the "dearest" thus addressed was her husband. "Because," Lady Anna continued, "poor Mary does seem so anxious we should go to Cruttwell Court. She has some craze about a young artist and her pictures. Really, Mary is so very obscure in her letters, poor darling! But the gist of the matter is, she wishes to awaken my interest in this girl, and induce us to take her out to Florence next winter."

Mr. Cowper-Smith laid aside his spectacles, turned the magazine over on his knee, and said:

"Well, my dear, what do you wish? I will go to Dryborough if you like; but somehow, the last visit has left behind a disagreeable impression. It is more than I can stand patiently to see that old tyrant riding rough-shod over your sister. But there is nothing to prevent *your* going for a few days —if you like, that is. Please yourself, my dear, and *I* shall be pleased."

This was invariably the conclusion at which Mr. Cowper-Smith arrived when appealed to by his wife. If one sister had secured a home and a husband with a bad temper and a fine fortune, the other, far earlier in life, had secured a husband with a far larger fortune and a really good, easy-going temper. Mr. Smith was plain Mr. Smith, when Lady Anna accepted his proposal; that plain name was in her eyes a decided drawback, and she hastened to make it "double-barrelled." Mr. Smith was questioned delicately as to his ancestry, but the inquiry was not pursued too far.

"No one grand ever belonged to me," he said. "My father and grandfather were good working men; and my mother, she was the daughter of a Dissenting minister named Cooper."

Lady Anna caught at the name, and ignored its connection with a chapel.

"Cowper!—the poet Cowper's family perhaps, dearest. Do call yourself Cowper-Smith. It sounds so pretty and poetical! So I will address my next letter to you: 'John Cowper-Smith, Esq.'"

Lady Anna kept her word; she addressed the letter with the double name, and when Mr. Smith replied to it he said: "I scarcely knew my grand name, and you have spelt it wrong. My mother's name was Cooper."

Lady Anna took no notice of this. The marriage was announced in the *Morning Post* between Lady Anna, eldest daughter of the Earl of Fernclyffe, and Mr. Cowper-Smith. The spelling was never altered, and the second "o" was exchanged for the "w," to the great satisfaction of the bride.

A very easy luxurious life was in store for Lady Anna Cowper-Smith. When her father died, and her sister, Lady Mary, was, as we have seen, thrown upon the world, and the Irish estates grew yearly less and less remunerative, Lady Anna was perfectly prosperous. The great cotton-factory still continued to roll in its thousands and tens of thousands to the Smiths; and although Mr. Cowper-Smith soon retired on his inherited fortune, the business still went on, and Smith and Co.'s cottons were in as much demand as ever in the market.

Mr. Cowper-Smith was never ashamed of his position. He was far too simple-hearted, and far too much of "nature's gentleman" to be pretentious. He was one of those Englishmen—true to the core, honest and loyal—of whom, when we meet them abroad or at home, we may well be proud. There are, alas, too many pretentious, self-asserting men, who have made their wealth by trade and are ashamed to own it; who buy "ancestors" from picture-dealers, and hang them up in gaudy dining-rooms, as grandmothers or great-aunts; whose whole lives are in some sense a sham, and whose wives and daughters, even more than their sons, help to build up the paste-board castle of "family" and "inheritance" that exists only in their own imaginations. It is therefore refreshing to meet men like Mr. Cowper-Smith, who never for a moment allowed any false statement to be made about his antecedents, and yet had not that want of tact which sometimes forces, on those who care or do not care to know, that our guest or host has worked for his living, and that his father before him had done the same.

"Well, dearest, I think I shall go to Cruttwell for a few days. I really have not seen Mary for two years now; and as we are going to Florence in October——"

"You have quite made up your mind to winter in Florence then?" Mr. Cowper-Smith said.

"Really, dearest, how can you ask that question? You know you are so tired of the Riviera, and I cannot face an English winter; and besides, we must decide, or that house will be engaged in the Piazza d'Azeglio. Really, dearest, you must lose no time in telling me if you mean to stay here all the winter."

"Well, well, my dear, I've no objection to Florence, I am sure; but we were cold enough at Cannes last winter—you said so yourself—and then there is little Peggy."

"I wish, dearest, you would call her Daisy, or Margaret. I *do* so dislike Peggy."

"Well, Margaret, then—my mother's name, so I ought to like it. Surely the child should have more regular teaching."

"Trust that to *me*, dearest. *I* know what I am

doing. Daisy speaks French and Italian wonderfully; she is totally unfitted for school, or a dreadful Higher Education governess. I found Miss Perkyns a terrible mistake: ask Percival's opinion. You are always ready to take what *he* says as gospel. Certainly my own delicate chest is inherited by our little pearl—our only treasure !" Lady Anna said with a sigh; "given to us so late in life—our aftermath. No risk should be incurred about *her*. As to myself!" Lady Anna sighed, and her husband hastened to say:

" My dear, I am quite contented that you should have another winter abroad. There are our two large houses shut up half the year, which seems a pity, rather; but as you wish it, let us decide to go to Florence."

It was decided already—and perhaps Mr. Cowper-Smith knew it, as he returned to his magazine, fitted his glasses on his nose—a short feature which required some skill in balancing the pince-nez securely—and with a sigh dropped the conversation.

Lady Anna turned to her writing-table and wrote two letters immediately; one was addressed to the Lady Mary Beauchamp, Cruttwell Court, Surrey; the other to Signor Bernini, the agent at Florence; and both letters were, with some of less importance, consigned to the bag, when the collection was made by the butler for the post.

There could not be a greater contrast than that afforded by the huge modern mansion, near the great commercial town where Mr. Cowper-Smith's money had been coined, and the old-world, low-roofed, many-gabled home of the Beauchamps.

Money, that great factor, was perhaps a little too apparent in Willesford Hall and its surroundings. Nevertheless, though everything was costly and of intrinsic value, everything was also in good taste. Mr. Cowper-Smith disliked gimcracks and "trifles," so that the suites of rooms were all furnished regardless of expense. He grudged nothing that could please his wife, and had entire dependence on her taste, and as years went on he always hoped that Lady Anna would like the neighbourhood better. But the contrary seemed to be the case. Her birth gave her a certain position in the county—that mystic word, which implies so much in provincial society; but she was obliged to make herself generally agreeable to the "town," and many of the townspeople were connections, not to say relations, of her husband, and, she was well aware, could recall the elder Mr. Smith and his homely excellent wife—nay, some could go back to the days of the previous generation, when the head of the Smiths' flourishing concern was but a humble office-boy, who had, so tradition said, come into the large manufacturing town without employment, with his jacket out at elbows, and his feet without stockings beneath his ragged boots. It was scarcely better in London, where Mr. Cowper-Smith had a fine house in Hyde Park. Lady Anna was not on the crest of the wave, and this was a vexation to her. It might have been different in Viceregal circles in Dublin, where her ancestry was so well known, and her brother courted by a certain party who sympathized with him about his diminished and diminishing income, and were agreed to trace his failing fortunes to one cause—whether rightly or wrongly is not our business here.

Thus it came about that the yearly migration to Italy or the Riviera, becoming now so fashionable, suited Lady Anna's views exactly. For the last five or six seasons Willesford Hall had been left to the housekeeper and a few servants from October to June, and the London house was only used as a stage on the journey to and from the Continent, for a few weeks at a time. It is plain that this kind of life removes the weight of responsibilities and home duties; and there is a charm in it, especially for those who, like Lady Anna, dislike what she called the prosaic and matter-of-fact side of existence.

"When Daisy is grown up," she said, "and I must present her at Court, we will turn into humdrum stay-at-homes; just take three months of London in the season, and live the rest of the year at Willesford, if my health permits, which is, to say the least of it, very doubtful."

This remark had been made in a supplementary fashion, long after Mr. Cowper-Smith had forgotten what had passed about Florence, and he was too deeply engrossed with a paper in the *Nineteenth*

Century, on political economy, to notice the remark, or make any rejoinder.

And now voices were heard in the hall, and Lady Anna went hastily out, exclaiming:

"Is that you, my darling Daisy?"

"Yes, mother."

"I hope you have not tired yourself and ridden too far; you look so pale."

"I met Percival; he rode with me, and he *would* go over Grayfell."

"How very wrong! It is much too far. Really, Percival, I shall be very angry if you tempt this child to any over-exertion."

The young man thus addressed only smiled—a very bright pleasant smile—and said:

"Trust me, Aunt Anna, I never let that child do too much. The mistake with her, is that she always does too little."

Daisy, or Margaret, or Peggy Cowper-Smith was wearily dragging one foot after the other up the wide staircase, an attendant on one side, and another following. These were a maid and what is called, in the polite language of the present day, a lady-help. Miss Cromwell filled rather an anomalous position in the large establishment. She could hardly be called a governess, for Margaret was not allowed to study; nor a companion, for a woman of eight-and-twenty can hardly be called a companion for a child of fourteen. But Miss Cromwell was supposed to be always on the watch to discover if Margaret were tired, or dull, or if she wanted amusement, or if she had any wish, in short, ungratified.

The child's naturally sweet disposition was proof against all the attention lavished on her. It seemed impossible to spoil her, though every care was taken to do so. She had very delicate health, and had never known anything of the vigour and joyousness of childhood. Some people, who knew her, said she resembled her aunt, Lady Mary Beauchamp; and indeed there was a far stronger likeness between the aunt and niece, than between mother and daughter. Daisy was not a child to be generally interesting or popular; she was very quiet and shy, disliked nothing so much as to be talked about by her mother, in the presence of strangers, and liked nothing better than to sit on her father's knee, and feel his arm round her, enjoying the unspoken sympathy that existed between them.

As Daisy's little figure, in its beautifully-fitting habit, vanished out of sight, Lady Anna turned to her nephew, and said:

" Did Daisy get breathless while she was riding to-day?"

" I did not notice it," was the reply; " she ought to be in the fresh air much more. Such is my humble opinion."

" Percival, I have decided to go to Florence; I am sure it will be best for the child and for me. Will you join us for part of the winter?"

"I will think about it," he said indifferently; "perhaps after Christmas I may come out, but I am not sure. By-the-bye, have you heard anything from the Beauchamps lately?"

"I have written to Aunt Mary to-day, to say I will pay her a little visit. Will you be my travelling companion?"

"No, thanks; I do not wish to put myself into the claws of that old beast—I beg your pardon, old lion—Mr. Beauchamp! Not if I know it."

"But you need not see much of him, Percival. Do think of it, there's a dear fellow! I shall only be away a week."

"I saw Lysaght the other day in London," Percival said. "He was inquiring about the old man and his gout. I told him that gouty leg might carry him off before long; and he was not sorry."

"*Very* shocking! I am afraid he is not a satisfactory person."

"Oh yes! He is a good fellow in his way; a rough diamond perhaps, but of the first water all the same," he said. "He is literary and has had weak lungs, so he ought to be interesting, you know——" Percival Clyffe stopped. "I dare say it is idle gossip, but Lysaght had heard some rumours which were not altogether pleasant, rumours which make his prospects of inheriting Cruttwell a little doubtful."

"Do you mean there is a son?"

Percival nodded, but added:

"*Was* a son is the more correct rendering."

"And did he leave any children? Dear me! how distressing for poor dear Mary, if true!"

"I could believe anything of Mr. Beauchamp. I dare say it may be a cock-and-bull story, but Lysaght was told it in good faith. However, he vowed me to secrecy, and I had better not say any more."

"That is ridiculous after saying so much," Lady Anna said. "But please yourself; only do manage to travel with me next Tuesday. I have just written to Mary to fix that day, and I shall be starting by the ten o'clock train."

"I will see about it," was the reply, as Percival Clyffe strolled away, declining afternoon tea, and saying he should be back again in time for dinner.

Percival Clyffe was the son of a younger brother of Lord Fernclyffe, and had been thrown on the world at an early age. His uncle was, as we know, in no position to help him; and the very slender portion of the son of a younger son was with difficulty eked out to provide for the finishing of his school career at Harrow, and the three years at Oxford which had followed it. Percival had gone in for honours, but had not taken any, either in Moderations or the Final Schools. Then he read for the Bar, and had been called, as so many are called, to wait for briefs which never came, and to incur expenses for chambers and dinners, which it was rather hard to meet, and which came fast enough. Percival Clyffe was not insensible to the comforts of

Willesford Hall, and he knew he could turn up there and find a welcome whenever he wished to do so.

He and his little cousin Peggy were fast friends, and, next to her father, Percival was dearest to her in the world. He laughed at her and teased her, and performed all offices which fall by right to the brothers in large families. But Peggy had no brothers and no young companions, and thus, if it had not been for Percival, she would never have known what a little wholesome chaff meant, and would have been even more subdued and quiet in her manner. Sometimes there arose in this child's mind a suspicion that she was very much unlike other children, or girls of her age. The occasional garden-parties or afternoon teas which her mother planned for her especial benefit, when two or three daughters of neighbours were invited to come and spend the afternoon with Margaret, were always a failure. She could not play tennis; she was not allowed to sit on the lawn for fear of cold; she was muffled in shawls, while the other girls frisked about in pretty white dresses, and, except for the little court some of them saw fit to pay her, as Lady Anna's daughter, and the heiress of immense wealth, she was left very much to herself.

"They don't care for me, mother," she would say, "and I am sure I don't care for them. Don't ask them again. I don't want young companions; they only bore me."

"Then I am sure I will not ask them again,

darling. You are, of course, very superior to them —so thoughtful, and far beyond your age."

"Oh! *please* don't, mother," would be the rejoinder; "and pray—pray never say so to anyone, because it is not true. I *know* it is not true."

"That is only your modesty, darling. You have a mind far beyond your years; and it is all the more delightful to me, because your health has made the routine of study impossible."

Lady Anna was one of those people whose swans are very white swans indeed; and if she had possessed ten children instead of one, there would probably not have been a goose amongst them. A certain high appreciation of herself, and everything belonging to her, was a characteristic of Lady Anna. Her love for, and admiration of her pale, fragile little Margaret was perhaps the reflection of her own self-love and self-satisfaction. The mere fact of belonging to her raised everything to a pinnacle of excellence; and, although she was bored at times by her husband's plain-speaking and constant desire to *be* what he *seemed*, and not to pretend to *seem* what he was not, she gave him his meed of praise. Was he not hers, and was not her imprimatur set upon him, as upon everything else which belonged to her? Percival Clyffe did not escape the same high valuation—I will not say wholly from the same reason, but certainly in great measure it sprang from it.

"*My* nephew" was surely above the nephews of

half a dozen other people whom Lady Anna would name; and Percival, like his little cousin, sometimes shrank from his aunt's praise, when it was scattered broadcast in his presence. But then he had a jest always at command to turn the sweeping current of admiration away from himself—a weapon which poor little Margaret did not possess and could not use.

"So we shall be alone together next week, Peggy?" Mr. Cowper-Smith said, when his little daughter came to spend her accustomed hour with her father. "We shall not grumble at that, shall we?"

"*No*, dear father," Daisy said emphatically; "it will be delightful. Not that we want to get rid of mother," she added in a half-apologetic tone, "but mother wants so much to see Aunt Mary; so it is all right."

"Yes, yes, of course it is. Tell me, Peggy, do you like the idea of a winter in Florence?"

"If I were asked, I should say I would rather stay here, father; but of course there are many things I should like in Florence. Oh, would you ask mother not to make me come in, when she has receptions, as she did at Cannes last winter? I always felt so shy and so miserable."

"You shan't be made miserable, my Peggy, if your old father can prevent it. I dare say mother thinks it amuses you, and, as you are not a grown-up or come-out young lady, you have only to sit and watch other people; you are not expected to talk. Now, shall we read something? Have you got any book to read to me, or shall I read to you? We are supposed to improve each other's minds, you know, when we spend this hour together."

But Peggy answered:

"I like talking best, father; have you heard any more of that poor man's children?"

"What children, my dear?"

"The children of that man whom you tried at the Sessions, and he was found guilty, and sent to prison for a year."

"Oh, that fellow who snared the game—a regular old hand at poaching. He deserved his sentence."

"But, father, Parsons says the woman and the children will starve while he is in prison."

"What does Parsons know about it?"

"Her sister-in-law is Parsons' cousin, and she *has* had so many troubles! Could you send them some money? Parsons will see that they get it."

"Ah, my Peggy, it is against my principles to give to beggars."

"But they are *not* beggars, father. Parsons says the poor woman has worked hard to keep the children, but now she is ill and broken-hearted. Father, please help her!"

The earnestness of his little daughter, as she fixed her large gentian-coloured eyes on him, touched Mr. Cowper-Smith.

"*Do* help her, father! She cannot help her husband's poaching, and it was for her sake he snared the last hare. She was ill, and he wanted to tempt her appetite."

"Tut, tut, my dear! that's a very poor story. Honest men do not thieve to feed their sick wives. Besides, as far as I can make out, it was that fellow's wild conduct which brought his family so low. It is hard, I know, when the innocent suffer for the guilty, but it cannot be helped; and it is a part of his just punishment when a man sees what misery his ill-doing has brought upon his family."

"I have been talking to Percival about it, father. He says there are thousands of people, like this man, tempted to sin by want; and that rich people like us don't wish to think about it, and don't care. Why have we such heaps of money, father—more, a great deal, as Percival says, than we want—and people in Ironstown—thousands—can scarcely get food?"

"My dear, you are too young yet to understand the condition of this country. Don't trouble your head about it. A great deal more is done now for poor struggling folk than was done even when I was young. No wonder you look pale and thin, if you worry yourself about these questions. Wiser heads than yours or mine are puzzled."

Daisy clasped her small white hands round her father's arm, and said:

"If you *could* give me a little money, Parsons could let Mrs. Fletcher have it. Oh, father, the baby is ill, and another little boy is a cripple, and—" (Daisy's voice faltered) "and——"

Mr. Cowper-Smith put his hand into his pocket, and brought out a handful of gold and silver.

"Here," he said, "rather than you should fret, my Peggy, count it and take it."

"What! all? Oh, father!"

She sprang up with an alacrity very unlike her usual movements, and, bringing a little ornamental table near her father's chair, said:

"Let me count it here."

"Very well. Don't make a mistake. Now, then, put the sovereigns in one heap, the half-sovereigns in another, and the florins and shillings and sixpences by themselves."

Daisy's pale face flushed crimson with delight as she handled the treasure. The whole amounted to seven pounds fifteen shillings and sixpence. It was put safely in a large blue envelope taken from her father's table, and then, with a fervent kiss and "*Thank you*, dear father!" Daisy went away, stopping at the door to smile and kiss her hand once more in token of gratitude.

"It is for your sake, Peggy. Remember, it is contrary to my principles, rather; it's for your sake."

Then, when the child was gone, Mr. Cowper-Smith fell into a long fit of meditation, from which he roused himself to ring the bell; and finding there was yet time for a ride before the late eight o'clock dinner, he ordered his horse round, and very soon was riding in the direction of Ironstown.

"Perhaps it is as well" (he thought) "we are going to Florence. Things like this take such a hold on the child's mind. Percival puts them into her head, I believe. Let people work for their bread. My father did it, and so did I, till there was no need for it. It is a false benevolence, depend upon it, this indiscriminate charity. The seven pounds the child has got from me will do no real good. I put my name on every subscription-list when I am asked, and never grudge it, but to worry over the family of an ill-conditioned fellow like that Fletcher is not in me. If they are well kept while he is in prison, he will try it on again. But, bless my little Peggy! what an angel she is! I wish she were less like one. I am afraid of hearing her wings rustle. Well, if she took flight and left me it would break my heart. What would a kingdom be to me without her? I would rather break stones on the road than lose her. I wonder if we are going the right way to keep her. I can't interfere with her mother; she always knows best, or thinks she does; but *I* think the child is kept too much away from girls of her own age. I will just see if I can find Barbara at home, and if I do, I will take upon myself to invite her girls to Willesford next week."

Barbara, otherwise Mrs. Smith, with no prefix, was the wife of one of the working partners in the firm of Smith, Smith, Bolton and Smith, who lived in the heart of the great commercial town, where, after half an hour's quick trotting, Mr. Cowper-Smith found himself. He received many respectful salutations as he rode up the principal street, and turning into a broad square, stopped before a red brick house mellowed by smoke, of that very respectable class of residence which only falls short of a mansion when described in an agent's list.

His arrival had been seen from the window of the dining-room, where the family were assembled at tea. Mrs. Smith hastily rose from her place at the head of the long table, and, telling her eldest girl to preside in her absence, was hastening out into the hall, when her husband, who was dividing his attention between a mutton-chop and the *Ironstown Evening News*, called out:

"What are you doing, Bab? Don't go and toady the great man for coming at this time to suit his convenience."

"I must go, James. Sit still, children," as one or two of the young Smiths were slipping down from their chairs, Will calling out:

"Let me go and hold the horse, father."

"And get sixpence for your pains," was the reply. "Be quiet; you are not an errand-boy, are you?"

A man had been summoned by Mr. Cowper-Smith to take charge of the horse; and Mrs. Smith met her husband's cousin in the hall, just as the maid-servant had admitted him.

"Oh! Cousin John! do come in! How are you?

And how is Cousin Anna, and poor little Margaret? Do come in."

Mrs. Smith led the way into the sitting-room on the side of the hall opposite the dining-room. The drawing-room was upstairs, and seldom used.

"Poor little Margaret!" Mr. Cowper-Smith disliked to hear that adjective applied to his darling.

"Margaret is very well, thank you. She had a good ride to-day over the moor. She would be glad to see her cousins next week. Will Wednesday suit? I'll send a carriage for them; and they can spend a long day—indeed, two days—if you can spare them."

"You are very kind, I am sure, Cousin John. Which two would you like? Barbara and Rose are nearest in age to your poor child. *How* is she? —I mean, is she stronger?"

"Oh, I hope so," Mr. Cowper-Smith said indifferently; "I hope so. Girls are often ailing at her age—growing fast, and all that."

"Yes; I know that. But poor Margaret has never been like other children. Dr. Bradfield was saying the other day he thought it a wonder she was alive."

Mr. Cowper-Smith hit his riding-boot impatiently with his whip.

"Dr. Bradfield has no business to talk about his patients to other people," he said; "so you may tell him."

"But we are not 'other people,'" Mrs. Smith persisted; "we are relations, and relations who care a *great deal* about poor, dear little Peggy, as I know you call her. A very sweet child she is. My little Bella said only the other day, ' Mamma, I should so like to play with dear Margaret sometimes. She is so pretty—like a snowdrop.' That is what Bella said. Wasn't it sweet of her?"

Mr. Cowper-Smith could well have been spared the simile, and said:

"Well—well, let your two girls be ready on Wednesday by ten o'clock, and stay till Friday. The carriage shall be here at ten. My wife will be away, and——"

"Ah!" thought Mrs. Smith, "the secret is out. If Lady Anna were at home no such invitation would be given."

" I *hope*," Mrs. Smith said, " I hope, John, Lady Anna approves of the girls being asked. I never wish to push—I hate to seem to push anywhere. Lady Blunt will tell you so. She said the other day——"

But Mr. Cowper-Smith did not wish to hear what Lady Blunt said—an authority Mrs. Smith was fond of quoting — the wife of a man who had been knighted for some service at the time of a royal visit—whom Lady Anna called a very " objectionable person."

" Well, well ; I shall tell Peggy the girls will come, and I hope this fine weather will last. Is James quite well ?"

" Yes, thank you. Shall I call him ? He is at

tea, and he is always very tired after a long day at the office; but I will call him."

"No, no; pray don't disturb him," Mr. Cowper-Smith said, for his cousin was decidedly less civil than his wife; and in another minute he had taken leave, and was riding at a quick trot out of the town again.

Barbara and Rose received the news of their invitation to Willesford with very decided dissatisfaction.

"Oh, mother! we shall *hate* it!" Rose said.

"I simply shan't go!" exclaimed Barbara. "I don't choose to be patronized by Lady Anna."

"Go—go where?" asked Mr. Smith, between two mouthfuls of currant tart, which had followed the chops. "Where are you going?"

"A nice visit to Willesford. John came to invite them. They ought to be delighted! but delighted or not, you will have to go," said Mrs. Smith with decision. "Your dear little cousin will be so pleased;" and with a doleful shake of her head Mrs. Smith resumed her seat, adding, "You may not have her long; you may soon lose her."

Mr. Smith laughed in a very provoking way.

"Lose her! well, they can't lose what they never got," he said. "It's a joke, though, about her ladyship. John dare not have invited the girls if she had been at home. However, no more nonsense," he said, as Barbara began a murmur of discontent. "You'll have to go, and make the best of it."

Poor Mrs. Smith was certainly no favourite with

her cousin's wife. She could not help asserting herself, when at rare intervals they met. She certainly was devoid of tact, and, it may frankly be said, was not *au courant* with the courtesies of ordinary society. Thus, she had told Lady Anna, on her return from Cannes in the spring, that she was sorry to see her looking so very far from well, and that she had aged considerably, adding, by way of consolation, "like the rest of us." She invariably spoke of "poor sweet little Margaret" in a tone which implied she was doomed. She made unpleasant comparisons between her own lot—as the mother of a large family, condemned to a town life—with that of those who had country houses at their disposal, and every advantage for their children.

She often quoted, as I have said, the opinion of Lady Blunt, who declared that the county were ridiculously exclusive, and gave themselves airs, which was of course a matter of supreme indifference to Lady Blunt and to herself. In fact, Mrs. Smith was not happy in the choice of subjects, or the way in which she treated them, and Lady Anna looked upon the very occasional visits which were exchanged as moments of penance, when she had some difficulty in retaining the calm aristocratic indifference which befitted her.

There certainly is no bitterness more bitter than that which is engendered by family feuds. In this instance the strained relations could hardly be dignified with such a name, but the feeling between the Smiths of Marlborough Square and the Cowper-Smiths of Willesford Hall could never be cordial. Alas! that truth should compel me to say that there was a strain of what might be called "vulgarity" in Lady Anna herself. She had shown it in those far-off days, when she insisted on her husband's second name; she had shown it by the perpetual desire—which all who knew her observed—to bring her own family superiority prominently forward. Lady Anna could *not* take people as they were, she must have some imprimatur with them. She was sincerely attached to her husband, and his perfect honesty and lack of pretension had won her in her young days to accept his proposal of marriage. She, like her sister, had seen a great deal of the misery caused by means which were insufficient to meet the supposed requirements of rank and fashion. And when her old father represented to her that on inquiry he found the Smiths were rolling in riches, and that John was a good honest fellow—adding that the days were over when the nobility could afford to scoff at trade—Lady Anna agreed with him; and being determined to make the best of even her husband's name, by the addition of his mother's, she was fairly well satisfied. But Lady Anna was not noble enough to rise quite above the disadvantages which were tied to her marriage. Immense as the advantages confessedly were, the disadvantages were as a drop of bitterness in the sweetness of the cup, and the keen edge of satisfaction was thereby a little blunted.

CHAPTER III.

AN ENCLOSURE.

THE picture of the fisher-boy — with the glowing sunset sky behind him—had been framed according to Lady Mary's promise, and was a conspicuous object in the drawing-room at the Court, which had been put into order to receive Lady Anna Cowper-Smith.

Lady Mary always rather dreaded her sister's visits. It was so hard to prevent a collision with Mr. Beauchamp, and Lady Anna's requirements were manifold. Lady Mary felt very much as a subject feels when Royalty is expected. A maid and a man were always in attendance, and, as is invariably the case with the servants of people like the Cowper-Smiths, far more *exigeant* than their masters and mistresses.

So it came to pass that Lady Anna's maid and footman were a source of considerable anxiety to the good old-fashioned housekeeper at the Court, and to the much-enduring Preston, who, besides constant attendance on his master, was supposed to exercise the same authority over the men-servants as Mrs. Ball exercised over the maids of the household.

A very modest household it was, and "company," strictly speaking, was unknown at the Court; thus the arrival of such a grand person as Lady Anna Cowper-Smith caused some trouble, and not a little anxious care and vexation.

Lady Mary went through the rooms several times to inspect them, and herself arranged her sister's writing-desk, and put upon it a large supply of paper, and vases of flowers on the table. The old-fashioned chintz curtains were pulled further back from the two rather small windows with their thick frames, and her own maid was summoned to get fresh chair-backs for the easy-chairs, and another footstool was sent for to replace a well-worn one under the writing-table.

"Lady Anna likes to see everything very nice," her sister said; "you know, Grace, everything at Willesford is so beautiful."

"Yes, so I have heard your ladyship say," Grace replied; "but to my thinking there's an *air* about the Court, which makes *all* the difference. The Court," Grace continued, "*seems* the residence of real gentry, though of course we know her ladyship is of the highest family, as your sister, but——"

Lady Mary was silent for a minute, and then said gravely:

"Take care to encourage no gossip in the house-keeper's room, Grace, and remember my sister's servants are to be treated with courtesy and kindness."

Grace took the hint and said no more then, but any good resolutions she might have made were blown to the winds by the fine airs of Mrs. Parsons, who made a good many disagreeable remarks about the *low* ceilings and the small windows, and wondered how gentry could exist without plate-glass; "the windows at Willesford were just the same as if they were open, the plate-glass was that enormous, and as clear as crystal!"

The arrival of Lady Mary's sister made some excitement in Dryborough, as well as in the Court itself. Mrs. Birley consulted Mrs. Ponsonby as to the best time to call, whether the very day after Lady Anna's arrival, or later a day or two.

"I do not wish to seem *too* anxious to call," she said; "Miss Castigan and the Miss Townleys are certain to be in a hurry to go up to the Court, and Mrs. Wardlaw will go of course, as Adelaide is made so much of by Lady Mary."

Mrs. Ponsonby, who was the essence of good nature, round and rosy like her daughter—to whom she bore the likeness of a full-blown rose to a half-opened bud—only said:

"Please yourself, Mrs. Birley; and I am sure you will please my cousins. We are not expected to stand on ceremony at Dryborough."

Mrs. Birley laughed, and said:

"No, indeed. Hugh thinks us all very much behind the time, and says he hopes I shall send his sisters to school. But I do not see how it is to be arranged. They must go on at Miss Castigan's—with Susie and Nina Wardlaw. My husband finds the boys so expensive—Oxford bills do run up so frightfully—and then there are Joe and Percy coming on—the girls will have to be content; and I tell Hugh what was good enough for Hester—whom he thinks perfection—must be good enough for his sisters."

Mrs. Ponsonby avoided any direct reply to part of this speech. Her eyes were opening, by slow degrees, to the fact that the intimacy between Hester and Hugh was becoming rather pronounced.

Easy-going and good-tempered as she was, Mrs. Ponsonby did not altogether like the idea of Hester entertaining any serious liking for the Rector's son, and was already looking forward to the end of the long vacation with some eagerness.

While the matrons were discussing the important question as to the proper time to pay their respects to Lady Anna Cowper-Smith, Hester and Adelaide were occupied with the same subject. The two girls were together in the little room at the back of Mrs. Wardlaw's house which was given to Adelaide for her own purposes. It opened out of her bedroom, and was hardly more than a closet with a window in it. But it was *her own*, and here she painted, and dreamed, and read a variety of books which her step-father lent her—history, biography, plays, poetry—

here she wrote what Miss Castigan called "themes" on many subjects. Adelaide had filled several large books of lined paper with a great variety of extracts —"chips" they might well be called—from the workshop of many a labourer in literature past and present—chiefly past—for current literature was slow in reaching Dryborough, as everything else was slow, and a book had its day in London before Dryborough had realized that it was one of those productions which "everyone *ought* to read."

This obligation we have all felt laid upon us sometimes, and have fulfilled it as a duty, perhaps, more than as a pleasure.

Adelaide was lying back in a small folding-chair, Hester balancing herself on the narrow window-seat, with her head turned in the direction which commanded a view of the Rectory lawn. Mr. Wardlaw's house was in the street, but the back looked upon a narrow strip of garden, which was separated by a low wall from a field where two cows and a rough pony—the property of Mr. Birley—were feeding. Beyond, again, was a narrow belt of the inevitable firs, and through a gap in them was seen the view of the lawn at the Rectory, separated by a low park railing from the field and the narrow plantation of firs.

Hester was as usual bright and happy-looking. She did not trouble herself with the deep questions of life. They had, perhaps, never been as yet brought before her. She went to church on Sundays, and had read the Psalms every morning with her mother since she had left school. But there was nothing in the least awakening or inspiring in what might be termed the religious atmosphere of Dryborough, and Hester had no aspiration for anything beyond what was within her reach. She had naturally a sweet temper and a happy disposition. She loved her mother, and she loved Adelaide with that admiring love which girls of nineteen are so often ready to bestow at the shrine of some idol. Lately, she had begun to feel that Adelaide had a rival near the throne of her heart, and, even now, as she sat in what had been to her for several years the most delightful converse, and interchange of endearments with Adelaide, her eyes were ever and anon directed to the gap between the fir-trees, where, on the Rectory lawn, a figure was outstretched in white flannels, a straw hat on his forehead, and a pipe in his mouth, from which, every now and then, a little cloud of smoke was lazily puffed.

Adelaide was not conscious of any distraction on Hester's part; she was too much occupied with her own affairs, and with the dim hope rising in her horizon, like a gleam of a bright dawning, which had been awakened by the note lying on the floor by her chair. It was from Lady Mary, and ran thus:

"MY DEAR ADELAIDE,

"My sister, Lady Anna Cowper-Smith, arrived last evening. She admires your picture very much;

and though she says she is not a judge of art, she would like to possess it. My sister has taken a house in Florence for the winter, and I am hoping that she may ask you to accompany her there. She has a very sweet, delicate little girl of fourteen, for whose sake chiefly she winters in Italy. It has struck me you might be a companion to her, and pursue your art studies also.

"Will you come up to dinner this evening, with Hester and my cousin, Mrs. Ponsonby? Mr. Beauchamp is confined to his room to-day, and therefore will not dine with us. It will be only ourselves.

"Yours affectionately,
"MARY BEAUCHAMP."

"What dress shall I wear, Hester?" Adelaide said after a pause. "What are you going to wear?"

"White; my white embroidered muslin. Mother likes me best in white of an evening."

"You have so many dresses," Adelaide said. "I have so few. But I shall wear the old-gold, with the brown velvet skirt. Shall I?"

"You look like yourself, and no one else, in it. But I think——" Hester paused. "I think, as Cousin Anna has never seen you, perhaps—I think——"

"You think I look a guy in the old-gold gown? I know who put that into your head; but I do not care to rule my taste in dress by *that* standard."

"How can you say I think you anything but charming, in any gown, Adelaide?"

But Hester's face flushed crimson. It was quite true, as Adelaide had divined. Hugh Birley *had* used that very term when speaking of Adelaide's dress— "She makes herself a perfect guy!"

Adelaide folded her hands at the back of her head, tossing back as she did so the mass of dark hair from her low square forehead. It was a favourite attitude of hers, and it displayed the shape of her arms and delicately-formed wrists to anyone who cared to look.

Hester left her seat by the window, and took up a position at Adelaide's feet on the floor. Clasping her hands on Adelaide's knees, and looking up reproachfully into her face, she said:

"Don't be vexed with me, darling. I do want you to make the *best* impression on Cousin Anna. It is very unselfish of me; for, if you go to Florence for the winter, what will become of me without you? *Don't* be vexed with me. Wear your old-gold gown. And I will come and gather your hair into the knot you like best, low on your neck, and lend you those lovely Venetian pins mother gave me."

"No; I don't want borrowed goods, thanks, Hester." Then one arm came down from behind her head, and Adelaide threw it round Hester's neck. "You are very dear and good to me," she added. "I will wear what you like. Even let my hair be scraped up to the top of my head, if it pleases you. Shall I wear my blue cashmere?"

"Yes; that will do beautifully. Let me get it out and see."

So the dress was fetched from a deep drawer, and shaken out by Hester, the lace ruffles at the elbow pinched, and the baggy sleeves smoothed down; while the Venetian collar falling from the low square-cut neck was subjected to a similar process. Hester was inwardly regretting that the blue was so faint and faded in hue; but still was saying to herself, "What did it matter when Adelaide was *not* like other girls, and never would be? She had her own style of beauty, and it was the same whatever gown she wore."

"There," she said, "you will look charming in this! And may I come and dress you at six o'clock?"

"You may dress me now, if you like. I shall stay up here till it is time to go to the Court."

"But some visitors may come—Miss Castigan or Mrs. Birley."

"That is not at all likely. But I dare say you would prefer going to the Rectory to have a game of tennis."

Hester glanced at the lawn through the trees, and said indifferently:

"I dare say mother may like it best if I go home to tea. I will come back about half-past five; it is scarcely four now. Good-bye, darling;" and then Hester left her friend to her meditations.

These were not altogether untroubled ones. Adelaide had that self-consciousness which so commonly accompanies temperaments like hers. It was too much her custom to wonder what people would think of her. Her paintings, her dress, all passed in review before her mental vision; and the judgment that others would be likely to pass tormented her sometimes, very needlessly. For it is true that often, while we are wondering *what* people are thinking of us, they may not be thinking of us at all.

Adelaide had been sitting just as Hester had left her, for some time, when there was a gentle tap at the door, and Mrs. Wardlaw came in.

"I am glad you are to dine at the Court to-night, dear. Can I help you to dress? Can I lend you any chain or brooch?"

Adelaide sprang up.

"No, mother, thanks; I never wear ornaments, you know. Sit down, mother; you look tired."

"I am always more or less tired," gentle Mrs. Wardlaw said, accepting the seat Adelaide offered. "I should like to look at Lady Anna's letter again, if I may."

"Hester put it on the table, I think; oh yes, here it is!"

Mrs. Wardlaw read the few lines again and said:

"It would be a delightful plan for you, dear; your father is quite as glad you should go as I am.

Florence is a city of pictures, and I have no doubt you will get great advantages there."

Adelaide was now on the perch on the window-ledge Hester had vacated. She was twisting the tassel of the blind in her fingers, and looking through the fir-trees absently, for she saw nothing to interest her, as Hester had done, in the Rectory garden.

"I do hope you will go, dear," Mrs. Wardlaw said again. "I have always felt, with your unusual gifts and powers, Dryborough was a sad banishment for you. Yes, I think we may really consider this Florence plan is arranged."

"I don't think so at all," Adelaide said, with some vehemence; "I have yet to see Lady Anna Cowper-Smith, and it is just as likely as not she may not take to me, or I to her! You all seem very pleased to get rid of me, I must say; and, mother, I do not think you ought to say I have gifts and all that. It is more than likely that it is a mistake, and I am a very ordinary person indeed."

"Nonsense, Adelaide! you would not like anyone else to say that. No one can be a better judge than a scholar like your father, and he knows what you are. Now Nina and Susie, dear children, and Hester Ponsonby are, of course, far from clever; but *you*— no one can look at you and not be sure that there is something very far superior to the ordinary girl of twenty about you. What dress are you going to wear? Do take pains to appear to the best advantage."

Adelaide laughed a little bitterly.

"Everyone seems mightily concerned about my dress," she said; "it seems as if my general appearance were not altogether satisfactory to my friends. Hester chose my most appropriate garment — the blue cashmere; it is on the bed in the next room. You can see it if you like, if you are uneasy about my appearance."

Mrs. Wardlaw gave a sigh of relief at the mention of the blue cashmere. She, too, had dreaded the "old-gold," with its very large sleeves, short waist, and scant skirt.

"That will do beautifully," she said; "and I must try to scrape together enough to fit you out nicely for Florence. We must ask what is likely to be most worn there, and most useful."

"Dear mother, you speak as if it were quite a settled thing. Remember I have yet to be seen, and my measure taken, and—oh! *how* I hate it!" Adelaide exclaimed with sudden passion, which brought the colour to her face and the tears to her eyes. "Yes, I hate having my picture forced on Lady Anna, and myself too! It is all a scheme —kindly meant, I know—but I hate to be schemed about. Dear little mother! don't look so vexed."

And then Adelaide became infinitely tender and gentle, and held her mother in a close embrace, and said:

"I will do anything to please you, sweetest of mothers. And of course Florence—going to Florence is like the fulfilment of a dream. I have longed to go—to see the Pitti, and the Uffizi, and the sculpture. Only there are times when I wish I could go independently, and not be indebted to anyone. However—who knows?—I may sell the copies I make of the pictures, and then I shall be able to pay every expense, and do many nice things for you and Nina and Susie."

Mrs. Wardlaw was quite satisfied now, and said:

"You are full of energy and spirit, my darling, very like your dear father; if I ever say anything you do not like, you know it is all out of love and appreciation for you. I want you to have every possible advantage."

"I know it, dear mother," Adelaide said; "you are only too kind to me. I wish I deserved it better."

Hester returned, faithful to her promise, to give the finishing touches to Adelaide's toilette. She found Nina and Susie watching their sister with great interest, and when she came in, dressed in her simple and becoming evening dress of white muslin, the two girls went into raptures, and openly expressed their admiration.

"It must be nice to go out to dinner," Nina sighed, as she watched Hester and Adelaide set off; "and to put on pretty dresses every night as some people do. I wonder whether we shall ever look like Hester?"

"That I am sure we never shall," said Susie. "She is pretty to begin with, and you and I are dowdy little things; father thinks so, I know. He always calls me Jenny Wren."

"That is only his fun," Nina said. "Anyone who is well dressed can look tolerably pretty. Well, I must begin to practise and be content. After all, things might be worse," Nina added philosophically, as she turned to the piano, and began to rattle off scales and exercises in the mechanical fashion which her mistress approved. For Miss Castigan's musical training was of the old school of air and variations, with an occasional sonata by Dussek or Haydn.

The warm August evening was favourable for a walk to the Court, and Mrs. Ponsonby had but a few steps to take from her gate to the Lodge. The Rectory came next, standing back from the road, and then, a few hundred yards nearer the town, was Mr. Wardlaw's house. Mrs. Ponsonby had thrown a light Shetland veil over her head; she had lately discarded caps, and wore her hair—which was neither plentiful nor of any particular hue—in the fashion which Adelaide described as "scraped up to the top of the head." The two girls had only shawls thrown over them, and therefore, on arriving at the Court, there was no preparation necessary, before entering the drawing-room.

Lady Mary was alone, and received her guests in her usual quiet manner.

She was never demonstrative in her greeting, and

there was nothing in the way in which she introduced Adelaide, a few minutes later, to her tall and handsome sister, which would have led anyone to think she had an especial interest in her. Yet the reverse was really the case, and it was with some anxiety that she tried to read in her sister's face what impression Adelaide had made.

"I have not seen you," Lady Anna began, "since you were a little girl, I think. The last time I came to Cruttwell, you were under some ban from scarlet fever. And, Hester, you were away from home, I think."

"Oh yes; I remember," Mrs. Ponsonby said. "We had fled from infection, and, after all, Susie Wardlaw had not scarlet fever—it was only rose-rash; but the scare was the same."

"How well you look, my dear Grace!" Lady Anna said; "so bright and happy: and Hester is exactly like you. It is quite amusing to see two people look so ridiculously happy."

"Well," Mrs. Ponsonby said, "it is well for me that I take life as I find it. I dare say there are cares with money as well as cares without it. You must know what the first sort of care means, Anna."

Lady Anna sighed.

"Perhaps I know others also," she said; "a precious, delicate child, like mine, must ever be a care!"

It was not till after dinner that Lady Anna addressed Adelaide in any especial manner. Then she swept her train of lovely pearl-gray silk across the room to the place where Adelaide—dreading the remarks she knew were imminent about her future—had withdrawn behind a curtain, which shaded the deep, old-fashioned bay-window where she sat from observation.

"I find," Lady Anna began, settling herself in a low chair just outside Adelaide's retreat—"I find that pretty water-colour picture is for sale; if you will allow me, I shall like to be the purchaser. Tell me frankly what I should pay you for it."

Adelaide had winced under this speech as if she had been touched on some sore place, and her most stiff and reserved manner came over her at once.

"I never sold a picture," she said, in a constrained voice. "I have no idea of the value of this one, except"—with a little laugh, which was not natural —"except the value of the frame, which seems to me a great deal too good for the picture."

"Oh!" Lady Anna said coolly. "Everything has its proper value, and in purely business matters it is better to be quite frank. I should think," Lady Anna said, turning her head towards the old oak cupboard with glass doors against which the "Fisher-Boy" was leaning, "I fancy five guineas might be the right price. I think many little pictures of the sort in the Exhibitions are marked at this sum, and I am sure this is superior to most of its class."

Adelaide felt a strong inclination to start up and

leave her position in the window, but Lady Anna blocked the way, and she must step over, or upon, the rich folds of that gray silk train, if she attempted to do so.

"I shall take the picture to my dear child," Lady Anna said; "she always expects me to bring her a present, even after a short absence. You may have heard Lady Mary speak of Margaret: she is very fragile and delicate, and quite unable to study like other girls of her age; but she is so very thoughtful and superior in all ways, that mere routine knowledge is of no importance. Certainly not, if by the attainment of it her health should suffer. We are always obliged to pass our winters abroad on her account, and on mine."

Lady Anna here gave a little cough, which always irritated Mrs. Smith at Ironstown. She was so irreverent as to call it "a regular made-up cough, which anybody could imitate if they chose."

"I am not at all strong, and my dear child's is inherited delicacy. Have you ever been in Italy, Miss Wardlaw?"

"My name is Millington," Adelaide said sharply. "No; I have never been anywhere. Once or twice to London, and two or three times to a seaside place, Eastbourne and Southsea, with my mother and the children. My travels have not been extensive."

"That is a pity," said Lady Anna, moving her fan gently, in a languid fashion; "for there is nothing like travelling for education in art, and, indeed, in almost everything."

"I don't doubt it is a great advantage," Adelaide said, rallying; "but, like many other advantages, it has been denied me."

"You are young yet," Lady Anna replied, with a smile which was meant to be consoling. "There is plenty of time before you. I dare say you will travel when the right time comes."

The right time had evidently *not* come then. Not a word did Lady Anna say about the proposed visit to Florence. She meandered on for a few minutes longer, about the picturesque old Court, the gateway and the castle, and said she felt inclined to envy her sister the possession of such a dear old place, while she was condemned to very *new* surroundings. Willesford had been, it is true, raised on the site of an old mansion, but, greatly to her distress, Mr. Cowper-Smith had pulled down the entire house, and erected the modern one in its place.

Very soon Lady Anna drew herself upright in the little chair, which was far too small for her, and her voluminous garments, as they swept away, finally upset the chair, and made Hester, who had been on the watch, spring forward to put it on its legs again.

"Well, what did she say, Adelaide?" Hester asked.

"Nothing," was the reply.

"Nothing about Florence?"

"No; not a word about any invitation to go with her; and I am glad, on the whole. It would take a great deal to compensate for her patronage and her self-assertion. Who could believe she was Lady Mary's sister? Surely there never was such a contrast since the world began."

Hester saw Adelaide was vexed, and had been rubbed the wrong way, but she ventured to say:

"I think, dearest, it would be worth while to put up with anything, for the sake of Florence. You, with your genius for painting, *ought* to have every advantage."

"Oh dear!" Adelaide said; "how tired I am of hearing that! I shall do very well; and if I can sell the 'Fisher-Boy' for five guineas—which Lady Anna assures me is the ordinary value of such little pictures—I may sell others, save a little fortune, and then—then—you and I, Hester, will take an independent journey together. To be sure, we shall be a pair of old maids by the time this object is attained; but that won't matter; we shall be all the more free to do as we choose."

Hester gave a little laugh, and then said:

"We won't wait as long as that, Adelaide; and I don't think I mean to be an old maid. We will both have *very* nice husbands to pay our expenses for us, and frisk about wherever we choose."

"Ah, I forgot," Adelaide said. "Your views in life are changing. Mine are not. I never intend to marry if anybody asks me, and I am pretty sure no one *will* ask me."

"Oh, Adelaide! you know better than that! The

only difficulty would be to find anybody half good enough for you."

"Well, let us go into the garden. It is such a lovely evening, and I like twilight. We can go round this way and get our shawls in the hall. The three elders are having a delightful gossip together; it would be a pity to disturb them."

The two girls then quietly emerged from their hiding-place, and crossing the end of the room to a door, which opened into a little ante-room, they went out to enjoy each other's society in the old garden.

Passing under the window of Mr. Beauchamp's bedroom, they heard his voice raised in loud angry tones, answered now and then by a murmur from the much-enduring Preston.

"Listen, Hester! Would you like a husband like that? Even gay young Oxford men in flannels and blazers, with the college arms worked on the left side, *may* get the gout in old age, and may be like that. There! He has flung something out of the open window in his rage."

As she spoke a book fell at Hester's feet with its face on the terrace-path and its back broken. Hester picked it up, and raising her head, saw Preston at the window.

"Shall I give it to one of the servants to bring upstairs?" she asked.

"No, miss, thank you. I'll run down for it."

Then there was a sound of muttering, like the grumble of thunder after the storm had burst. For

Mr. Beauchamp generally quieted down after an ebullition of temper, and the next minute Preston's dapper figure appeared, coming round from the back of the house.

"Poor book!" Hester said. "It is battered to pieces."

"It just missed my head, Miss Ponsonby; and it might have hit yours. Dear me! what a thing it is to have a temper like that! And all because I was reading haphazard about the duty of forgiveness. I am sure I didn't know what was coming; half the time I am thinking of something else as I read. The long articles in the *Times*—lor! it *is* a penance! But there, I must go back. I shall not try stories any more. It doesn't answer. There are apt to be hometruths in them which certain people don't fancy."

"Poor Preston!" Adelaide exclaimed; "he ought to be canonized as a martyr when he dies. I suppose that is the mission of tyrants like the old Squire—to make those about him miracles of patience. Lady Mary is one, I am sure, and Preston not far behind her."

The next day Adelaide received an envelope decorated with an imposing cipher and shield. The quartering of that shield had cost Lady Anna some trouble, Mr. Cowper-Smith declaring his arms were a cotton-spool, and a steam-engine or a tall chimney was his crest! He would not lend himself to any nonsense about the Cowper family, and he refused to allow a coat-of-arms to be manufactured.

But Lady Anna found Mr. James Smith more amenable. Indeed, he declared that he had found in the Heralds' Office the arms of the Smiths of the North Riding, and had no hesitation in adopting them. Hence the imposing and yet delicately engraved arms, surmounted by the cipher A.C.S., which caused some excitement, when it arrived on Lady Anna's envelope, especially in Nina and Susie's minds.

The letter arrived when the family were at dinner, and Adelaide's countenance was eagerly watched while she opened it.

"Do give me the crest for Molly Pearson!" Susie exclaimed.

"Oh! there's another on the note-paper," said Nina. "Let me have it, please, Adelaide."

"What does Lady Anna say?" Mrs. Wardlaw asked anxiously.

"You can read the note, mother; it is not very interesting;" and Adelaide tossed the envelope across to her mother.

A very clean and crisp Bank of England note was enclosed in a sheet of very thick canvas notepaper, and within were these words:

"DEAR MISS MILLINGTON,

"I enclose five pounds for the pretty picture, which I am delighted to possess.

"Yours truly,

"ANNA COWPER-SMITH."

AN ENCLOSURE. 71

"Is *that* all?" Mrs. Wardlaw said. "Well, I am glad about the picture."

"What picture?" Mr. Wardlaw asked. He seldom joined in any general conversation, and was always dreamy and absent when a question was asked him. "What picture?" he repeated.

"Let father see the interesting letter; and you may keep its contents, mother, till I want it."

Adelaide spoke indifferently, but her heart was sore. The dream of Florence was over. The five pounds was a reality, no doubt, and not a vision. There is always a pleasant sensation caused by earning money by exertion. The first-fruits of labour are always sweet, and Adelaide was not insensible to this; but she would have been glad had the money come from anybody else.

"You must answer the note, dear," her mother said, "and acknowledge the receipt of the money. What will you say?"

"'Thank you,'" Adelaide replied; "won't that be enough? Yes, Susie, you may have the grand paper, and give the cipher to Molly."

Adelaide was leaving the room, when Mr. Wardlaw said: "Come into my study presently, Adelaide; I want you to copy some notes for me."

"Not notes like Lady Anna's, I hope, father," was the reply. "Yes, I will come."

"Don't trouble yourself about that woman and her patronage, my dear," Mr. Wardlaw said, before he gave Adelaide the sheet of foolscap, and put the book before her. "You will find your level at last. All the Lady Annas in the kingdom cannot prevent real power from finding its proper outcome. You will not end your days in Dryborough; a bright career is before you, I hope."

"It is kind of you, father, to be so hopeful; but if Dryborough is good enough for *you*, surely it ought to be for *me*."

"Ah!" Mr. Wardlaw said, with a sigh, "my day is over. It is a miserable thing to look back on a lifetime, and see nothing but failures marking the backward path, like so many milestones. I have made shipwreck, and I am stranded here—as well here, as anywhere; and your dear mother, gentle and uncomplaining, is an example to me."

"And to *me*," Adelaide said. "When I think of mother I am ashamed of my discontent. Now I will forget Lady Anna Cowper-Smith, and only remember her when I spend that five pounds for my poor 'Fisher-Boy.'"

Mr. Wardlaw leaned back in his chair and watched Adelaide, as she set herself to the task before her, with kindly interest and affection. Her neat, clear handwriting was a great boon to him, and she was of use as an amanuensis. As he was looking at her, he saw her hastily brush away a tear which seemed likely to drop on the paper; but he said nothing, for he knew Adelaide always shrank from attracting notice, when under any strong emotion. He therefore made no further remark, but, taking up a book, was soon buried in its contents.

CHAPTER IV.

THE TIDE TURNS.

PERCIVAL CLYFFE entirely approved of the invitation to Barbara and Rose Smith; and, taking the place of an elder brother of the house, he contrived to make his young cousins so happy, that instead of being glad when their two days' visit was over, they were only delighted to stop for another two!

Miss Cromwell had to exercise her authority about Daisy over-exerting herself, and pursued her with wraps according to tradition, while Mrs. Gray, the nurse, relaxed her discipline.

"The child is ever so much better, Miss Cromwell, when she is allowed to be natural," Mrs. Gray said. "It does my heart good to hear her laugh. Look at her now!"

Margaret was on the lawn, actually playing the forbidden tennis, and trying to instruct her father how to "score." Rose and Percival Clyffe were on the opposite side, and Mr. Cowper-Smith's vain attempts to get the ball over the net caused much amusement.

Lady Anna had left home on Monday. The two

girls had arrived on Wednesday, and now Saturday had come and they were to stay over Sunday.

The weather was lovely, and the town-bred children forgot all their misgivings and dislike to the grandeur of Willesford, in pure enjoyment of the country life of a large country house. As soon as the game of tennis was over Miss Cromwell advanced with the inevitable wraps, and summoned the three girls to schoolroom tea.

They went off gaily, Rose with her arm round Daisy's waist.

"We'll have another game on Monday, father—won't we?" she said, turning back to kiss her father.

"Yes, my Peggy; as many as you like."

"I shall not be here," Percival said. "I am going southwards early on Monday. I ought to be in chambers now."

"Don't hurry!" Mr. Cowper-Smith said heartily; "you are always welcome here. Anna will be back on Wednesday. I do not think she is exactly pleased with me about inviting these two girls. Nice girls, aren't they, now?"

"Yes, indeed!" said Percival warmly; "and it is the best thing in the world for Daisy to have them with her. They are natural and unaffected—wonderfully so, considering——"

"Yes, yes; I know what you mean. Their mother is a very tiresome person—poor Barbara! she is irritating, I confess, and Anna can't put up with her. But now about the girls. I think I shall suggest that we take one of them to Florence as a companion for Peggy. What do you say?"

"A capital idea—it would do the Smiths a kindness, and be a benefit to Margaret!"

"Rose is the one nearest in age—and such a merry creature; but I don't know who is to propose it."

"Let Daisy propose it herself," Percival said; "her mother never refuses her anything. I rather think of going to look her up at Cruttwell. I have not been there for years, and I can put up in Dryborough, and pay a casual visit. Aunt Anna wished me to escort her thither, and take up my abode with her at the Court uninvited. That old bear would have growled then! but he cannot object to a visit of ceremony to my aunts."

"Poor Mary!" Mr. Cowper-Smith said; "she must have a sorry time of it; but as we make our bed, so we have to lie on it. Hers is a precious uneasy one, poor thing! Yes, Percival, go to the Court, and just feel the way about little Rose. Peggy writes to her mother every day, and I will get her to mention the plan, and then you can back it up. The child is like a different creature, with young ones about her. But I am afraid your aunt will never give her consent. Still, we can but try— we can but try. I will go and consult Peggy before the letters go to the post. It is nearly half-past five, I see."

Mr. Cowper-Smith left Percival to his own meditations and a cigarette, which he puffed in a leisurely fashion, lying back on the easy garden-seat, and thinking rather ruefully of his return to London, where he had nothing particular to do, and where waiting for briefs became more and more irksome as time went on. Birth and a long line of noble ancestors were good things in their way, but the fortunes realized in murky Ironstown were surely better.

"If things don't look up soon," Percival Clyffe was saying to himself, "I shall throw up the Bar and ask James Smith to give me a berth, and I dare say if I sink my small capital he would take me into the concern. But what are my few hundreds in comparison with their tens of thousands? They would not have me if I asked them, and I am not sure that I wish to ask them."

By this it will be seen that Mr. Percival Clyffe was in a very undecided frame of mind.

Lady Mary Beauchamp felt she had not succeeded in her plan for Adelaide. Her sister had evidently not taken to her. She had bought the picture, and there the matter ended.

The last day but one of Lady Anna's visit had come, and the two sisters were in the drawing-room after dinner. It had been a trying day, for Mr. Beauchamp's attack of gout had proved a very severe one, and Mr. Townley had paid more than a daily visit, and had looked grave about his patient.

"I am sorry, dear Nan," Lady Mary was saying,

"that I have seen so little of you the last two days ; but, you know, I could not help it. Did you have a nice little luncheon at the Cottage ?"

" Oh yes, dear ! it was *quite* a nice little luncheon. Grace manages wonderfully with small means ; and Hester is a nice girl."

" Adelaide Millington was there, was she not ?"

" Yes ; she seems very intimate with Hester."

Then there was a pause.

" She does not strike me as a very attractive girl," Lady Anna said. " Clever, I dare say, but self-opinionated and very conceited. Of course, living in a place like this, views of life must be terribly narrow."

" I do not think," Lady Mary said gently, " that Adelaide is conceited. She is rather apt to under-value her paintings, and dislikes praise."

" Does she ?" was Lady Anna's rejoinder.

Lady Anna was by no means inclined to look with a favourable eye on Adelaide, and Lady Mary was meditating whether or not she should pursue the subject further, when the door opened, and the butler announced :

" Mr. Percival Clyffe."

" My dear Percy ! What a pleasant surprise !" Lady Anna exclaimed. " When did you come ?"

" I am very glad to see you, Percival," Lady Mary said. " I am sorry to say my husband is very much worse, so that I am afraid I cannot ask you to stay in the house."

"I have put up at the Crown, thanks, Aunt Mary. I have just dined there; and I thought I would come up and bring Aunt Anna the latest news from home."

"That is very good of you, Percy. How is Daisy?"

"Perfectly well. She has had Barbara and Rose Smith staying with her; and they have all been as merry as possible."

"I was rather sorry to hear the Smiths had been at Willesford; they are too rough for Daisy. Poor children, they are uncouth in their manners; and no wonder! And, really, Daisy does *not* like young people."

"Margaret is very fond of Rose," Percival said, going straight to the point. "She would like to have her as a companion for the winter at Florence."

Lady Anna laughed—not a pleasant laugh—and said: "Dear child! I am afraid the wish is not spontaneous. It has been suggested to her that Rose would like it—probably by Rose herself, instigated by her mother."

"Indeed you are quite wrong, Aunt Anna. As far as I know, Rose is ignorant of the scheme. But, seriously, I think you could not do better. I hope you will consent to take that nice merry girl with you to Italy."

"I am afraid I must disappoint your hopes, Percy. Mrs. Gray and Miss Cromwell are quite indispensable. My only fear is that Miss Cromwell will not be able to leave England. She is anxious about her mother. I am a little surprised to find that those two girls were invited to Willesford without consulting me. My dear husband is so impulsive, I shall hear of his inviting the head-gardener's girls to associate with Daisy next! But now tell us about your own plans, Percy."

"I have nothing to tell you of any importance," he said. "I dare say you may hear I have gone off cattle-ranching before long, or diamond-mine hunting, or something of the sort. You look very pale and tired, Aunt Mary; I hope you are going away for change soon."

"That is very improbable," Lady Mary replied. "Dr. Townley has mentioned that the Bath waters might benefit Mr. Beauchamp; but I am afraid to advise a journey——"

"You don't want the Bath waters, Aunt Mary; it is you I am thinking about. I am sure Aunt Anna agrees with me that you should get some change and rest."

Lady Mary smiled — the patient smile which seemed to put all idea of a change in her condition at an end.

"I can never leave my husband," she said; "and should not entertain the idea for a moment. It is kind of you to interest yourself about your old auntie, Percy."

"You are killing yourself—that's all," Percival said; "and I call it awfully hard."

As he spoke a very peremptory summons came from Lady Mary's maid:

"Mr. Beauchamp wishes to see your ladyship immediately. Preston has just sent down a message."

Lady Mary was gone before there was time to make any remark, and Percival said:

"She really looks very ill. She is aged ten years since I saw her!"

"It is the wear and tear of living with that irascible old man. But he really seems much worse; this last attack affected his head. Poor dear Mary, it will be a happy thing for her when her release comes!"

"Lysaght is a fortunate man to came into this fine old place," Percival said. "I should not mind standing in his shoes."

"I wonder if there will be any hitch," Lady Anna said. "You hinted at something of the kind the other day."

"Have you questioned Aunt Mary about it?" Percival asked.

"My dear Percival, it is utterly impossible to get anything out of poor Mary. I think I never knew anybody so soft and gentle as she seems, with such a power of resistance! You simply can't make her say a word about her troubles, nor against that old bear—her husband! Really, the last few days he might have been the tenderest and best husband in the world, if I had judged by her anxiety and ceaseless attention to him."

"You cannot have had a very cheerful visit," Percival said.

"Not very. But I am not sure that Mr. Beauchamp's presence would have made it more cheerful—probably the reverse. It is a lovely evening; shall we stroll down the park and pay the Ponsonbys a visit?"

"The Ponsonbys? Oh yes, I remember now. Mrs. Ponsonby is a cousin of somebody belonging to us. And she came to live at Dryborough to be near Aunt Mary. Yes; I should like to make her acquaintance; let us go by all means."

"I must ring for Parsons to bring my cloak. It is such a perfect evening; and the harvest moon makes it almost as light as day!"

Parsons answered the summons despatched to her by the footman, and soon came into the hall with a white and gold opera cloak and a pair of thicker slippers.

"You will find the dew falling, my lady; and you should put on a hat."

"No; throw a veil over my head, that will be best; and just gather up my train, Parsons. That will do; now, Percival."

Then the grand lady, her white and gold cloak shining in the moonlight, stepped out into the glorious summer night, sweet with the fragrance of the late roses over the old porch, and the subtle charm of the mysterious murmur in the fir-trees— "the murmur of far seas"—which, in the hush and stillness of all around, makes a melody like the chime of waves on a level strand.

When Lady Anna and Percival had gone half-way down the drive, the sound of voices made them pause.

"Who can be here, at this time?" Lady Anna said.

The question was soon answered by Hester and Adelaide coming out from under the dark branches of the firs into the drive, on which the rays of the full moon lay unchequered by any shadow.

"We thought it was such a lovely night, Cousin Anna," Hester said. "So we came out into the park for a stroll; the full moon is so bright it is almost like day! Were you coming to see mother? Do come!"

"Yes. We were on our way to introduce a new cousin; this is Hester Ponsonby, Percival."

"I am very glad to claim such a desirable cousin," Percival said, warmly shaking Hester's offered hand. "And is this another cousin?"

Lady Anna then turned towards Adelaide, and said:

"Miss Millington—Mr. Percival Clyffe."

Adelaide returned Percival's bow, and, Hester walking on with Lady Anna, she was left a little behind with him.

Adelaide was dressed in the much-abused "old-gold dress," with its large sleeves and loose bodice. She had been spending an evening at the Cottage, where Mrs. Ponsonby was entertaining Mrs. Birley and Miss Townley. Hester had persuaded Adelaide to come out into the garden, and then they had been tempted to pass through the old gateway into the park.

Hester had a great deal to tell Adelaide; for before Hugh Birley had gone away that week to join a reading-party, which his father had jocosely said he hoped would not prove a tennis-party, he had made Hester understand that he loved her and her alone, and that nothing but the sternest sense of duty and obedience to his father's commands could have torn him away.

Adelaide was fresh from this confidence of her friend's when Lady Anna and Percival had appeared, and she had been meditating much on the difference between herself and Hester. Hester was welcome to the Hugh Birleys of the world; but, nevertheless, there was that unspoken longing, which I believe exists in every woman's heart, for the exclusive possession of one to love and cherish her, sympathize and care for her, and her alone.

The wide-spreading cornfields, golden-brown in the sunlight, are very fair to the eye; but, as the poet has said, the possession of one loaf is what the hungry man needs. The little crystal stream where thirst may be quenched is more to the weary traveller than rushing cataracts, and rolling rivers.

On their first introduction Percival had only given

Adelaide a passing glance, but at this moment she paused and said: "That is the nightjar. It is a sound which seems to belong to Surrey."

As she spoke she raised her head listening, and the moon shone full on her face, illuminating it with that pale light which refines everything with its pure radiance. The great masses of Adelaide's dark hair, swept back from her level brow, made it, by way of contrast, intensely white, while the somewhat irregular outline of her nose and chin was softened and chastened.

Percival was looking at her with the sort of half-inquiring, half-surprised sensation which we have all experienced when brought face to face for the first time with someone who, from no particular reason, stirs our inner consciousness—a personality that makes itself *felt*—a something new, and something which, if only from the sense of novelty, is pleasant.

Adelaide in her quaint dress, with her eyes raised, and her beautifully-formed hands clasped upon a bit of heather which Hester had gathered amongst the bracken under the fir-trees, made the impression on Percival I have described.

"She is like no one else," he said to himself. "I wonder who she is, and what she does?" Then aloud he asked: "Do you live at Dryborough?"

Her name had escaped him, for he had really not listened to his aunt's introduction, as he bowed in response, in the mechanical fashion usual on such occasions.

"Yes, I live here, in a house just beyond Mrs. Ponsonby's, nearer the town."

"Dryborough is a quiet little place, I should think. I came from the Junction to-day in the omnibus, and I was the only passenger. The people at the Crown Inn rushed out to welcome me, and the landlord seemed delighted when I ordered a room, and announced my intention of staying here for a day or two. I am sure guests must be rare at the Crown Inn."

"Perhaps that is fortunate for those who honour it with their patronage," Adelaide rejoined. "They get more attention, you know."

"That is what I was trying to impress on you," Percival said. "I am afraid I failed to make myself intelligible."

"No; I understood you perfectly," was the reply.

They were under the old gateway now, and at the gate of Mrs. Ponsonby's cottage was seen the gleaming of Lady Anna's gold and white cloak. Adelaide quickened her pace a little, and Lady Anna said:

"It must be delightful to be able to live such a thoroughly unconventional life as you all do here. The quiet of the country is most refreshing. Don't you find it so, Percival?"

"Yes; but Willesford is as quiet."

"My dear boy, the high-road to Ironstown lies just outside our gates: who would care to pass through them in evening dress after dinner? There would be common people about, and tramps, and Ironstown vehicles passing."

"I dare say, if we were to extend our walk to the Junction on the other side of the town, we should meet tramps and carts and the like. What do you say?" Percival asked, turning to Hester. "And I suppose 'common people' have as much right as we have to come forth on warm moonlight nights, and get what air there may be stirring."

"I should think so!" came in a low earnest voice from Adelaide.

"Well, let us go round to the drawing-room," Lady Anna said, "and I will introduce you to your cousin—another cousin, I ought to say."

The arrival of Lady Anna made some commotion in Mrs. Ponsonby's drawing-room. Mrs. Birley was flustered, and poor Miss Townley quite overcome by the grand apparition of the opera-cloak and the rustle of the long pearl-gray train which followed Lady Anna with a sound conveying the idea of importance.

Mrs. Ponsonby gave Lady Anna a sounding kiss, and was altogether effusive in her welcome.

"So kind of you to come, Anna. Hester, ring for more hot water and bread-and-butter. You know Mrs. Birley, Anna, and Miss Townley, our good doctor's sister? Dryborough could hardly do without her. She is next best to the doctor himself!"

"Oh! really, Mrs. Ponsonby! You *are* too kind," said Miss Townley, fluttering under the compliment paid her in the presence of the grand lady, and inwardly wishing her sister had been present to hear her praises thus loudly chanted. Her sister was wont to say she meddled too much with the patients, and talked a great deal more about complaints than was seemly for a young unmarried woman.

Percival, meanwhile, had been standing a little behind, and waited for his welcome, which he feared might be, perhaps, disagreeably effusive.

" I hope she is not going to kiss me !" he thought, as Mrs. Ponsonby bore down upon him, and, taking both his hands in hers, went over the genealogy of the Clyffes, till she satisfied herself as to Percival's precise claim to cousinship.

" Of course ! poor Donald's boy ! He and I were great friends in our youth. Poor fellow ! he married imprudently—a young thing with no fortune: a good family, I believe ; but younger sons of peers— especially Irish peers—*must* think of money. So much the worse for them ! You are very like your father. I am delighted to see you. You are staying at the Court, of course, or I should be quite offended at your not coming to the Cottage !"

Percival did not attempt to enlighten Mrs. Ponsonby as to the fact that he was sleeping at the Crown Inn; he merely replied, as he at last succeeded in freeing his hands from the grasp of his warm-hearted cousin, that he had only arrived that afternoon at Dryborough.

"How kind to come so soon—you have seen Hester? Now, then, we will have tea."

Lady Anna had settled herself and her train in an easy-chair, and lay back in it with proper aristocratic calmness, as she talked to Mrs. Birley and Miss Townley.

A pretty little conservatory opened out of the room, full of bright flowers, where three or four fairy lamps were shining like glow-worms amongst the plants. Mrs. Ponsonby had lighted them for the express gratification of showing them, as something new and wonderful, to Mrs. Birley. Adelaide, who had felt very much *de trop*, as she was the last to enter the room, took refuge in the conservatory, and hoped to remain hidden till Lady Anna and Percival had departed.

"It is just as well she did not invite me to go to Florence with her," she was saying to herself, as she plucked a leaf of sweet-scented geranium, and pinned it with the sprig of heather in the band of her gown. "What I should have suffered from her patronage—a perpetual blister!—I would not go with her if she asked me. I wonder how long they will stay! How they chatter!—at least Mrs. Ponsonby and Hester are chattering! Lady Anna would not condescend to do anything so vulgar. How she drawls out her words to impress poor Miss Townley and Mrs. Birley with a sense of her own superiority. I wish I could escape; no one would notice my absence. I think I will try."

Then she went to the door of the conservatory, and found it blocked by Percival. Before she could ask him to move aside and let her pass, she caught her name, and Hester's voice saying:

"Adelaide is so clever; she paints beautifully!"

The words were addressed to Percival, and she felt the hot colour flush her face.

"How stupid of Hester! I wish she would leave me alone!"

But Hester, not knowing Adelaide was near, went on.

"We have been hoping Lady Anna might propose taking Adelaide to Florence. Cousin Mary is so fond of her; and, of course, there are no advantages for anyone like her in this dull old place. It does very well for people like me, you know, but Adelaide is so wonderfully clever."

"Hester, will you let me pass, please? I must go home; it is getting late, and mother will be expecting me."

The voice was one of suppressed vexation, and Hester laughingly said:

"How could I tell you were in the conservatory, Adelaide? Well, for once, a listener has heard nothing but good of herself."

"Please do not be so foolish, Hester. Perhaps it would be better to hear what is true about one's self, than what is pure fiction."

Percival listened to this little passage of arms between the two girls with great amusement, and he was beginning to say something to the effect that it was very easy to take Hester's remarks as absolute truth, but Adelaide had, on his moving aside, slipped past, and without waiting to say good-night to any-one, she had snatched her shawl from the hall, and was gone.

The next day was wet, and there were no strolls in the park, and no tennis at the Rectory, to which Mrs. Birley had invited Hester, Adelaide, and Percival. Mr. Beauchamp was still very ill, and Percival found the day rather long and dull.

He had read the papers and a shilling novel Lady Anna had bought to beguile her journey; and after luncheon there seemed nothing else to do.

A very prolonged yawn made Lady Anna turn round from the writing-table—where her always busy pen had been employed in writing letters to pass the time on this wet day—and say:

"It is a fearful downpour. I am so sorry, Percival. I had hoped to have driven with you to Corsham to call on the Probyns. But it is out of the question."

Percival folded his hands at the back of his head, stretched, and said:

"Where is the picture you say you bought of Miss—what is her name? I've got mixed about her. Hester said her mother is Mrs. Wardlaw."

"Oh, Adelaide Millington, you mean! Yes; her mother married twice; she is the child of the first marriage. Parsons has laid hands on the picture to pack it. Would you ring, please? I rather want this note taken to Miss Millington."

"Give it to me," Percival said, starting up; "I don't mind the rain, and I want something to do."

"Oh, I really can't let you run the risk of getting rheumatic fever, Percival; it is such heavy rain."

But Percival took no other notice of this remark than to take the note from the writing-table, saying, as he left the room:

"Any answer?"

"Well, yes. I wrote to ask Miss Millington to come up and speak to me; you need not wait for her reply. Of course she will be only too glad to come."

"I should not say it was ever safe to count upon that young lady's actions or sentiments. She strikes me as having a will of her own," Percival said, as he left the room.

In the hall he met Lady Mary.

"My dear Percy, I am so sorry to have seen so little of you, and this is such a wretched day. I am going to try and spend an hour with your Aunt Anna now. Where are you going in this deluge?"

"Turning messenger for Aunt Anna. I have a note in my pocket for Miss Millington."

"Why should you go out in the rain?" but Percival was gone.

He was soon at the Wardlaws' door, and admitted by a maid to the little parlour to the right of the passage, which was empty, and where he waited for some minutes. He had leisure to examine the room—a small square room, but not without signs of taste. The best was made of it, and the space left in the middle, by pushing the table into the corner, made it seem larger than it really was. Percival was in the act of looking at the pictures hung round the room, when he started almost guiltily as the door opened and Adelaide came in. She had been summoned from her room by her sister coming to announce the arrival of a gentleman, who wanted to see her.

"It must be mother he wants, or father, perhaps," Adelaide had said.

"No; Sarah says he asked for Miss Millington." So Adelaide had smoothed her hair, taken off her painting-apron, and now presented herself to Percival in a blue serge gown made in her favourite loose style, the collar and sleeves turned up with crimson. Her face glowed with surprise, and perhaps pleasure, which made Percival forget his embarrassment, and put him at ease.

"I have brought you a note from my aunt, Lady Anna," he said; "she asked me to wait for an answer. I can take a verbal one, if you please."

Adelaide's face, as she read the note, was a study. She was silent for a few minutes, and then, looking up, she saw Percival was watching her intently.

"Will you say I will come up to the Court as soon as I can, please? Lady Anna wishes to see me—she is to spend the winter at Florence, and she asks me whether I should like to accompany her. I hardly know in what capacity."

"As her friend, whose society will be a gain to her and to Margaret, I should think," Percival said.

"How can you judge?" was the quick reply. "You have had no experience of what my society may be."

"Very little, I know; but I suppose it is allowable and reasonable to judge of the value of anything by first impressions?"

Adelaide smiled, and shook her head.

"It is never safe, though it may be allowable."

"I hope, if I may venture to say so," Percival continued, "that you will go to Florence with my aunt. I have a very dear little cousin, whom you would like, I know. She has so little to vary her life and interest at home, that I am sure it will be doing her a kindness, if you join the party."

Again Adelaide shook her head incredulously, and said:

"I don't think you should answer for your cousin; probably she would rather be without me than with me—especially as, from what Lady Mary has said, she is the one object of care and devotion from her father and mother."

"Yes, and very tired she gets of it," Percival said; "she has had two young cousins with her, in her mother's absence, and it was wonderful to see how she enjoyed their society. If you will allow me, Miss Millington, I will wait till you are ready, and then walk up the park with you, and do my best to shelter you from the rain. It is a regular downpour, and you must protect yourself by a waterproof."

Adelaide hesitated a minute, and then went to get ready. Mrs. Wardlaw was just coming out of her husband's library, and Adelaide put the note into her mother's hand.

"Shall I go, mother?"

"From Lady Anna—is it about Florence?"

"Yes; she asks me if I will go there and improve myself in art! I don't feel sure about it. I don't think I really want to go; she will patronize me so dreadfully!"

"My darling, it is what you have wished for so long; what your father and I have desired for you, with your gifts—and——"

"Very well, go and talk to Mr. Clyffe while I get ready; only pray, mother, don't say anything to him about my gifts—he will only laugh at you."

Mrs. Wardlaw could not resist turning back to the library with the news, and Mr. Wardlaw said:

"Go! of course she must go; let nothing stand in the way, my dear."

"*I* don't wish to put any obstacles in the way; it is Adelaide who has misgivings."

"Nonsense! she ought to be only too glad to go. I envy her. I think there is nothing I should like better than to find myself standing on the Ponte

Vecchio once more, or watching a sunset from San Miniato."

"Mr. Clyffe brought the note," Mrs. Wardlaw said; "shall I bring him in to see you?"

"Yes, by all means," Mr. Wardlaw replied; "my fire is welcome on this dull wet day, and this room looks more cheerful than your parlour."

Mr. Wardlaw was quite right; and Percival Clyffe, as he sank down into the depths of a most luxurious chair, thought the master of the house took good care to have the best of it for himself.

The shelves were well lined with books—books to suit every taste, by dead authors mostly; but there were some exceptions, and the *Edinburgh* and *Quarterly*, with some more modern magazines, had a shelf to themselves. A large bay window looked into the garden, and the view from it was very much the same as that which Adelaide had from her room on the floor above.

"What a delightful room!" Percival could not help saying.

"Yes, a student's room, with no ornaments except a picture or two. That is a fine engraving of the San Sisto, and I am proud of Adelaide's little sea-piece. She has considerable gifts, which want cultivation, of course. There is nothing like study of the greatest masters in any branch of art or literature."

"Except the study of men and women," Percival said quietly.

Mr. Wardlaw looked at him with his keen deep-set eyes.

"Ah! you are a philosopher, I see. Well, I agree with you, though I confess the study of the works of the giants of the past, in literature and art, is more attractive to me than the contemplation of the pigmies of our own time. Adelaide's mother tells me there is a hope that she may have the advantage of seeing Florence, by Lady Anna Cowper-Smith's kindness. We shall gratefully accept the offer, and here comes Adelaide to say what she feels on the subject."

Adelaide was equipped for her walk in the rain, and after a few minutes' more conversation, and the pardonable vanity with which Mr. Wardlaw exhibited an edition of Shakespeare's plays which he had edited, Percival asked Adelaide if she were ready to brave the storm. Mrs. Wardlaw went with them to the door, and Nina and Susie watched—from the parlour window—their sister walk quickly up the road, carefully shielded by Percival's large umbrella.

When Percival Clyffe came to Dryborough the day before, he had told himself his chief object was to persuade Lady Anna that Rose Smith would be a charming companion for Daisy during the winter.

How was it that he had changed his mind, and only once had advocated Rose's claims and Mr. Cowper-Smith's wishes? He was almost provoked with himself, when he remembered how he had by no means exercised his influence in the direction which Mr. Cowper-Smith had expected.

The next morning Lady Anna's daily letters to Willesford heralded her return on that evening, and the train which the carriage was to meet was specified. There was a postscript to Daisy's letter:

"I have secured the society of a charming young lady, who will spend the winter at Florence with us. She will study art, and she will be such a fresh element in your life, my darling. I am sure both you and dear papa will delight in her. She is very clever, and I think you, my sweet Daisy, will thank Aunt Mary for introducing her to me."

"Oh, father!" Daisy said, as she ran to her father with her mother's letter; "mother says nothing about Rose. She has got another young lady to come with us to Florence."

Mr. Cowper-Smith understood his wife's tactics at once.

"Ah!" he said emphatically, "I see."

"Does mother tell you anything about this young lady?"

"No, my dear; not a word. Well, let us hope it will answer, and we will take Rose with us another time."

"I am so sorry, and Percival will be sorry, too. He liked Rose so much, and he said she was just the right sister for me. I wonder what Percival thinks?"

"The tide may have turned, my dear. Perhaps

Percival is also so much taken by this young lady at Dryborough that he has forgotten all about Rose."

"But he promised to try and persuade mother to let her come. He promised, father!"

"Well, well; we must make the best of it, my Peggy."

For Mr. Cowper-Smith was far too loyal to let his little daughter have any suspicion that it was only when Rose Smith was suggested as a *compagnon de voyage* that Adelaide Millington had been invited to take that place.

"Poor Anna!" he said to himself, not to Daisy— "poor Anna! she cannot forget that my people are tradespeople; and the wonder is she ever married me."

CHAPTER V.

EN ROUTE.

" When the desire cometh it is a tree of life."

Adelaide had attained her desire, and on one bright October day she had left Dryborough behind her, and was fairly launched upon the world.

It has become a very common experience in these days to cross the Channel, pass through the far from interesting country between Calais and Bâle, and, taking Milan as a resting-place, go forward to sunny Italy.

There is almost a distinction nowadays in those people who have never travelled—to whom the snowy Alps and rolling hills of Tuscany are only known after the dim uncertain fashion which photographs, letters and descriptions by the pen and tongue leave upon the mind. There are so few who have not, at any rate, "done" the customary Continental route by the help of Gaze or Cook, or, in a better and more dignified fashion, by couriers, and other luxurious appendages which wealth can command. And I need not say Lady Anna Cowper-Smith was amongst the latter class. The suite which embarked at

Calais by the *Invicta* was almost like a royal one. There were degrees and certain gradations of rank even here. Lady Anna and Daisy, and her own maid and Mrs. Gray, travelled in one of the best appointed sleeping-carriages. Mr. Cowper-Smith, who could not forego the consolation of a pipe, travelled in a first-class smoking-carriage. Miss Cromwell and Adelaide were in an ordinary first-class compartment; while the long train of attendants were in a second-class carriage, which they filled with all the loose bags and bundles and small boxes which were not committed to the officials for registration.

The journey could not have been performed with less trouble and less adventure. Travelling has become so prosaic now, that even ordinary folk, who have to think of their own registration tickets, and wake up out of an uneasy slumber at the frontier station and see their boxes marked with a bit of white chalk, though but seldom opened, find nothing very exciting in it. Everything goes in a certain groove; and, whether jogging along through France or at an easy pace through Switzerland and Italy, there are no surprises and no startling sensations, as far as the mere act of travelling is concerned.

The party reached Bâle in the early dawn of the fine October morning, and then what a bevy of dishevelled passengers turned out on the platform for breakfast, and that very important operation after a night journey through dusty France—a morning wash!

Mr. Cowper-Smith was the only person who

thought about Miss Cromwell and Adelaide. He came to the door of their carriage and helped them to descend from the high steps, and took them in to breakfast.

Lady Anna was already seated at the table, her white hands, with their many rings, folded before her, as she leaned back composedly, waiting for what she had ordered through the courier, and looking with sublime indifference on the crowd of less dignified passengers. Lady Anna, to use a common expression, had not "turned a hair," and, indeed, there was no need for her to do so. She had slept comfortably, her maid had performed her usual duties, and, in point of fact, she had no more trouble than in her own house at home.

Little Daisy sat next her mother, and called across the table, " Here we are, father!" as he came into the room with Miss Cromwell and Adelaide.

" Good morning, my darling. I hope you are well looked after. Had you a good night?"

" Oh, yes, dear father; I thought I was in my own bed at home."

" Don't talk across the table, my sweet one," Lady Anna said, for she saw the eyes of several people directed to Daisy. " Here comes our breakfast; now, you must eat some of this chicken."

" Oh, I can't, mammy dear; not so early. I only want coffee. I *can't* eat chicken."

" My darling, you must try. You have a long day before you."

Here an unfortunate spinster lady, who still wore the gray handkerchief, pinned under her chin, in which she had passed the night on an "Oreiller" hired for one franc in a second-class carriage, ventured to say:

"You had better try, dear, to do as your mamma wishes. There is nothing like eating good food to help through a long journey."

To this remark Lady Anna made no rejoinder, but there was an expression on her face which effectually prevented the poor little lady from volunteering any more advice.

When at last Lady Anna pushed back her chair, and walked slowly out of the restaurant, a stout English traveller, who had had varied experience of journeys in many countries, stopped in the dissection of a cutlet, to say to the little spinster:

"My lady gives herself airs, doesn't she? I can spot English swells abroad in a moment, by their manners. They don't do the nation credit, I must say. What harm would it have done her to smile, anyhow, when you spoke, instead of looking like a bit of granite at you?"

"Oh, I don't mind," was the reply. "I was sorry to see that little girl look so delicate, as if she would not live to get back to England."

The words smote Mr. Cowper-Smith with a sharp pang. He was seated on the same side of the table as the poor little lady, beyond Miss Cromwell and Adelaide, so that the speaker had not noticed him. He gave a deep sigh, pushed away his plate, and, telling Miss Cromwell and Adelaide not to hurry, there was plenty of time, went to look for his wife and child with a heavy heart.

"Dearest," Lady Anna said, "will you kindly tell Miss Millington and Miss Cromwell that they are to travel with us as far as Milan? Mrs. Gray and Parsons will change places with them. And, dearest, do not invite conversation at those public tables; it is so embarrassing."

"Invite conversation! What do you mean? Surely I may speak to my own child and ask her how she has spent the night!"

"You know what I mean, dearest," was the reply. "I do hope Miss Millington is going to be a more cheerful companion. She looks so gloomy this morning."

They were soon off again. Who shall tell what are the different influences, upon different people, as the train passes through the low wooded hills which lie just beyond Bâle, with glimpses here and there of the snowy peaks of the distant Bernese Oberland? Then on to Lucerne, and thence by the side of the lake, shut in by mountains which rise in ever-increasing majesty on every side. Pilatus, dark, proud, and solemn in the morning light, which wakes no smile from him, as it does from the grassy slopes sweeping down to the very edge of the water, and the laughing cataracts leaping gaily from rocky heights, to find their home in those deep blue waters.

Onwards, and then upwards goes the train, beginning to ascend what seem immeasurable heights, in and out of tunnels which are a triumph of engineering skill. Onwards and upwards, through darkness into light, from dazzling radiance into darkness again. A village church is passed on a level with the windows of the carriage: children are playing in the little square before it; then it is soon lost to sight as the train enters a tunnel, and is next seen far, far below, like a child's toy in the old Dutch villages of long ago.

It was in the St. Gothard Pass that Adelaide and Daisy began a friendship which was to be firmer and more tender than either of them thought of then; for Daisy pressed close to Adelaide, and said:

"Isn't it wonderful and beautiful, Miss Millington? The great mountains, and the waterfalls, and the snow—the white, pure snow! Did you ever see mountains like these before?"

"Never," Adelaide said—"never, except in dreams."

"I have seen the Alpes-Maritimes from Cannes, and the blue Esterels, but I never went near them. Now we seem to be amongst the mountains, climbing up to their tops."

Presently Daisy's hand was slipped into Adelaide's, and she said:

"I shall write to my cousin Percy, and tell him all about this journey, and that you and I enjoyed it together. He will be glad, I know. He wanted Rose Smith, my cousin, to come, and I was very much vexed when mother told father you were coming instead; but I think, after all, you will be best. I love the picture of the fisher-boy, and I made Parsons put it at the bottom of one of the big boxes. I shall hang it up in my room at Florence.'

Miss Cromwell had fallen asleep again; Lady Anna was reading, only looking up now and then to make some remark about the stifling atmosphere of the longest tunnel, and to insist on Daisy burying her face in a handkerchief saturated with eau-de-cologne, forbidding her to speak a word.

At the top of the pass an excellent *table d'hôte* was provided, and this time Daisy was hungry, and did full justice to the bill of fare. Her father was delighted, and when she said, " Oh, father, I never liked a journey half as much before !" the cloud which the well-intentioned words of the little spinster lady had called up on his face vanished, and he answered brightly:

" I am glad of that, my dear. I shall come into your carriage now, and we will look at the Italian lakes together."

The examination of the luggage at the frontier of Chiasso did not affect the comfort of people like the Cowper-Smiths. Parsons and Miss Cromwell and the courier and manservant followed the luggage and the rugs and hold-alls into the great *salle des bagages*, having the keys in their possession. It was left to humbler folk to trot after porters, carrying their small boxes and bags, and to stand patiently till their turn for examination came. Then the welcome mark in white chalk made on each package relieved all anxiety, and the crowd of passengers flocked back.

Lady Anna surveyed them from her vantage-ground with supreme satisfaction, and wondered what could be the pleasure of travelling second-class, and enduring so many hardships.

The glow of the evening light, rosy and beautiful, was on the mountains as they passed Como and Lugano; but the evening closed in quickly after Chiasso, and it was nearly dark when the Hotel Cavour at Milan was reached, where rooms had been engaged.

There was just time the next morning for Adelaide and Miss Cromwell to see the cathedral—the first vast cathedral which Adelaide had ever seen. The marvellous beauty of the marble tracery of the roof against the pure blue of the Italian sky fascinated her. She stood on the wide Piazza, gazing up at it with admiring wonder.

"Come, Miss Millington," Mr. Cowper-Smith said; "we have not too much time. We must go inside, for there is some old saint buried below the nave, so Murray says. You can look down at his shrine; and you may see him, I believe, if you pay for the sight."

"No, thank you," Adelaide said. "I do not want to see Saint Carlo Borromeo. Where is the great Cenacolo of Leonardo da Vinci?"

"I am sure I don't know," Mr. Cowper-Smith

said; "but we must ask. This is a grand place," he said, looking up with a critical eye; "but I think York Minster is bigger. Come, Miss Cromwell."

Miss Cromwell was gazing with curious eyes on the shrine of Saint Carlo, and scarcely looked up at the marvellous beauty of the forest of pillars and the soaring grace and beauty of the roof.

Adelaide walked on as if in a dream, and followed her companion to the carriage, and drove with them to the ancient Church of Saint Ambrogio, to see the celebrated picture in the deserted refectory of the convent adjoining the Church of Santa Maria delle Grazie, which has proved a disappointment to so many whose expectations have been raised—the half-effaced sad remains of what had been once so beautiful made Adelaide exclaim, saying: "Is that all?"

"Yes," said Mr. Cowper-Smith, referring to his Murray. "Yes; it is little better than a patch now. I can't conceive how people can try to copy it. There's scarcely anything left to copy. You would not want to try that, Miss Millington. But we have no time to lose; we must get back to the hotel."

"Yes," said Miss Cromwell, who was beginning to be uneasy as to what Lady Anna would say at their prolonged absence; "we had better go back to the hotel. The train leaves at twelve o'clock."

"You are right; we have no time to lose," Mr. Cowper-Smith replied.

But Adelaide had returned to look once more at the picture.

"Is that all?" she repeated, and yet she half repented her first judgment. There *was* something still there. Surely that outstretched hand of the Lord, and the expression in it, and in the turn of His head, seemed to make the pathetic words almost audible: "One of you shall betray Me!" Ah, memorable words! "*One* of you!" And then the eager questioning of those anxious men: "Lord, is it I?"

These thoughts passed through Adelaide's mind more quickly than I can write them; and as she walked backwards from the faded picture, with a longing, lingering gaze, she came in contact with some one close behind her.

"I beg your pardon," she said, turning round and colouring deeply, as she faced a man rather below the average height, whose black hair was streaked with gray.

A young lady was with him, gaily dressed, and with that air about her which we know as "fast."

"What a horrid old picture!" she said. "Surely you can't admire it, Godfrey; I think it is *frightful!*"

"You had better write a note for the next edition of 'Murray,'" was the reply. "But I would keep such opinions to myself, if I were you."

Adelaide had answered Mr. Cowper-Smith's frantic summons, and did not hear the rejoinder; but the man's face was a remarkable one, and she said to herself: " I should know him again anywhere."

"Come, Miss Millington, we shall get into disgrace. I thought you did not care for the old picture, and yet you were staring at it for ever so long. It was rather fun to see you backing on that gentleman; what a strange face he had."

"And did you notice how the lady was 'got up?'" Miss Cromwell said.

" Dressed smartly, do you mean ? Yes ; I thought she was very grand."

"I did not mean that sort of 'get up,'" said Miss Cromwell. " I meant that her eyes were darkened, and the roses on her cheeks not altogether natural."

" Painted up! Dear, dear !" Mr. Cowper-Smith said; "what a mistake women make who do that! I never could think well of a woman who paints her face. Perhaps it is partly from association with the story of a certain royal lady in the Bible. It is an odious practice—as all shams are odious. A sign of the times, I fear."

" It has been a sign of every time," Miss Cromwell said. "And I don't know that it is worse to darken eyes, and make lips like cherries, than to wear false hair or put in teeth—so many people do it now."

" Now, now! you are shooting wide of the mark," said Mr. Cowper-Smith. " If people feel their bald heads cold, I hold it is right to wear a wig. And, as to teeth, everyone is welcome to know mine were put in by a grand American dentist some years ago, and my digestion has been better ever since. But I ask what good can ever come from colouring cheeks and lips, and darkening eyes? No good, but positive harm, so the doctors say."

Miss Cromwell seldom ventured on an opinion; she now relapsed into silence, and Adelaide repeated to herself Miss Cromwell's words: "So many people do it now."

"Not people in Dryborough," she thought. "Imagine Lady Mary colouring her pale face, or darkening her eyebrows and eyes—it would be impossible!"

The day was less brilliant towards evening than its predecessors, and the great Lombardy plains looked bare and desolate. Modena and Bologna awoke some interest in Adelaide; but she got tired of looking out of the window, and before the train had begun to dart in and out of the long succession of short tunnels which lead at last by a gradual descent to Pistoja, she had fallen asleep, with little Daisy nestled close to her, with her head resting against her shoulder and her hand in hers.

When the train reached Florence rain was falling —a cold, chill rain—and there was a great deal of bustle at the station, and much pushing and jostling by the English travellers, who, like the swallows, were now returning in flocks to the sunny South.

The sunny South! the words seemed a mockery— rain pouring down, chill air blowing in from open doors, the *salle des bagages* full of anxious travellers who were giving up their registry tickets and receiving the luggage which had not been in their possession since it was taken from the cab at Victoria three days before!

Lady Anna Cowper-Smith commanded everyone to keep their seats till the last moment. She was so terribly afraid of Daisy getting a chill, and she said it would only retard matters if they descended to the platform. At last Mr. Cowper-Smith came to announce all was ready, and the servants had packed everything into one carriage, while another was ready for Lady Anna and Daisy, and Miss Cromwell and Adelaide.

"Oh! three will be enough in one carriage. Miss Millington, will you go with Parsons; and——"

But Miss Cromwell exclaimed:

"Oh no; I can go with Parsons, please."

"Well, don't stay parleying here, my dear; make haste."

Lady Anna never hurried, and she descended with grave dignity from the carriage, her book in her hand, and her little Russian-leather travelling-bag, supplied with every conceivable scent and "tablets" for Daisy, slung on her wrist. Adelaide was the last to leave the carriage, and forgetting the height of the step, which is a feature of railway-carriages in Italy, she fell with some violence on the platform.

In an instant she was lifted up, and by the flickering gaslight she saw the man whom she had stumbled against in Milan in the morning bending over her.

"Are you hurt? I hope you are not hurt! These steps are so dangerously high."

"Thanks," Adelaide said, "I am not hurt, only——"

"Shaken, let me take you to your friends."

"What *are you* doing, Godfrey? Do, pray, come, or we shall get no cab; there's such a crowd outside, this wet night. Godfrey!"

The voice was shrill and fretful, but it did not produce much effect on Adelaide's benefactor. He gave her his arm, which she was only too thankful to take, and asked her whose carriage he should call for.

"Oh, thanks! Mr. Cowper-Smith has engaged two or three carriages. We have such an enormous amount of luggage."

"Yes; I thought when I saw you all get in at Milan it must be royalty 'incog.,'" was the reply.

And then the strong manly voice, in its resonant English tones, shouted:

"Is Mr. Cowper-Smith's carriage here?"

The footman now came up, and said to Adelaide:

"Her ladyship could not wait, Miss Millington; you will please to come in the last fly with the luggage: this way!"

"Not very civil of her ladyship to leave you alone. Here,"—to the man,—"show us which cab you have engaged.'

But Adelaide withdrew her hand, and said:

"Good-night; and thank you very much."

"I shall see you safely into the cab," was the reply. "You had better take my arm again."

Then way was made, and following the tall footman, Adelaide found herself put into the cab with Mrs. Gray, the footman jumped in after her, and the cab drove off.

Mrs. Gray was not in the best of tempers. She began to grumble at the weather, and kept up a running commentary as to the folly of gentry leaving their own comfortable abodes for foreign places.

"Just as if Miss Daisy would not be ten hundred times better at home! Her ladyship is cracked about warmth and sunshine. There never was less of it than now in Florence!"

"Well," said the footman, "we don't look for sunshine at near ten o'clock at night in England, do we? For my part, I like to see the world."

"Her ladyship was fearfully put out that you did not follow her to the carriage, Miss Millington. What were you doing?" Mrs. Gray said.

"Talking to a gentleman, of course, who was a friend—was not he, Miss Millington?" answered the footman.

Adelaide became conscious that the footman and Mrs. Gray were treating her as very much on the same level as themselves. The footman's familiarity brought a rebuke from Mrs. Gray.

"Hush now, Sam; you forget yourself."

Poor Adelaide had given herself a severe shake with her fall; she was very tired, but she tried to say, with becoming dignity:

"My foot slipped as I left the carriage, and that gentleman kindly helped me to rise." Here her voice faltered, and in her heart was the cry: "Oh, I wish I had never, never come! How could I be so foolish? I knew what Lady Anna was. I shall not stay. I will go home as soon as possible. What would Hester say if she knew I was treated like this by impertinent servants! and mother and father—how angry they would be!"

"Dear me, Miss Millington, I hope you have not injured yourself," Mrs. Gray said. "Those high steps are dreadful to get up and down; it is a wonder I did not fall, I am sure. What a long drive it is! I wonder whether we shall ever get there."

They were, though they did not know it, in the Piazza d'Azeglio, and the cab stopped.

"Che numero?" the driver asked. "Signora, che numero?"

"What number? I am not sure," Adelaide said. "You will see the other carriages at the right door."

The cabman only repeated his question with many flourishes of his whip, and gestures such as Italians only can make.

"Thirteen—thirteen—tell him thirteen, Miss."

Adelaide was taxing her memory in vain for thirteen. She knew her numbers in Italian, and, if allowed time, she could surely bring forth thirteen from the treasure-house of her memory. But, as the cabman got more and more vociferous, so did the truant number get further away from her lips.

"Dieci—Tre—dieci!"

"Si, si," said the man, with the prolonged "a—a—a—" which it is impossible to express in writing. "Si, si, Signora. Tredici—tredici. Si, si!"

At this moment the other two carriages, which had discharged their passengers and luggage, passed by. A series of exclamations and gesticulations followed between the men, and with a cry of "Tredici, Tredici," the cab jogged off to the further side of the piazza, and finally stopped before a large door, which at a touch of the bell opened in the middle, and Mrs. Gray said:

"You had better go in, Miss Millington, and I will stay with Sam, to see all the small things are right."

Adelaide stumbled up three stone steps, and came to a second glass door, which was also open, and then what?

It seemed to her utter darkness, but presently she became aware of a dim light shining down from above, and she could discern a flight of wide stone stairs before her.

She went up cautiously. The voices of Mrs. Gray and Sam at the door below echoed through the house with a hollow noise, and presently the light from the upper regions grew stronger. When she turned for the third time, she saw a woman holding a lamp, and inviting her to come up higher.

Assunta had been left in charge of the house by her Italian master and mistress, and belonged to it as much as the furniture did.

"Chi è là—la Signorina!—venga presto."

It was by no means easy for Adelaide to make haste, and she came up the stairs so slowly that Assunta ran lightly down, and seizing one of her hands, drew it within her arm, saying:

"Molta fatica, signorina; povera signorina!"

At last the topmost step was gained, and Adelaide found Mr. Cowper-Smith in the wide lobby, just within the door, trying to unfasten a hamper, from which Lady Anna wanted at once to get some champagne for Daisy.

Adelaide heard a voice from some unseen quarter saying:

"Where are the other servants and Miss Millington? Really, it is very inconvenient."

"Where am I to sleep?" Adelaide asked of Mr. Cowper-Smith. "I am so tired."

Miss Cromwell now came forward.

"Lady Anna does not think the house as large as she expected, and dislikes the stairs—but it is very spacious, and well furnished. You look very tired. Lady Anna was vexed that you kept her waiting at the station."

"I had a fall," Adelaide said. "I was almost

stunned at first. I think you might have come back to see if anything was the matter."

"Come back! You don't know Lady Anna if you think she would have waited a moment. Mr. Cowper-Smith did want to return to the platform, but it was not allowed; we are all under orders here."

"*I* am not," said Adelaide proudly; "and you will soon see that I am independent."

"I beg your pardon; I did not mean to offend you," Miss Cromwell said. "What I mean is, we all need patience; and, with Daisy for an example, we ought to be patient. It is wonderful to see how sweet and gentle she is to-night, when everyone is cross and tired."

"Oh, do take me to my room!" Adelaide said in a despairing voice. "Which way?"

"Your room is through these doors; it is at the back of the house, but it is very nice. Mine has to be near Daisy, at the other side of the corridor. Lady Anna is already beginning to speak of giving up this *piano* as too high; and Mr. Cowper-Smith is remonstrating, for, having engaged it till May, he will have to pay for it, if he does not stay. This is your room; shall I help you to undress—shall I bring you something? You must have a cup of tea Mrs. Gray and Sam have the spirit-lamp in their basket, and I can soon fetch it."

Miss Cromwell was really sorry to see how pale and weary Adelaide looked; and added:

"I am sorry I did not see you fall."

"Good-night; never mind. I shall be all right in the morning. I have some biscuits and claret left if I want them. Good-night."

This was a very different first night in Florence from what Adelaide had often pictured. The rain made a ceaseless patter on the loggia below her room, and the wind sighed in the trees outside. Adelaide opened the shutters, and tried to peer out, but it was very dark, and nothing was to be seen. Presently the sound of a clock striking made her listen.

The sound was deep-toned, and musical; she was quite sorry when the last of the ten strokes was told out; very soon the sound of that bell from the Campanile became familiar, and would be one of the memories of Florence in after-time.

The sound sleep of youth did not forsake her, and she was awakened by the church bells ringing for the early mass, before the sun had risen. It was a clear, fair morning, and there was not a cloud in the sky.

Adelaide sprang up, and then, feeling stiff from her fall, thought she would lie down again. But the spell was broken; the voices of the bells from many church-towers seemed to call her to awake. She rose, and throwing open the large French window, looked out.

Innumerable drops were shimmering like diamonds on the branches of two tall trees before her windows; it was the clear shining after the rain.

"I wish I was in the old city of Florence; this all

looks so new, and what a tangle of a garden below, and——"

As she leaned out, she caught sight of the tower of the Palazzo Vecchio, raising its flower-shaped head high in the clear sky.

"I must go out. I wonder if they will mind. But I really must go and see the Arno."

She was soon dressed, and then she went softly out into the corridor from which her room opened. The kitchen department was on the opposite side, and there she saw Assunta plaiting the braids of her raven hair before a small glass, singing in a low voice as she did so.

She caught sight of Adelaide, and came towards her smiling, as she thrust the thick pin through her plaits.

"Buon giorno, signorina; ha ella bisogna di me?"

Adelaide only shook her head, and pointed to the door.

"Dove conduce—questa—strada?"

"Alla Piazza della Santissima Annunziata." Then, seeing Adelaide had difficulty in understanding her, she said: "I speak a little English, signora."

"I wish to go to the bridge, the Ponte Vecchio."

"A—a—a. You go down the Via de' Servi, and then on to the Piazza Duomo, and on to Via Tornabuoni, and then come to Lung' Arno."

The directions were not very lucid, but Assunta

accompanied them with many gestures, and smiled, and nodded, and looked so happy, that Adelaide felt quite cheered.

"Tante grazie!" she said.

"Posso farle una buona tazza di caffè, Signorina."

And Assunta hastened to take a pot from the wood fire, and poured out steaming coffee with one hand, and with the other some milk.

Adelaide was greatly refreshed with the coffee, but declined the hard roll into which Assunta set her strong white teeth with great appetite. She had risen early, she said, to be ready for the servants of the signor, who were asleep upstairs, on the top floor; there was a little room prepared for them; for the servants of the English signors wanted more than their masters. The signora was very grand, and did not admire the *piano*, as everyone did. The salon was beautiful—such pictures and china—and it was all good enough for her master, the old Marchese— why not for English signoras? The house was grand, and yet the signora did only frown and shake her head. Well! she, Assunta, knew full well that the Piazza d'Azeglio was more to English taste than the old houses. Of course there were hotels—Paoli's and others—very good—but Piazza d'Azeglio was cheerful and bright. Antonio, the *chef*, would come at seven. And Adelaide made out that Antonio was to fill the office of cook, and that he had been, like Assunta, in the service of the old Marchese.

Was the signorina going out alone? and Assunta gave her shoulder a significant shrug.

Adelaide, however, paid no heed to this, and ran down the stone stairs, eager to find herself in the streets of old Florence. The heights of Fiesole were before her, and the noble curve of Monte Morello to her left. She walked straight down the long road till she came to the Piazza of the Annunziata, and there she stopped.

It was yet early, and the donkeys and mules, laden with country produce, were coming into the town. The women wore brilliant handkerchiefs over their dark hair, and short coloured skirts, and bright kerchiefs crossed over their shoulders. There was a great deal of chatter in a high-pitched key, and every now and then a peasant woman disappeared within the shadow of the door of the church, and, leaving her merchandise outside, went to say her prayers before that silver shrine of the Madonna which is of fabulous cost, and of world-wide fame, and is perpetually replenished with the votive hearts, of purest silver and of every size, hung in glass cases round the shrine. When these become too numerous, they are melted down, and the silver is remodelled for lamps, or candlesticks for the shrine.

Adelaide followed several peasant women and children through the vestibule of the church, where Andrea del Sarto's most precious frescoes are protected by glass, and entered the church itself.

The bright morning light had no free access there. All was shadowy and dim, and the candles at the many altars burned with a dull yellow light.

So have men's devices and dogmas obscured the full shining of the Sun of Righteousness. So have a long succession of vain traditions shadowed the beauty of the Son of God, as *seen* in the face of Christ. But Adelaide, who had never, perhaps, been touched, as yet, in her spiritual being, stood in wonder, as she watched the devotion written on the faces of the women, and children, and rough peasants, who were kneeling before the silver shrine. The dark eyes of one woman—whence tears were dropping now and then—arrested her. A child knelt by her, with her little brown hands clasped, and her lips moving as her mother's moved. Presently, a prayer from the very depths of that sad heart broke forth. And, as the woman covered her face, Adelaide heard an audible,

"Santa Maria! ah, Santa Maria, ora pro me!"

The pain and misery expressed in that cry wrung from a heavy heart made Adelaide hasten out again to the sunny Piazza, then through the narrow Via de' Servi, till she came to the Duomo, with the dazzling purity of the marble of the new facciata shining with an almost transparent brightness, and Giotto's Campanile raising its stately head to the sky. There was a busy crowd here, all full of life and life's concerns. It seemed as if the dimness and the pathos were left behind in the Church of the Annunziata, and that this was the common life of men and women in Florence—careless and happy, and forgetful of all, save the present and its needs.

Adelaide would not pass inside the Duomo now; she felt compelled to press onward to the Arno, that river whose very name seems to possess a subtle charm. The blue sky overhead! the morning sunshine! it seemed as if she could not exchange these again for the gloom and heaviness which would probably hang over the interior of the Duomo, as it had hung over the interior of the Church of the Annunziata. Adelaide felt strangely moved by the novelty of all around her—the unfamiliar cries—the soft Italian tongue spoken on all sides.

No, not on all—for an English voice made her turn her head quickly as she came to the Strozzi Palace, where flowers, fresh from the hands of the flower-merchant, were being heaped in brilliant masses, contrasting with the old stone-work—centuries old—as youth, radiant and joyful, contrasts with age.

"How much are those roses?" For Florence is seldom without its roses, and, though less abundant than in spring, the autumn bloom is rich and full.

Adelaide recognised the voice, and saw the dark-haired man who had been so helpful to her at the station the evening before, now too busy bargaining for his roses, and some large bunches of chrysanthemums and marguerites, to notice her. She passed quickly on down the Tornabuoni, till at the corner of the Lung' Arno the Ponte di Trinità was before her, the Arno smiling as it flowed beneath the arches with a rippling murmur, swelled by the heavy rains of the last few days.

On all sides how beautiful it was! Distant hills and loftier mountains, valleys and slopes studded with villas, and all under the canopy of an Italian sky, clear, and with a depth of colour unknown in our northern climates. Adelaide leaned mid-way on the parapet and tried to take it all in—soaring campaniles and domes, belfry towers, and high-pitched roofs, and irregular gables of every height springing from the river-side; wonderful in eyes which had never looked on any scene more striking than Dryborough.

Adelaide had been twice to London, it is true, but mist and rain had obscured all the picturesque beauty of our own river-banks, flanked by the gray old buttresses of Westminster Abbey, and the lofty clock-tower of the Houses of Parliament.

Here was Florence, then, at last! no dream, but a reality; and Adelaide exclaimed aloud, with a deep sigh of satisfied delight: " It *is* beautiful!"

This time her voice was heard, and she saw a few paces from her on the bridge her acquaintance of the previous night. He raised his hat and drew a little nearer, the flowers he had bought in his hand.

" I trust you have not suffered from your fall," he said; " I hope not, as you are out so early."

Adelaide's manner became stiff and constrained at

once. English reserve taught her that she must not talk to a stranger without an introduction. And then how odd he must think it, to see her out by herself at that time in the morning. She answered his question in a self-conscious manner, which made her bring out her words in a short, almost sharp tone :

" Thanks, I am very well ;" and then she moved off, a little uncertain which way to turn, and beginning to wonder how long it would take to get back to the Piazza d'Azeglio. The little indecision in her movements was not lost on her friend of the railway-station, and he said :

" I think if you will allow me I can show you a short way to the Piazza d'Azeglio. I ought to say I am not altogether unknown — certainly not by report—to Lady Anna Cowper-Smith. My name is Godfrey Lysaght. I saw Lady Anna's name on the luggage yesterday when I was standing in the Salle, and I heard the direction given to drive to the Piazza d'Azeglio. You were with Lady Anna, I know."

" Yes," Adelaide replied ; " yes—I am staying with her. I must make haste back, for it is getting late."

" This way then," he said ; "along Lung' Arno Acciajoli, and you will get what I suppose will be your first sight of the great tower at the end of the porticoes of the Uffizi. It is one of the finest views in Florence."

Adelaide walked along silently, looking through

the arches by the Arno bank, at the river, and the opposite heights of San Miniato, without turning her head towards her companion.

His name conveyed no very distinct idea to her, though she fancied she had heard it somewhere. But she felt uneasy, and had none of the *savoir faire* which enables some people to carry off embarrassment. Presently her companion said:

"Stop one moment, and look this way now."

Adelaide did as she was told, and there before her was the long paved court which lies below the Uffizi, with the white marble statues of Florentine heroes on either side, and at the end the marvellous tower of the Palazzo Vecchio, soaring into the blue sky above the Piazza della Signoria, and forming a picture, perfect in beauty and interest.

"Here is a goodly company of painters, poets, and statesmen on either side," Mr. Lysaght said; "but you will have plenty of time to examine them at your leisure. Some will strike you at once like the faces of old friends—Dante, and Petrarch, and the saintly Archbishop Antonino."

"Is she stupid after all?" Mr. Lysaght was thinking; "she makes no sign of interest, and it is impossible to see her face with this monstrous hat shading it!—That is the place where Savonarola suffered," Mr. Lysaght said, after a few moments' pause. "He was brought down from his cell in that tower to meet his death just where that white pigeon is flying in and out. A

PALAZZO VECCHIO, FLORENCE.

Reformer before the Reformation, and, unlike many Reformers, the idol of the people, and holding them spell-bound for a time. Of course the breath of popular applause is fickle as the wind, and that square resounded with groans and execrations when they led him out to die. I think I must bid you good-morning now," Mr. Lysaght said; " I am staying at Paoli's Hotel with my sister, Mrs. Murchison, and it must be getting near breakfast-time. If you cross the Piazza della Signoria you will easily find your way ; or shall I call a carriage for you? The fare is only one franc to any part of Florence within the gates."

" Thanks," Adelaide said, hesitating a little ; "perhaps I had better have a carriage, as everything is so strange to me, and," she added under her breath, "so beautiful."

Mr. Lysaght called one of the little open carriages which are so numerous in Florence, and then, directing the man to 13, Piazza d'Azeglio, he bowed and departed. As Adelaide was swiftly borne along she seemed to awake as it were from a dream. " How stupid I must have seemed, and what must he think of me? He seems to know Florence well. I wonder when I shall see him again ? He might tell me about the galleries and studios, for I must not forget I have come here with an express purpose, which I *must* carry out, whatever happens."

CHAPTER VI.

COMPLICATIONS.

LADY ANNA COWPER-SMITH was so much engrossed with her own concerns, that Adelaide found herself treated with a little wholesome indifference.

What was the study of art, when compared with the mighty question engrossing Lady Anna's mind, of enlarging her borders and getting possession of both floors or *piani* in the house? It was impossible, she said, for her and Daisy to get out as often as was necessary if those terrible stairs were to be encountered every time. The first *piano* must be obtained, or the second must be given up. Thus it became a question of throwing away the rent of the second *piano* and removing to other quarters or an hotel, or applying for possession of the whole house.

Fortune favoured Lady Anna. The inhabitants of the first *piano* were suddenly called to Rome by the illness of a relative there, and were glad to find such rich English people to take possession of their rooms and another maidservant. Within a week, therefore, Lady Anna had established herself and Margaret, and Mrs. Gray and Parsons, on the first floor; while the spacious rooms above were left to Miss Cromwell and Adelaide and the servants; Sam having expressed his disapproval of being asked to sleep in a "garret"—he was sure Mr. Fielding (the butler at Willesford) "would not approve of his being so put upon."

"We shall have room for our guests now; for I hope Percival will come out, and I shall invite Mrs. Ponsonby and Hester to do so in the spring. We ought to have had a villa on the Fiesole side; but, failing that, through ignorance and want of due inquiry, we shall do very *fairly* well."

This remark was made at luncheon, and Mr. Cowper-Smith was heard to murmur something about the Villa Palmieri, and that perhaps Lady Anna was wishing she could be "fairly comfortable" there.

"Will you send for Fielding, dearest? Sam can hardly get through all the waiting. Fielding felt rather hurt at not being included in our party. Will you give orders, dearest, for another servant to go to the housekeeper at Lancaster Gate, and for Fielding to come here?"

"Dear, dear! how many more people? We shall be getting a perfect crowd in Florence! However, it is as you like, my dear. Yes, I'll write to old Fielding; but I think he had better be labelled 'Florence,' or he may find himself at Frankfort instead."

"He will get on very well. He went with us, if you remember, to Hyères one winter."

"I hear Florence is frightfully cold in winter," Mr. Cowper-Smith said. "We shall have to keep good fires."

"It is deliciously warm to-day," Lady Anna rejoined. "Daisy has had a charming drive this morning. You will see, dearest, about the carriage? I *must* have one entirely at my command."

"Yes, yes; I have arranged that, and I am to see the horses to-day."

"Pray ensure our having a steady coachman, for it would be frightful to be driven by an inexperienced hand."

Mr. Cowper-Smith pushed back his chair and was leaving the room, when Daisy ran after him, and, standing on tip-toe, whispered something in his ear:

"Adelaide wants to begin painting. Do ask how she is to get to the galleries and a studio!"

Then a fervent embrace was exchanged between father and daughter, and Mr. Cowper-Smith departed. Presently he put his head back into the room: "I suppose you would not like little Rose Smith to come out with Fielding?"

"My dearest! what a notion! No, indeed! I should not dream of proposing anything so preposterous!"

"It could easily be managed," Mr. Cowper-Smith said, as he finally left the room. "I thought in your opinion it was 'the more the merrier.'"

Lady Anna had just finished eating a peach, and was leaning back in her chair, satisfied that things were now in a fair way of being comfortably arranged.

"By-the-bye, Miss Millington," she said, "have you made any inquiries about painting?"

"No," Adelaide said; "I cannot do so alone. I thought perhaps one day you would be so kind as to go with me to a studio, in the Viale Principe Amadeo."

"Yes, we will certainly see about it when we are settled. There is plenty of time."

"Adelaide is taking my portrait, mother—oh! I forgot it was a secret," as Adelaide gave Daisy a warning look.

"Pray don't tire yourself with sitting for a portrait, my darling. Miss Cromwell, you should have asked whether I approved it. Dr. Brocklehurst was so very decided about over-fatigue."

"But, mother, I *like* it so much; and Miss Cromwell reads, and we *do* so enjoy ourselves. Pray let me go on sitting."

"Well, we must be very careful. And are you using oil-paints, Miss Millington?"

"No; I am only trying a little water-colour sketch."

"Very well. I must forbid oils, as the smell is so unwholesome; only be very careful, Miss Cromwell, that Daisy is not over-fatigued."

Daisy had possessed herself of Adelaide's hand.

and they went together to the upper floor, Miss Cromwell waiting to receive a great many orders from Lady Anna.

The little room next Adelaide's bedroom was now given to her for a sitting-room, and here the portrait was in progress. Adelaide had indeed no reason to complain of the accommodation offered her, and she told herself she had everything she could wish for, *but*—an important "but"—sympathy! She missed Hester and her mother, and the admiration they had lavished on her performances. She missed gentle Lady Mary, and if it had not been for Daisy she would have felt more lonely; and she began to hunger for the interest and praise which, when she had them, she was sometimes inclined to resent.

Adelaide had paid her visits to the Uffizi and Pitti Palace, and had taken that cursory glance at the pictures which on a first visit is almost inevitable.

Miss Cromwell had been her companion, and had hurried her on without allowing her time to make up her mind *which* picture she should try to copy. For it had come to "trying" now. Some of the best works on the easels in the "tribune" at the Uffizi had struck her as almost identical with the original, and the question arose: "Shall I ever do as well?" One little dark-eyed student had produced what seemed to Adelaide a very faithful copy of the Madonna del Cardellino, and she meditated over it rather sadly, and a sigh escaped her.

The little artist turned quickly, and smiled, and Adelaide said :

"Com' è bello!" To her surprise the answer was in English.

"Yes; one of the loveliest pictures in the world. I don't mean mine," she said, laughing. "How can a copy, even the best, be the same as the reality?"

"Yours is very like the original."

"Like! ah! the same and not the same. The spirit of Raffaelle is in that picture; and mine—mine —well—I paint for my living!"

"Have you made up your mind which picture you will copy, Adelaide?" Daisy asked, when she had nestled comfortably in a chair, while Adelaide was arranging her colours and wiping her brushes.

"No; besides, I must get a *permesso* first; and somehow I feel rather afraid of beginning in public."

"I hope I shall be allowed to go to the galleries soon. Mother thinks I should get too tired—but I should not. That beautiful picture with the bird and the Lord's hand softly touching it! Ah! I *should* love to have that copied. Do try, Adelaide! all for *me*, you know—my very own. The photograph is lovely, but I should like it coloured."

"You shall have a copy when I can make a fair one," Adelaide said. "Now please turn your head on one side, and put your hand under your chin. Yes, that is right."

"I suppose Miss Cromwell is not coming to read

to-day. I don't mind; I like talking to you. Isn't it nice that Percival is coming at Christmas? I do long for Percival. We had such a happy time at Willesford while mother was gone to see Aunt Mary. Do you know, I have felt better ever since. I had set myself against girls of my age, and was so shy and stupid. But Barbara and Rose were so nice; and of course I wished to have Rose here in Florence, and then you came instead—and I *could* not like anyone better than I like you. So it is all right—for *me* at least. Rose was, I know, disappointed, and I often wish father had not told her about it, till he was sure she was coming. Adelaide, do you know *why* all the pictures here in Florence are pictures of sacred things? Now, no one in England paints the Madonna, and lovely little angels, and saints. I went to the Academy when we came back from Cannes, and most of the pictures were of smart ladies, and stories out of novels; and in Paris, at the Salon, they were all so awful, and of such dreadful things, that mother took me away—I could not bear to look at them. I can't quite understand it, can you? I mean how it is people don't paint beautiful Madonnas, and Apostles, and saints now?"

"I suppose it is," Adelaide said, "that in the days when there were few books, and artists only painted for churches and monasteries, they represented what was wanted to teach the people about the life of our Lord and the disciples, and thus to fasten on their minds the story of the childhood of

Jesus, and the sufferings of those who suffered for His sake—the martyrs and prophets, and all that happened in the Bible history. Art was then the great teacher—people learned by the eye when there were no books, or at least very few."

"Fancy the world without books! and without the Bible! I cannot fancy it—can you, Adelaide?"

"I cannot fancy life without books of any kind," Adelaide said indifferently.

"But the Bible is *the* book. It is the most beautiful book to *read*. Don't you know what I mean?"

Adelaide was always honest, and she did not like even to this child—I ought to say, especially to this child—to profess anything she did not really feel.

If she had been pressed for an answer, she would have said the Bible was not the most beautiful book to her, and that there were many she read oftener, and with greater pleasure.

Daisy watched Adelaide's face as she mixed some more colours on her palette, and repeated her question.

"Don't you know what I mean?"

"Yes, dear, I know what *you* mean," she replied. "Do try and sit still, just for a few minutes."

"But you like me to talk; you said so the other day. You said it brought out my expression; didn't you?"

"Yes; but I am now trying to get your arm right. Arms and hands are so troublesome."

They were indeed, to judge by results. If the

fisher-boy's arm was stiff and wooden, what was Daisy's? And, if it had been held out straight, it would have been longer than herself! Had Adelaide been trained in an art-school, she would have been taught to study models of hands, feet, and arms; and she would have been led to the study of anatomy and the right understanding of the framework of the figure, which cannot be dispensed with, if anything good is to be achieved in "the art that can immortalize."

She had just determined to get rid of Daisy's hand and arm, by concealing them by some drapery drawn over them, when Miss Cromwell appeared.

"There are visitors downstairs," she said. "A Mr. Lysaght and his sister. I could not catch her name. She is a very fashionable personage indeed."

Presently Sam's footsteps were heard; and he came to say:

"Miss Millington is to go down to the drawing-room on the first *piano*."

The order was given in rather a peremptory fashion, and Adelaide's colour rose as she said:

"Will you tell Lady Anna that I am very much engaged with Miss Margaret's portrait?"

Sam looked doubtful about delivering this message; and Miss Cromwell said:

"Oh, you really had better go downstairs. Lady Anna won't like it if you don't! Pray go."

But Adelaide still went on painting, and took no further notice of the summons. Sam departed; and

Daisy, who had watched Adelaide's face, and saw that she looked annoyed, said:

"Perhaps mother thinks you would like to see the visitors. I will sit very still while you are gone, and Miss Cromwell will read to me. I won't move, I promise, if you go for a few minutes."

"I don't wish to go, dear," Adelaide said; and she thought how she disliked the idea of Mr. Lysaght hearing her sent for, as if she were a child, or worse, a dependent!

"I am a guest, it is true; but I am not a welcome one. Lady Mary, kind as she meant to be, made a mistake; but I made a greater in coming here."

Again steps were heard coming along the corridor, and voices and laughter; and the door opened to admit Mrs. Murchison, who came gaily in, saying:

"As you would not come down to see me, I have come to see you. I am so fond of painting, but not figures; I sketch." Then Mrs. Murchison greeted Daisy with a kiss, and going to the rather high window, looked out.

"Why, this is like the view birds must have from their nests," she said, "over the tree-tops. You can see Fiesole. I cannot go into raptures about Florence. Godfrey made me go up to Fiesole the other day; but the church was so damp and musty, it made him cough. We are here for his health: he has had something wrong with his lungs." Then Mrs. Murchison turned from the window, talking all the time. "Ah! this is a portrait—gold hair and blue eyes. It is meant for you, little Daisy, I suppose. You see, I know your name already. Well, as far as eyes and hair are concerned, it is like you; don't think me rude, Miss Millington; you know we artists are allowed to criticize each other. But, I am afraid, the figure is out of drawing. The child's head is much too small in proportion to the figure. I see you have put a convenient bit of—lace, is it?—over the arm and hand. I am up to all these little dodges. I made a sketch last evening, of San Miniato and the Arno from our windows, and gave the cleverest turn, to hide a boat which did not please me, by putting a larger one just before it. It is a pretty sketch, and a good sunset sky. I hope you will come and see us. Ah! here is Godfrey at last. He and Lady Anna have been talking secrets, and were so glad to dispose of me!"

Mrs. Murchison's chatter, rapid and discursive, fairly bewildered Adelaide. She smarted too, as all sensitive people do smart, under the lash of her criticism—delivered, it is true, in a jocose fashion, but from a vantage-ground of superiority that was in itself irritating.

Before Mr. Lysaght had time to speak—for the ascent up the stairs had made him breathless—his sister attacked him to come and look at Miss Millington's picture—a portrait of Lady Anna's little girl.

In a moment Adelaide had swept the block from the easel, and, turning it with its face to the wall, said: "The portrait is not finished. I do not wish anyone to see it."

Poor Adelaide's voice showed that she was annoyed, and her face grew crimson. She was grateful to Mr. Lysaght for taking no notice of his sister's remark or her own; and then Lady Anna came rustling in. There was always a rustle when she moved, though her movements were abundantly dignified and slow. Still, she never failed to be heard as well as seen.

"I have ordered tea in the drawing-room on this floor. Shall we all migrate there? This little room is only used by Miss Millington for her painting. . . Now, my darling Daisy, come with us. You have been here quite long enough. Miss Millington, please remember that Daisy is not to exceed half an hour, sitting as a study for your picture."

"These are beautiful rooms!" Mrs. Murchison exclaimed; "and I believe we should have been better here than by the Arno. What a suite!—one, two, three, four, five rooms, and what enchanting old mirrors and pictures and dear little beds! How different from our ugly erections in England, where, instead of being made subordinate in rooms, the beds stare you in the face. You are very fortunate, Lady Anna, to have secured two such *piani*. But you cannot use all the rooms, surely."

"No; but after Christmas I expect some friends to visit us. My cousin and her daughter and my nephew Percival Clyffe may turn up any day. You know him, I think."

"I don't, but Godfrey does. They are both briefless barristers; and I think it is as well Godfrey gets no briefs. He is not strong enough. I have really come out to take care of him; and he is not half grateful to me. Godfrey, look at this old bit of Sèvres china. I wonder the people left anything so precious about."

Lady Anna smiled.

"You must not think many little decorations belong to the old Marchese. I cannot live in bare rooms; and last year at Cannes I was rather celebrated for having the prettiest and most home-like rooms in the Belle Vue Hotel. We always buy things on the spot, and get rid of them when we leave a place. I have spent two mornings already in the shops here."

"To some purpose," sighed Mrs. Murchison. "Poor people like me must be content with hanging up a few bits of Liberty silk, and some cheap Florentine crockery."

When Lady Anna and Mrs. Murchison had got into the drawing-room, which was on the further side of the corridor, Sam had arrived with tea.

"Where is Godfrey?" Mrs. Murchison exclaimed. "I thought he was following us. He must have gone downstairs by mistake. Perhaps he is making friends with your little girl. How dreadfully delicate she looks! What advice have you had for her?"

This was a little too familiar for Lady Anna's taste, and she was thinking that Percival Clyffe's friend was fairly agreeable; but his sister was *not* a very desirable acquaintance—a person to be repressed and not encouraged, or she might become troublesome.

" My daughter is stronger than she was, or we should have resorted to the Riviera for this winter. There is more to interest her father in Florence, and he is, of course, our first consideration."

Lady Anna really believed in this last assertion, and those who deceive themselves, generally contrive to deceive other people.

" Shall I give you sugar, Mrs. Murchison?"

" No, thanks. Why, Godfrey, where have you been?—flirting with Miss Millington, and renewing your first acquaintance at the station? For you know, Lady Anna, my brother performed the office of knight errant to Miss Millington, and kept me waiting at the station on the night of our arrival in Florence, till I got quite savage with him."

" Really!" was all Lady Anna vouchsafed in reply. " This is a pleasant room, Mr. Lysaght, is it not? I prefer it to the l ower *piano*. But I could not undergo the fatigue of mounting those stairs very often. When my cousin arrives this suite will be given up to her and her daughter. Where is Daisy—my little girl?" Lady Anna asked.

" She is trying to persuade Miss Millington to come and join us, apparently with no effect."

Lady Anna's brow clouded, and her face assumed an expression which those who knew her well always understood. She turned to the footman, who was handing the cakes to Mrs. Murchison.

"Tell Mrs. Gray to let Miss Cowper-Smith know I wish her to come into the drawing-room."

This seemed a very roundabout way of capturing Daisy, and Mr. Lysaght said:

"Shall I call her, Lady Anna? She is close at hand in the next room."

"Oh, I will not trouble you," Lady Anna said, rising herself, and going to the door which communicated with the next room. For in Florence all rooms communicate with each other by the little doors cleverly contrived, painted or papered like the wall, and only noticeable by the brass handle, which, when turned, opens the door."

"Margaret, my love!"

"Yes, mother."

"Come to tea, and talk to Mr. Lysaght and Mrs. Murchison."

"Mother! I want Adelaide to come, and she won't. I have been trying to make her, and so did Mr. Lysaght. *Do* ask her to come!"

But Lady Anna had possessed herself of Daisy's hand, and gently drew her with her into the room; Adelaide meanwhile escaping to her own apartment, at the further end of the long suite of rooms.

"I think it is a pity you did not go, Miss Millington," Miss Cromwell said. " You let Lady Anna get the upper hand: for myself, I know that I must submit, but you are really different, and quite independent. And how patronizing and disagreeable that Mrs. Murchison was! I never saw a brother and sister so different: one so frivolous and 'made up,' and the other so solemn and grave."

Adelaide did not feel disposed to enter into any further discussion about Mr. Lysaght and his sister with Miss Cromwell, and, taking out her writing-case, went on with her letters—one to Hester and the other to her mother.

Hester's letters were very long and intricate; full of happiness and joyful anticipation. From Hester's account the Squire was not really better; but Lady Mary would not say much about him, even to her mother. Mr. Birley had gone up to the Court twice, but he had refused to see him, and Mr. Birley said it was really very shocking that he would not see his own clergyman—for Dr. Townley considered his condition very critical.

"It will really be a merciful release," Hester said, using a stereotyped expression; "and if he does not die soon, Cousin Mary will be the first to go."

The next morning found Adelaide once more at the Uffizi, and she was recognised by the little bright-eyed artist, who was putting her finishing touches to "The Madonna del Cardellino," and listening to the criticisms of an old man, who haunted the galleries, and considered himself a judge of art:

"A little too much shadow here," he was saying; "and a few touches would put the arm right."

The artist nodded and smiled, and then, as the old man passed on, she said: "He always has some improvements to suggest; it pleases him and does not vex me. But I think I shall not follow them this time."

"I am longing to begin," Adelaide said. "Will you tell me where to get the necessary *permesso?*"

"Oh, yes; I will go with you, if you like. But, perhaps"—then there was a pause—"perhaps it would be as well to begin with something simple. I am going to the Accademia, to copy the head of Savonarola by Fra Bartolommeo, next week. If you like, we could work together there. There are two little angels of Andrea del Sarto's which many artists find tolerably easy. Would you like to try them? I shall be there on Monday early. The light so soon fades at this time of year; so it is well to get a long morning."

"I do not know where to get a proper easel and canvas. Will you help me to do so, and give me the address of the shop where to buy them?"

The little artist tore a leaf from a note-book, and wrote down the names of two shops—one in the Borgo Lorenzo, the other in the Via Pucci—where the artists' requisites could be bought.

"You are English, I suppose?" Adelaide said, for though a slight foreign accent, and the quick gestures of her small hands, seemed almost to point to an

Italian birth, she spoke English with perfect ease and fluency.

"My father was English," she answered, "my mother Italian. I will write my address on this paper," and she wrote, "Lucia Campbell, Piazza Cavour." "I must bid you good-bye now. Buon giorno, a rivederci!" And then, gathering up her brushes and palettes, she tripped away.

Adelaide was left alone, standing before the picture, and presently the old man returned who had spoken to Lucia about her painting.

"You are admiring that copy. You would admire it still more, signorina, if you knew, as I know, that the artist keeps a family by her brave exertions —a sickly mother, a blind brother, and, for years, a father also, but she is rid of that encumbrance— he died a few years ago. She is a wonderful little girl. But I wish she had just touched that arm. Yes; it is a mistake to have such a broad light there; but young folks are always slow to take advice from their elders! I *was* a painter," the old man said, with a deep sigh, "till God was pleased to afflict me, and take away the use of my right arm. See, signorina," he said, pointing to it, "it is withered and helpless. Yes, it has been a bitter trial. Well, God knows best—God knows best!" he said, as he took a pinch of snuff from an ancient tortoiseshell box with silver hinges, and went to another room to offer criticisms which no one heeded.

The figure of Andrea Maura was well known in the

galleries of Florence, and he was looked upon as a harmless old man, who believed he had been once an artist himself, second only to "The Faultless Painter." But no one else shared his faith. Tradition said he had never sold any of his pictures, and that they existed only in his imagination. He lived in the glories of his past, and no one really cared to dispel the illusion. It is well for some of us that nothing can take away happy memories of our past, even when they are touched by the sadness of contrast with the present. There are few who would give up the beauty of a distant time, even if it is true, as the poet says—

> "That the Past must always win
> A beauty from its being far,
> And orb into the perfect star
> We saw not when we walked therein."

When in those solemn galleries at Florence, Adelaide forgot her inharmonious surroundings at the Piazza d'Azeglio. What did it matter that Lady Anna patronized her, and that she was daily made to feel more and more that a kindness had been done her, for which she was to be grateful, but never to allow her gratitude to be mingled with any demonstration of affection?

The Lady Annas of the world always manage to take off the keen edge of appreciation of the favours they bestow, by levying a tax on them; and perhaps a little feeling of jealousy was rising in the mother's heart as she saw how Margaret clung to Adelaide and cared more for her society than for that of anyone else.

Several masters were engaged for Daisy. Italian, French, and German must be spoken by a girl who was to occupy Daisy's position in society; but she was not to be teased with grammar, or exercises, or dictation. She was to be helped to read and converse, but not worried in any way. As to music, a violin-master was engaged; but, like the other professors, so many restrictions were laid on him that, though he liked to receive fees for his lessons, he felt almost as if he were taking them as a gift.

But no restrictions can crush a real love of, and even genius for music. Daisy made her violin speak, and, though her fingers wanted the practice her mother denied them, her bow never scraped. The purest tones came to delight the ear of the little enthusiastic signor, who was ready at the same time to tear his hair with vexation that the signora was so blind, so deaf, so stupid, as to limit Daisy's lessons to playing airs, and forbid exercises as too exhausting.

It was a large but poorly furnished *piano* in the Piazza Cavour where Lucia Campbell lived and laboured for those who were dependent on her. She was the only support of her mother and blind brother, and a querulous sister who professed to perform all the household duties, but did so very inefficiently and with but a bad grace. She had about her all the depression of an Englishwoman who, under adverse circumstances, can take no bright view of life, looks on duty as drudgery, and pines for what is denied her.

Lucia, on the contrary, had all the fire and buoyancy of the Italian nature. She was satisfied with very little, and was content with a dinner of herbs, like most of her country-people. If only the salads and macaroni had been seasoned with love, Lucia would have been quite happy to live on cold cauliflower served with oil and salt, and other compounds made up from the vegetable world.

It was one bright morning when November was close at hand that Lucia received her fee for the copy of the Madonna del Cardellino. Her spirits were as bright as the morning, and she was singing as she went about her household duties—duties which Marietta undertook, but never performed.

"Come, Marietta," she said, "make haste and help Giovanni to dress while I finish the clearance of this room. Oh, what dust! I must get a broom."

"I swept the floor yesterday: my back ached so I could scarcely stand up afterwards. You have no pity—none, Lucia!"

"Pity! Yes, I have pity, you poor child! I can only say, 'Patienza; better times will come for you.'"

"I don't think it; it is all mother's talk. It is nonsense to expect we shall ever get any money from that grandfather who hated our father. He will hate us for his sake."

"Well, then, we will go on earning money. I

have enough now to pay our rent up to May, and I will give you a fine new gown, Marietta, and something over our expenses—oh! mi fa tanto piacere!—for I got another commission to draw Savonarola's head. It is joy to me to paint him!'

'Joy! I think it is a hideous picture!"

" Non fa niente, piccina mia!" Lucia replied.

And now a shrill and high-pitched voice was heard, and a dark-eyed woman with a sallow skin, and yet with the remains of beauty of a certain type, came in, saying in English which had a more decided Italian accent than her daughters':

" Do not speak Italian! I do tell you fifty times a day to keep going your English! Your father did say if you talk Italian you have no chance. Look on me! Do I not speak English? Do I not try to obey the wishes of your poor, poor father? And *you*—you——"

Signora Campbell's voice broke down into a sort of angry wail and into Italian *malgré lui*, and became so voluble and excited that it was difficult to guess her meaning and catch now and then such words as "Lo dico per vostro bene! Volete tacere!"—the last injunction being wholly unnecessary as far as her daughters were concerned, who knew by experience that any remonstrance only made the torrent of their mother's speeches flow more fiercely.

It was after all but words. Signora Campbell forgot to be angry quite as quickly as she remembered to pour forth her indignation on her girls, and blind Giovanni coming in now to ask for his coffee and morning mess of macaroni, she busied herself in preparing breakfast.

Giovanni was a thin, fragile-looking boy of eighteen; his sisters were older. Lucia was twenty-two; Marietta twenty. By common consent Giovanni was treated as the baby, and his infirmities endeared him to his sisters, though they were a vexation to his mother. She was always throwing out hints that if only her poor afflicted one had been like other boys there would be some hope of future good for him. As it was, how could he ever make his way, or take his right position?

What that right position was, neither Lucia nor Marietta exactly knew. Lucia had gone through many terrible scenes in her early youth, caused by the perpetual misconduct of her father. At last his intemperance brought about a state of imbecility and irritability, which rendered every one about him miserable. The little old man in the galleries spoke the truth when he told Adelaide that his death was a happy deliverance to his children. In a short interval of sanity and something like a return to natural affection before his death, Lucia's father had committed to her a sealed letter, making her solemnly swear that she would never reveal its existence, or open it, till she could obey the instructions which he gave her in another envelope addressed to her, and never to be revealed to her mother till the moment came for opening the sealed packet.

Lucia put both packets away, and really felt no strong temptation to tell either her mother or sister what had passed between her and her father. She looked upon the whole thing as one of her father's frequent hallucinations; and engrossed with her work and her brave efforts to keep her mother and brother and sister in tolerable comfort, she may be said almost to have forgotten the two packets, which were carefully locked up in a small desk, which her father had given her when only a little girl.

Of course, her mother's hints about Giovanni's future and an implacable grandfather sometimes awoke conjectures in her mind. But all that she really knew of her parents was the fact that her father, when under age, had married her mother, who had been a singer, in no very high place in the professional world, and who soon after her own birth had lost her voice, never to regain it, thus cutting off her means of earning her living; while her father, growing reckless, had wasted a small fortune inherited from his mother, and had, by his intemperate habits, reduced himself and his family to the very verge of starvation.

Signora Campbell had taught music, at very low terms, and had also professed to teach English to her own countrywomen. But in no way was she a success; and had it not been for Lucia's exertions, absolute want would have stared the family in the face.

Lucia's taste for art had developed at an early age, and her copy of one of the pictures in the Accademia had attracted the notice of an artist. He had seen her latent power, and had taken her as a pupil in his studio, with no fee. Lucia made herself useful to him in many ways, and fully repaid his kindness. The old man died some three or four years before this time, and Lucia had gained sufficient skill to obtain work as a copyist.

The American and English visitors at Florence make a continuous demand for copies of the well-known pictures, and certain dealers are the medium, who pay the artist a fixed percentage on the sums for which the pictures are sold. But in some rare instances the copyist gets a commission direct, perhaps through the kindness of a friend, or perhaps through a copy from his hand attracting notice in one of the galleries, when still on the easel.

This commission which Lucia had obtained to copy Savonarola's portrait in the Accademia was a case in point. Godfrey Lysaght had seen the admirable copy of the Madonna in the Uffizi, and had entered into conversation with the artist.

The commission had been given, and a liberal price offered, and Lucia, full of hope and pleasure at having a direct commission, on this bright morning finished her domestic duties, and prepared to set off to the Accademia.

"If it is an English gentleman with whom you speak, Lucia, mind you speak English. You are so ready to speak Italian, and I would have you all remember your poor departed father was English. Ah! how he did praise *my* power of speech in his own tongue long ago—long ago! Ah! ah!"

"We all speak the English language like natives, Madre mia, do we not, Giovanni?" Lucia said, laughing and bending over her blind brother to kiss him. "Say now, Giovanni carissimo, is there anything I can do for you before I go?"

Giovanni shook his head.

"No, sorella mia, no, except"—Giovanni put his arm round his sister's neck and drew her head close to his face—"except to promise you will take me to the English Church on Sunday."

"Si, si, darling, I will take you, unless you have coughed all night, and the wind is cold. A rivederci; and here is your violin, I have put in the new string.'

Then she was gone, and with her the sunshine went out of the room.

Marietta and her mother began to wrangle about some trifling matter, and instead of sitting down to the mending of her own wardrobe, which was sorely needed, Marietta took up a Tauchnitz volume, which was in a torn and dilapidated condition, and with her feet on one chair, and leaning back in another, she soon forgot her promise to Lucia, that she would mend the great rent in her striped skirt, and not cover it with a gay-coloured upper-garment till this was done.

Signora Campbell made a hasty toilette, and very

soon set out with a little basket to the Mercato Vecchio to make purchases, indulging in a little bit of additional finery for herself, on account of the larger sum than usual that the bread-winner had put into her hand that morning. That brave little bread-winner, who was so happy to have her commission to execute! And it was only when she arrived at the Accademia that it struck her that the English girl with the deep-set, serious eyes and resolute mouth would be waiting for her.

Adelaide was waiting, all impatience, to begin. Her folding-easel and box of oil-paints and large canvas were already in the lobby, deposited there by a boy, who had been added to the staff of servants in the Piazza d'Azeglio, and who had been promptly buttoned up in a page's tight suit, which was altogether out of keeping with Carlo's dark olive skin and laughing wide mouth, his chin resting uneasily on the stiff collar, which seemed to him a badge of superiority, and therefore must be endured with a broad grin, however uneasy he felt.

CHAPTER VII.

SAN MINIATO.

THE *permesso* was obtained, and Adelaide found herself before the lovely cherubs of Andrea del Sarto, which have a wonderful charm about them. The half-unrolled scrolls, the uplifted fingers, the sweet childish faces with rosy lips half-opened, have attracted many artists, and have become almost as familiar by photographs and copies, as the sweet boy angels under the Madonna di San Sisto, and the two little cherubs reading from the same scroll at the foot of Raffaelle's Madonna del Baldacchino, in the gallery of the Pitti Palace.

"Yes, they are beautiful," Adelaide said; "and I think I can copy them. They will be a good beginning, and not difficult."

Lucia laughed.

"They are not too easy to reproduce," she said; "there is a great deal of drawing required to get those fat legs in their right position. You have got a very large canvas, but you can take off a corner. Don't put your easel in front of the picture, you will not catch the right light; here to the left is the place.

And where is your chalk? Ah! have you brought none? I can lend you mine. Now, if I were you, I would sketch in the figure on the right hand first, and then the other; you will get 'mixed' if you do both at once. I must leave you now, and go to my beloved Savonarola. Did you bring your luncheon with you? I always do. Addio."

And then Lucia was gone, and Adelaide was left alone in the long wide gallery, with her blank canvas, her easel, and her own thoughts.

Before she began to sketch out her first cherub she took a turn round the gallery, pausing before the Vision of Saint Bernard, by Fra Bartolommeo, and the Assumption by Perugino. She felt half inclined to move her easel and copy the two angels with their mandolines. The figures were more fully draped, and the arms would be easier. But what about the hands, instinct with life, as the beautifully-formed fingers played on the strings or handled the bow?

"Perhaps I had better hold to the cherubs," was Adelaide's final resolution; "they will not take very long to paint, and then I *must* try Albertinelli's 'Salutation,' in the Uffizi. There is plenty of time before I leave Florence. After all, it is worth having Lady Anna's patronage, to secure a quiet morning like this with all these pictures round me. It will be delightful to show what I have done to Hester, and Lady Mary shall see I have made the best use of the advantages she got for me."

So Adelaide returned to the contemplation of the

cherubs, and, seating herself on the high wooden stool, began that most important part of a study—whether from the life or from a cast—drawing in the outline of the figure.

As most novices would have done, she made her first cherub much too large, and the arm holding the scroll would come in the wrong place; the hand was much too near the knee, and the end of the scroll touched the foot, instead of reaching halfway down the chubby calf. Again and again Adelaide rubbed out the lines, and then resorted to that most delusive consolation—that in colouring she could make it right. Then there was the hand with the uplifted finger—it *would* come in the wrong place, for where the curly head of the least prominent of the two cherubs was sketched in, the forefinger of his companion touched his nose, instead of being just below the chin.

"It is wrong, somehow—it is all wrong," Adelaide sighed. "I think I will only make a study of the heads, and leave the figures. After all, it is the expression of the faces I want to get."

Then all the "bodies" were rubbed out, and the two heads and faces sketched in, with tolerable success.

"I will just put in the first flesh-tints, and stop for to-day," she thought.

There were several people in the gallery near—strangers who were passing through Florence on their way to Rome, and rushing through the galleries and churches at the utmost speed. Two or three artists had encamped before the great picture of the Assumption, and were busily at work.

Adelaide found some difficulty in mixing her flesh-tints; they were too pink, and too yellow, and then too gray. She scarcely liked to confess to herself how discouraged she felt; and when she passed through the room where Lucia was intent on Savonarola, she was surprised to see how rapidly the head was growing under her hand.

One of the passing visitors I have mentioned came up, and looked at the picture.

"What an ugly face! Oh! I see! It is that man whom Mrs. Oliphant writes about in the 'Makers of Florence.'"

"And George Eliot," said her companion. "Have you never read 'Romola?'"

"I am not sure. I fancy I found it dull; do move on. We shall never do San Marco, if you don't make haste."

"That is what people call *doing* Florence; then they proceed to do Pisa, and Siena, and Rome, and Naples."

Adelaide said this aloud, and Lucia turned her head. She had been far too much engrossed with her work to heed the chatter of the two girls, who had now passed on.

"Are you tired?" Lucia asked. "How have you got on?"

"Not very well. I have changed my mind, and I mean only to paint the heads of those angels or cherubs, whichever it is right to call them. You have only a head. It is much easier to accomplish that."

"Easy!" Lucia looked up. "When I sit down before this I feel I am almost helpless to produce what I see before me. Here is the gentleman who gave me the commission."

Godfrey Lysaght bowed gravely to both girls, and Lucia said: "You did not expect to see much done already, signor."

"No; I am not come even to look," he said. "I can trust you to accomplish this portrait in your own time, and in your best manner."

"No one could call that face beautiful," Adelaide said shortly.

"It is too massive to be strictly beautiful; but there is a peculiar charm in it, for me at least. Savonarola is the presiding spirit of Florence."

"Not before Dante!" Lucia said quickly; "not before Dante, signor. Dante must always hold his own place."

"Yes; but there is something less attractive to me in the personality of the lonely exile, whose love for the City of Flowers turned to bitterness, than in that of the man on whose lips the multitudes in the vast Duomo hung spell-bound, and who laid all their treasures at his feet, as proofs of the power that was in him."

"I know," Adelaide said, "it was a grand life; but he left nothing behind him to remain, like the 'Divine Commedia,' a monument of his genius for all time."

"We can never measure the power or effect of influence," Godfrey said. "A life like Savonarola's is its own monument, and may stir many humble hearts to devotion to God's service which Dante's splendid genius cannot reach. My sister is in a carriage waiting for me. Will you drive with us to San Miniato, and come back to luncheon to Paoli's? I fear I must not ask you to accompany us," Godfrey Lysaght said to Lucia.

"Oh no, signor; I have to work till daylight fails. I have my luncheon here," she said, pointing to a little basket, which contained a roll and an orange. "If you are going to San Miniato, do not forget to look at the sleeping cardinal in the side chapel. I often pay him a visit."

"Perhaps I ought to let Lady Anna know I am not coming home to luncheon," Adelaide said; "but I do not know whether it matters, for no one will miss me except Daisy."

"We can leave a message if you like, as we pass the Piazza d'Azeglio."

"I don't think it matters," Adelaide said; "thanks."

Mrs. Murchison was growing impatient, and greeted her brother with:

"What an age you have been, Godfrey! You seem fascinated by that little artist. Ah! Miss Millington, I am very glad to see you. Yes, come, by all means. You must be glad to get away from that stiff-and-starched Lady Anna. Goodness! how I

PIAZZA DELLA SIGNORIA, FLORENCE.

enjoyed shocking her! for she *was* shocked with me. I don't care two straws for people like her; and I hope you don't allow her to sit upon you, Miss Millington. Snub her well, and she won't try it on again. Godfrey, *do* pull the rug over your knees. The wind is cold; and though I suppose it is treason to say so of Florence, I consider it colder than England. We should have gone to the Riviera, only you were so set upon the beauties of Florence. I have had a long talk this morning with an old gentleman in the hotel. He evidently has a different opinion of me from Lady Anna. He actually complimented me on my knowledge of Italian history, and said he supposed I was an author; and if not, that I ought to be, for I expressed myself so lucidly! He is a learned professor, so I was much flattered. I shall take his advice, I think, and get my novel ready for the press, in spite of your scoffs, Godfrey; for you know you think I am incapable."

"I think you capable of many things, Theresa; but as to authorship, the field is too full of labourers to give new hands a chance."

"Oh, I don't know. There is always room for a brilliant society novel, with plenty of sensation, about dukes and marquises. You write yourself, so you should not grudge me a little scrap of your talent. Did you know he was an author, Miss Millington?"

"No," Adelaide said. "What does Mr. Lysaght write?"

"Oh, dull papers on religious and philanthropic

subjects. Godfrey has queer ideas, and so you will find out before long."

Adelaide watched the face opposite her with some interest as Mrs. Murchison thus sketched her brother's character in his presence.

"He is as steady as old Time," she went on, "and thinks heaps of things wicked which I think delightful; and yet we manage to jog on pretty well together. And I take care of him, and prevent him from killing himself, for which he ought to be grateful, don't you think so? He would poke about in the East End of London, and live in a hole in Whitechapel, if I consented. But I don't consent, so here we are; and very kind it is of me to take such good care of him. Now, Godfrey, you ought to say something pretty in return, or Miss Millington will think I am indulging in fictions."

Mr. Lysaght was too well used to his sister's chatter to pay much heed to it, or he might have rejoined that what kindness there was, was decidedly on his side. Mrs. Murchison was the widow of a young soldier who had fallen in one of "England's little wars;" and, finding it impossible to make the two ends of her income meet, Mr. Lysaght had taken her into his charge, and preserved her from running up bills and other extravagances, which, it must be confessed, was a brotherly act, more deserving of gratitude than her sisterly solicitude about his health, and preventing, as she said, his pursuing his labours of charity in Whitechapel.

A rumour had reached Mr. Lysaght, as Percival Clyffe had told Lady Anna, that his succession to the estate of Cruttwell was rendered doubtful by the fact that Mr. Beauchamp had a son who had married and left children. Where these children lived, or whether they existed at all, was yet an unsolved mystery, and Mr. Lysaght carefully kept the possibility to himself. Lady Anna had, however, questioned him on the day of his first visit to the Piazza d'Azeglio, and said that the account of "dear Mr. Beauchamp" was decidedly worse; adding that her sweet sister was a martyr, and yet, like many other martyrs, a saint who never allowed anyone even to pity her, but accepted her lot with the most beautiful resignation.

The drive to San Miniato on this lovely autumn day was delightful indeed. The zigzag road, which leads by slow degrees to the plateau before the Church of San Salvatore al Monte, opens out a more enchanting view of Florence at every turn.

The carriage was left below the church, and Adelaide lingered behind her companions to enjoy herself undisturbed by Mrs. Murchison's ceaseless rattle of small talk, which always had some reference to herself.

Fortunately for Adelaide, Mrs. Murchison joined company with the old Professor, whom she had fascinated at the hotel. He was seen labouring up the steep ascent, which leads by many steps through the cypress avenue to the plateau where she was standing. She greeted him with an enthusiasm which flattered him, and immediately began to air her superficial knowledge, gathered mostly from guide-books, about Michael Angelo's fortifications and the grandeur of the work which had thus made Florence memorable!

The Professor was short-sighted, and he may be forgiven for his belief that Mrs. Murchison's roses and cherry lips were the token of youth in its first bloom. He marvelled that one so young should be a widow, and looked upon Mrs. Murchison as a marvel of literary culture and youth and beauty combined.

It is often so. The counterfeit passes for real gold, and, while men are ready to accept it, we must not be too hard on the anxiety which many women show to keep up the delusion for themselves and others.

Mr. Lysaght was quite ready to leave his sister to her ancient admirer, and he fell back to join Adelaide. Only her eyes told her appreciation of the view stretched out on all sides. This suited Mr. Lysaght, and they walked silently through the thick walls of the fortification about which the Professor and Mrs. Murchison were so learnedly discoursing, to the gate which is kept by a *custode*, and, when opened, admits to the piazza of the Church of San Miniato.

From the marble steps of the old church Adelaide looked over that loveliest view, which remains a joy for ever, to those who gaze upon it, and make it a part of themselves henceforth. The widening Arno, the vineyards and olive-grounds, the encircling hills and distant Carrara Mountains, all bathed in the golden sunshine of this autumn day, with a canopy above of intensest blue, is a picture in itself of unequalled beauty.

But it is not in itself alone that every view of Florence has its peculiar charm. Memories of the buried past start to life: old wars and old conflicts; Florence besieged, and Florence victorious; the Medici triumphant and brought low in alternate succession; the genius of Michael Angelo, now defending the dismantled fortress of the Monte San Miniato, now with his chisel creating the giants in marble, which remain to this day in a grandeur unapproachable, combined with a grace that is inimitable. It is the story that every church and every palace tells in the City of Flowers which gives it a subtle charm—a charm which is like the afterglow of sunset, irradiating the present with the glory of the past—a glory which is chastened and subdued, for it seems to echo the words which are said to have fallen from the lips of the dying Bayard, that knight *sans peur et sans reproche*:

"All things pass away but the love of God. See, then, to it, that thou love and fear God above all things."

Mr. Lysaght was the first to speak.

"Shall we walk through the Campo Santo, or go into the church?"

"I should like to go into the church first."

As they turned to do so, they saw the Professor and Mrs. Murchison, the Professor waving his stick excitedly, and Mrs. Murchison smiling and nodding in reply. She was hearing a lecture on the likeness between San Zeno at Verona and San Miniato at Florence. The nods and wreathed smiles so appreciative of his erudition took the Professor's heart by storm, and "the lovely young creature" gathered from what he said more grains of superficial knowledge, which would serve her in good stead when aired at the *table d'hôte* at the hotel, and be another proof of her culture and historic lore!

"They seem to enjoy each other's society," Mr. Lysaght said. "Theresa has a taste for old fossils, or rather they always seem to have a taste for her."

"Mrs. Murchison is very clever, is she not?" Adelaide asked.

"She has very quick perceptions," was the answer, "and, like many women, catches up more from observation and listening to other people's talk than from books or study. It is an easy way of getting the reputation for culture! Theresa is careful not to get into deep waters, and I am often amused at the skill with which she skims the surface. This is a striking church," he said, abruptly changing the subject.

The first sight of the church of San Miniato awakes, perhaps, more surprise than pleasure. The pavement of the wide nave is marked by wreaths and crosses which show that it is a Campo Santo. The choir is raised above the open crypt, and wide marble stairs lead up to it, from right and left. On a first view, the real grandeur and beauty of the church is perhaps scarcely realized. The frescoes on the walls are a good deal defaced, and of no very especial interest.

"The Medici are here, as everywhere in Florence," Mr. Lysaght said; "you must look at the chapel, built for Piero de Medici, and at the beautiful screen and pulpit. This is your first look; you will find out many beauties for yourself on future visits, and you must get here if possible in the early morning, to see the windows at the back of the choir, which have a wonderful living gold colour when the sun strikes them; and you must get here also at sunset, for then the view through the open west door is something never to be forgotten. But here come my sister and the Professor, full of learned discussions. Let us turn into this side chapel—for there lies one of the most beautiful marble figures in Florence."

"You have been here before, then, often?"

"Yes, when I was very young, with my mother—a mother and a friend such as few men ever possessed."

Then he added in a low tone: "She died here, and lies in the English Cemetery. This chapel was one of her favourite resorts, and so it is mine. It is said of this man that he lived the life of an angel rather than of a man; he was only twenty-six when he died, four hundred years ago. The perfect repose of that face is, to my mind, almost unequalled, and it must have been, I always think, a faithful likeness. Sit down in the episcopal chair, if you like, and look at it at your leisure."

"Oh yes! here is the chapel built by—by—Rossellino." It was Mrs. Murchison's voice. "I do not think it is worth staying here. I do so want you, Professor Scoresby, to tell me about the Greek mosaic. It is called Greek, but is it? You will know, of course, and I want to be instructed."

"You do me too much honour," said the Professor, ambling away, but casting rather longing looks on the image of the young cardinal, as he lay with folded hands in his last long sleep. For centuries that serene face has been gazed on by many and many a traveller, who has now passed away into the eternal silence, into which Jacopo of Portugal passed in his early manhood. Careless eyes may miss the extreme beauty of this figure—the folded hands, the sweet calm lips on which a smile lingers, the easy repose of the stately head, a little turned naturally, as in profound slumber. Above is one of the most lovely of the Madonnas, with her child in her arms, apparently watching the sleeper below. The happy little cherubs who stand one at the head and the other at the feet of the monument have a smile on their faces, as if they wished everyone to feel that to die as Jacopo died was something to give thanks for. Only a short conflict here, in which he devoted the extraordinary gifts God had bestowed on him for His glory, and then the light of His eternal day, shining on him henceforth in His kingdom. Who would mourn for such? and to Adelaide's lips rose the words of the poetess, who lived and loved and died in Florence :

> "Not a tear o'er him must fall ;
> He giveth His belovèd sleep."

When Mrs. Murchison had fluttered away with her old Professor, Mr. Lysaght followed them, and Adelaide was left alone before the sleeping cardinal. There was not a sound to break the stillness when the footsteps of the rest of the party had passed out of hearing, and in that solemn church Adelaide seemed to awake more fully to what, since she had been in Florence, had begun to dawn upon her.

"I have come here to get humble," she thought. "I have had so many to care for me and to flatter me, and here I am alone, except for dear little Daisy. They have told me I was clever, and an artist, and—I know nothing, can do nothing. That frivolous Mrs. Murchison knows ten times as much. What old professor would care to talk to me? I may know, and feel a great deal more than I know; but I can't chatter as she does about painters and poets, and Florentine heroes and saints. As to my art, I will go back to the Accademia and begin those two cherubs once more, and then if

I fail utterly, I will never touch a brush again—never! Only to think of leaving behind a work like this—a beautiful monument of a beautiful life. To achieve something like that is worth living for; but for me——"

Adelaide left the chapel, and going down the nave, went out into the Campo Santo outside. The autumn bloom of the sweet monthly roses filled the air with fragrance; and amongst the pure white crosses of Carrara marble were kneeling, here and there, the friends of those who lay beneath, with offerings of flowery wreaths and crosses in their hands. The ruins of the old Palace of the Mozzi family form a boundary on one side; but all around is a scene of loveliness, which makes this last resting-place of the Florentines a God's-acre indeed.

As soon as Mrs. Murchison came, the charm seemed broken, and Adelaide withdrew into herself; and as they all walked down to the Piazza below the Church of San Salvatore, Mrs. Murchison rallied her on her gravity.

"She thinks me a silly little thing, I know," she said, addressing the Professor. "Well, I find plenty to amuse me in life, though I *can* talk of grave matters sometimes; but I do like a little fun."

Adelaide disliked being talked at, or talked of; and quickened her steps till she gained the stone balustrade from which the view of Florence most familiar to everyone by photographs and pictures is seen. Villas gleaming in the sunshine;—Fiesole rising majestically behind the noble outline of Mount Morello to the westward, and the valley widening eastward towards range upon range of lofty Apennines, the highest of them now just whitened by the first snow of winter. Immediately below were bridges and terraces, the stately tower of the Palazzo Vecchio, the Duomo on which Michael Angelo cast a loving look of farewell when summoned to Rome to work under the rival dome of Saint Peter, Giotto's Campanile, the spires of Santa Croce; and to the left, Santo Spirito, also with its dome, and countless other towers and palace-roofs, rising in every direction. And everywhere the cypress-spires, climbing up every hillside, in stately companies—those trees which, of all others, seem to belong to, and form part of, the land of monasteries and churches, pointing ever upwards; their depth of sombre green contrasting, as no other foliage can contrast, with the radiant sky above them.

The one o'clock *table d'hôte* was long over at Paoli's Hotel, and the sunny Arno was gay with many people in carriages or on foot, as Mrs. Murchison drove up to the door. The four late comers were, with some others, accommodated with the usual course at the end of the long table.

They were not the only late comers; and Mrs. Murchison talked across the table to some of her acquaintances; inquiring where they had been that morning, and whether the eccentric personage with the squint, in gray homespun, had been discovered—an injudicious question, answered by a stout man at some little distance in a grating voice:

"I guess she's my wife; and you bet she is worth two dozen of many a smart fine lady amongst you. A right good one is my wife."

"I am *sure* she is," said Mrs. Murchison. "She has a delightfully good-natured face. I long to make her acquaintance."

But the American gentleman would not be so propitiated.

"Tell you what, miss; it is a grand thing, I guess, to keep straight along the road; and a deal better to have crooked eyes than crooked ways."

If Mrs. Murchison blushed, as perhaps she might, the access of colour did not manifest itself. Her face always looked the same. But Mr. Lysaght said, in a low tone of angry remonstrance:

"I do wish you would be more cautious, Theresa, at any rate in public."

"But this is *not* public, Godfrey; is it, Professor Scoresby? Now, *isn't* he hard on me?"

To this the Professor said, with a bow:

"The young have to buy their experience, madam;" and he inwardly wondered if the lovely creature had noticed his eyes were not quite straight, and if when *he* was absent he was inquired about as that eccentric personage with a squint.

After luncheon Mrs. Murchison invited Adelaide

to ascend to the private sitting-room, which overlooked the Arno and the heights of San Miniato.

"That is Godfrey's corner," she said, pointing to a table covered with books and papers; and here is mine. This was my last sketch, at sunset, from this window."

"It is beautiful!" Adelaide said warmly. "The sky and the reflection in the river are lovely!"

"I am so glad you like it. How are you getting on with your painting?"

"Oh, pretty well! I have begun to copy the two cherubs of Andrea del Sarto in the Accademia. Have you copied any of the pictures?"

"No," Mrs. Murchison said, laughing. "To tell you the truth, I do *not* care for all these saints and angels with their gold rings round their heads. It is all very well to look at one or two; but I get sick of them; and as to Giotto and Cimabue, preserve me from them! I do not believe half the people who profess to care for them *do* care for them; and as to sitting down to copy any of them, in the first place it is hopeless to do so, and in the next I should not have the patience to do more than make a rapid sketch. I like to get everything done off quickly. Now, how long do you think I was at that sketch?"

"Indeed I cannot tell," Adelaide said.

"About two hours. I touched it up a little, of course, at another sitting. You had much better try to sketch, instead of copying old pictures. I play the violin a little, and I sing. I am a Jack-of-all-trades, you see. Are you musical?"

"No; that is, I don't play on any instrument. The children play."

"The children?" Mrs. Murchison said.

"My little step-sisters; they are fifteen and seventeen now, but we call them children."

"By-the-bye," Mrs. Murchison went on, "you live at Dryborough. Godfrey will live there one day. He is coming into property in that neighbourhood; quite in a roundabout way, but he is the heir all the same. His grandfather and Mr. Beauchamp's father were first cousins. His name is Beauchamp Lysaght, this is what the 'B' stands for. We shall be neighbours, perhaps; not that I could live in a dull place all the year. And perhaps Godfrey will marry, and I should not choose to play second fiddle, you know. Not that I think Godfrey *will* marry. His *views* are so extraordinary. He is religious, and philanthropical, and self-denying, and all the rest of it; and there are not many girls who would care to be tied to that sort of thing. Then he is far from strong, poor old fellow; and, as I told you, I have just saved his life by making him come here this winter. I don't say it was not one word for him and two for myself! I am *not* self-denying—quite the contrary. You look so grave and serious, I dare say I am shocking you just as I shocked Lady Anna. I can't help it: I never pretend to be what I am not which is a virtue in these days. I hate shams."

Adelaide was wondering if, indeed, those cherry lips and pencilled eyebrows, with the dark shadows beneath the eyes, which certainly made them wonderfully luminous, were to be reckoned amongst the shams of which Mrs. Murchison expressed her abhorrence.

The ripple of small talk went on ceaselessly, and Adelaide felt bewildered. She had never before met anyone like Mrs. Murchison. It was a new revelation to her—this free and easy chatter, which, though it made a good many detours, as it were, amongst the failings or peculiarities of her neighbours and friends, always came back to that most attractive subject—herself!

"Now," she said, after a pause, "now, tell me about yourself. You must have a bit of romance hidden somewhere; dear old Professor Scoresby said, 'That girl has a history.'"

Adelaide's swift blood rose to her face. "If I had, it could not be of any interest to strangers. As I have not a history, please let me sink at once into the commonplace person I am."

"Commonplace! No, that you are not. Commonplace people do not brave all remarks by wearing large sleeves to their gowns, baggy waists and very big hats. Of course, they are becoming to *you*, but poor little people like me would look absolute *frights* if they ventured on such garments."

"Really!" Adelaide said, with some heat. "I think people ought to please themselves about dress."

"No, no! my dear child. We have a duty to perform to our neighbours, and one of these duties is to make the very best of ourselves. Now, that is a new idea for you, I see; but mind you remember what I say."

"I think," Adelaide said, "I must be going home now. Lady Anna may not like my long absence, which is not explained. Therefore I will say goodbye, please."

"But can you find your way?"

"Oh yes; and if not, I can inquire it at the Library."

"You will probably find Godfrey and the old Professor at Vieusseux's. They frequent the reading-room there. Now, *do* forgive me, but you would look so nice in a high hat with a narrow brim! Those wide hats are *so* trying unless people are tall and can carry them off. Fancy little me in a large hat——"

The large hat had been lying on the table, where Adelaide had laid it, with her gloves and a large fur cape. Mrs. Murchison had snatched it up, and put it on her own head—cautiously, for the curled *toupée* was not precisely indigenous in its growth—and pirouetting round, said, as she glanced at herself in a long, rather dull mirror:

"After all, it is rather piquante. I declare I'll try one; only I am so much taller than you are, in spite of people calling me *petite*."

"Will you give me my hat, Mrs. Murchison,

please?" Adelaide said, in a low voice of suppressed vexation.

"Now, don't look so horribly serious, my dear child. I will say to you, as the dear old Professor said to me this morning, 'You look charming in anything!'"

But Adelaide did not laugh. Like all people of her temperament, she was very sensitive, and she had rather an unfortunate inability to see a joke. This is quite apart from a certain sense of humour, and quick perception of a position which is ludicrous. No one appreciated the wit of Shakespeare or George Eliot more keenly than Adelaide did, but what she called "vulgar tricks" or "silly jokes" at her own expense she never could tolerate. A great many of us are like Adelaide in this respect.

Now, as she went swiftly down the stairs of Paoli's Hotel she was saying to herself, "What an *idiot* Mrs. Murchison is! How can Mr. Lysaght put up with her?"

Happy it is for us that the point of vision differs in different people. For in the hall Adelaide brushed against the old Professor, who, having meditated on what pretext he could find for ascending to Mrs. Murchison's sitting-room, had decided that a volume of Villari would afford the best possible excuse for doing so, saying to himself, "How surprising it was to find a woman of such varied culture so brilliant and sparkling, so charmingly simple, and so full of the innocence of youth!"

The poor Professor had very short sight, which he helped by the aid of spectacles. But for his mental vision, alas! he had no such assistance, and was more at home in deciphering the contents of an old black-letter volume than in reading the character of a fascinating personage like Mrs. Murchison. Such masculine obtuseness is by no means uncommon.

Adelaide found herself in the Piazza Duomo just as the western sunshine had illuminated the pure white marble of the facciata, which looked almost transparent. The tame pigeons, taking every colour on their varied plumage, were pecking fearlessly at the very feet of the passers-by. Here and there a dove, as snowy as the marble pinnacle where it made its home, came swooping down amongst the rest, rising again in the glowing light on wings burnished like silver, and its feathers like wrought gold. The busy concourse of the people passes by, and the pigeons heed it not. They come down for their food, which is often thrown to them by the custodian who stands by Giotto's Tower, and by many others who haunt the Piazza and pass to and fro on business or pleasure. As Adelaide was looking at the radiant beauty of the Duomo, she was startled to see a line of black figures cross the surrounding whiteness. A procession of men in black robes and hoods were just returning from an errand of mercy.

The first four were bearing a litter with swift, even steps, empty now, to be deposited in the chapel of the Misericordia, whence, an hour before, it had been taken at a signal of the bell in the Campanile, which calls with its resonant voice to 'the Brothers of Mercy' to come to their headquarters opposite the Duomo, and prepare to set forth for the relief of someone who has had an accident, or who, sick and poor, is gently conveyed by them to a hospital.

"For six hundred years these men have performed this office, for the sick or wounded in Florence."

Adelaide turned at the sound of a voice near her, and saw Mr. Lysaght. She had been so engrossed with watching 'the Brothers of Mercy,' that he had come across, unperceived, from the door of the Duomo to the place where she stood.

"They look so strange in their black gowns, and only holes in the masks for their eyes," she said.

"That is to prevent recognition. They are often taken from the noblest families in Florence. One of the rules of their order is to take no remuneration but a cup of cold water. The great bell calls them from all parts of the city, and they come here for their orders."

"It is a beautiful work. How different from the rough way poor people are sometimes taken to our hospitals in England! Even in Dryborough I have seen a poor man who had fallen off a scaffold jolted along in a cart to the Cottage Hospital, which Lady Mary and two or three other ladies have lately established. We want Brothers of Mercy there, I am sure."

"May I walk home with you?" Godfrey Lysaght

said. "Have you looked at 'Sasso di Dante?' Here is the place where it is said 'passionate poor Dante did sit' to watch the building of some part of the cathedral. Whether true or not, it is a pleasant legend."

"I wish so many beautiful stories were not legends," Adelaide said. "I should like to believe they were all true."

"Even that the tree burst into leaf when San Zenobio's body, carried past, brushed against it. Well, we may comfort ourselves that there is truth underlying most legends. Often in death the good man's works, following him, call finer fruit and flowers to life, from apparently a hopeless stock."

Just as Godfrey had bid Adelaide good-bye at the door of the Piazza d'Azeglio, Lady Anna drove up in the carriage which Mr. Cowper-Smith had bought for her use while in Florence.

Adelaide waited till Lady Anna had alighted, expecting, perhaps, a remonstrance at her long absence. But there was none.

"She does not care enough about me to miss me," Adelaide thought, as she followed Lady Anna up the first flight of stairs to the drawing-room.

CHAPTER VIII.

AWAKENING.

"ADELAIDE'S letters are not so bright as I expected," Mrs. Wardlaw said to Hester Ponsonby one day. "I shall be glad when you go out to her; I think she misses you—and, indeed, all of us. Lady Anna is so very unlike Lady Mary."

"Yes," said Hester warmly; "it is the difference between a thoroughly selfish and a thoroughly unselfish person. Poor Cousin Mary does efface herself too much, perhaps, but it is the best extreme of the two. Mother says that yesterday, when she remonstrated with her about never taking any proper exercise and shutting herself up with that old creature, who does nothing but storm at her, she said, 'It will not be for long,' and she looked so sad, and ready to cry as she said it. Imagine crying about that old Squire!"

"My dear," said gentle Mrs. Wardlaw, "we do not always care the most for those who give us no trouble. I have often noticed that a mother loves a wayward, troublesome son better than those who never give her any anxiety. It is the same with sick, ailing children: the mothers always care most about them. And," said Mrs. Wardlaw, making a final climax, "even with husbands, the kind and thoughtful ones, like—like—" (she could not quite honestly say Mr. Wardlaw)—"like Mr. Birley or Mr. Cowper-Smith, are not mourned for half as long, as those who have worn out their wives by their bad temper and selfishness."

Hester laughed.

"Well, I hope I shall have no experience of the ill-tempered and selfish husbands. It is not very likely."

"You are engaged to Hugh Birley, my dear, are you not?"

"Well," Hester said, hesitating a little, "we are both determined to marry no one else. My mother will not consider it a positive engagement, and Mr. Birley says Hugh must not think of marrying till he has taken his degree and settled himself in the world. But we understand each other, and, though we do not correspond, we manage to hear about each other."

"That sort of engagement is not very satisfactory," Mrs. Wardlaw said; "but I dare say you know best."

Mrs. Wardlaw had so long been accustomed to think her husband and Adelaide "knew best," even yielding to both Nina and Susie's superior judgment sometimes, that she took the same optimist view of the world generally.

Gentle, clinging natures like Mrs. Wardlaw's are always content to take the lowest place. It never occurs to them that it is not their right place, and they feel, so to speak, more comfortable in it than in any other. It doubtless saves a great deal of worry, and that antagonism with the opinions and sentiments of our neighbours which discussion of burning questions brings about.

"It is so much pleasanter to agree than to disagree," Mrs. Wardlaw thought, and carried her thought into practice. "You know best," was always her placid way of settling any difficulty. "Your father knows best," "Adelaide knows best," and Nina and Susie understood that this meant that their mother had no more to say, but that the matter was settled.

"You know best, dear," Mrs. Wardlaw now said. Then she left the subject of Hugh Birley and returned to Adelaide. "She says nothing about her painting in this last letter. It is addressed to Mr. Wardlaw, and it is so interesting! I really think it ought to be published. I dare say the editor of the *Dryborough Weekly News* would be proud to print it in his paper. I will get Nina to copy it."

"Oh, I am sure Adelaide would not like her letter to be made public; that is why I never let anyone see that she writes to me. She always says handing on letters is like opening them when they are not meant for you."

'Oh, my dear! how shocking to hint at such a

thing! It is so very dishonest to open and read a letter addressed to someone else! If Adelaide has secrets with you, I am sure I do not wish to pry into them; but a letter about the antiquities of Florence and her favourite pictures in the gallery—surely there is no harm in wishing those who know her to read it, and see how clever she is. I am naturally proud of Adelaide; but perhaps you know best."

"I am sure Adelaide would hate to see her letter in print," Hester said decidedly; "I am certain of it! When did you see Cousin Mary last?"

"Not for some days. I do not like to intrude, and I know you and your mother are so often with her."

Although to the outer world there was no perceptible difference in Mr. Beauchamp's conduct to his wife, she was conscious of a change. He sometimes looked at her with wistful eyes, and one day surprised her by saying:

"How glad you will be when I am dead, Molly! You have been a patient, good wife to me, and I ought to be grateful."

"You have been so good to me," she said. "I owe you my home, and many comforts."

"You deserve more than I've done for you," said the Squire graciously. "You are well provided for at my death, and if this precious hundredth cousin of mine takes possession here, you will not lose much. You'll have enough to take a pretty little place all to yourself."

"We need not talk of that time yet, need we?" Lady Mary said gently. "You are better, and if we have a warm, mild winter, I hope you will soon be able to get out again."

"I shall never get out again," was the decided answer.

Then Lady Mary took his poor, distorted hand in hers, and stroked it gently.

"Look out!" he called sharply. "My thumb is very painful."

The momentary softness had passed, and Mr. Beauchamp became irascible again, and was hurling anathemas at Preston, who had just appeared, and had committed the offence of shutting the door with a click, which could hardly be called the "bang," which his master said it was.

Preston laid the letters which had just arrived on the table by Lady Mary's side, and Mr. Beauchamp was on the alert at once.

"Who are the letters from? Here! give them to me!"

"One is from Anna—I see the Florence postmark; and another is from Adelaide Millington."

"Let's hear what she has got to say. I wish she were here again. I like to see her flare up when I call her 'Addy.' There's fine stuff in her. What does she say?" he repeated querulously. "You might as well amuse me, shut up here as I am, like a bull in a net."

Lady Mary was glancing over Adelaide's letter,

looking out for anything which, when she came to it, it would be advisable to skip; but, afraid of exciting her husband's impatience, she began hurriedly :

"Dearest Lady Mary,

"It was delightful to get your last letter. You cannot think how I long for the next, and how disappointed I am when there is no letter for me.

"I have written to my father an account of what I have seen here, and enjoyed. I don't want to repeat the Guide-book style to you. There are so many printed 'walks about Florence'—the story of mine, written on this thin paper, would not be new to you.

"At first, I thought I should never really feel happy here; and, even now, I miss all the dear people at home, and all their interest in me and my little doings. Here, it is different. Lady Anna is very kind to have brought me at all, and I am very grateful to her; but I do not know her any better than I did when I came into the drawing-room at the Court, and you showed her my 'Fisher-boy' that day.

"Daisy treasures that picture. What a darling she is! and I think if she were allowed to lead a more child-like life, she would soon be bright and well, like other girls of her age. I have made the acquaintance of a Mr. Lysaght, who is a connection of yours. He is a very pleasant man, not like anyone I ever knew before."

"They'll make a nice pair," interrupted the Squire. "Little Addy will come here and be mistress—what do you say?"

Lady Mary had nothing to say to this. She was looking down the next page.

"What are you skipping for? Go on."

"I have begun to copy two little angels by Andrea del Sarto; but I do not get on very well. A girl who earns her living, and supports her mother and sister and a blind boy, her brother, by copying pictures, has made friends with me, and has given me some hints. Her name is Lucia Campbell. Her father was English, and her mother is an Italian; she was a singer, I think."

"What's her ladyship about, letting that girl associate with Italian singing women?—always a low set, always—— You must tell Addy to beware; she is just taken in—Italian singer, indeed! An Italian beggar is more like it."

Lady Mary hastily went on to the end of the letter, and missed some words of praise about Lucia which might be distasteful.

"I will read Anna's letter now, and see what she says; that may be amusing."

"Anna can't be amusing," was the answer, "except by her airs, which she plays off whenever she has the chance. She is very different from you, Molly. You are a gentlewoman, and my lady —well, I suppose I must allow she is born of the same parents, with a pedigree a mile long—no longer than the Beauchamps though—mind that! But there must be a strain of snobbishness somewhere that Anna has got, and you have missed. If you had married poor Smith, you would not have hung out your title on every possible occasion, just to show, as my lady does, that she did poor Smith a great honour by tacking it on his name. Cowper-Smith, indeed! He was plain John Smith, and never wanted to be anything better. Well, go on. What does her ladyship say?"

Lady Anna's letter might just as well have been written from Lancaster Gate or a fashionable quarter of Brighton. Florence simply meant to her a place where she could hold her own in society, drive to the Cascine, and receive the visits of the English families, who were beginning to congregate in Florence for the winter. Daisy's health and her own concerns filled the sheet of thin paper. Narrow streets with certain strong odours were an abomination to Lady Anna; hence the old quarters of Florence were as a sealed book to her. The little Church of San Martino, Dante's House, Michael Angelo's House, the Mercato Vecchio, the old Ghetto, all the associations of Oltr' Arno, the Via dei Bardi, and the Santo Spirito were a blank to her.

Of course as she drove along Lung' Arno, she looked about her, and, from her well-appointed carriage, surveyed, with something akin to pity, the visitors who, with Hare's books in their hands with the gold Mercury on the cover, were hastening to see all that could be seen in the City of Flowers.

Happy, eager girls, enjoying their first tour abroad; bustling mothers and spare spinsters, referring at every step to Baedeker or Murray—all this was a mystery to Lady Anna! Of course she paid a visit to the Pitti and the Uffizi and Accademia; but any enthusiasm that Daisy or Miss Cromwell showed was promptly repressed. It was a little vulgar to go into raptures about anything, though, of course, Lady Anna considered herself a lover of Art, and would gaze with her gold eye-glasses well-set on her arched nose at the Venus or the Niobe, and murmur something in a low voice about the marvellous folds of a drapery or the expression in an up-turned face. Sculpture is considered to stand on a higher level than painting; and for that reason, if for no other, Lady Anna was constrained to care more for it—or profess to care —which comes to the same thing.

" We have exchanged a good many visits already," Lady Mary read from the letter. " It was quite necessary to send for Fielding, though John did not think so. It was impossible for Sam, even with the best intentions, to do all that was required. We are pretty well off for servants. The chef understands the best Italian cuisine, and varies it with English dishes.

" Daisy shows remarkable quickness in her conversation lessons, and quite surprises Signor Benini and Madame de la Cour. She is reading a little history with Miss Cromwell, and I allow her to practise rather longer. I hope this winter will be more successful than the last. There is decidedly more variety than at Cannes; and John finds the reading-room at Vieusseux's a great resource. All the English papers and magazines are there, and the reading-room is pleasant. I have had several new books already: but really, with all that devolves on me, making arrangements, and seeing that everyone does their duty, I have but little leisure for reading. We have a very fair carriage ; but I don't know what 'The Park' would think of our horses They are not remarkable for high breeding !"

"All about herself, as usual," Mr. Beauchamp growled—"just like Anna."

Lady Mary skipped another page to a place where she saw Adelaide's name.

"Miss Millington has made an attempt to take Daisy's portrait. There is some merit in it ; but of course it would be difficult for an amateur to catch the ethereal beauty of my darling's face. Miss Mllington is copying a picture in the Accademia. We do not see very much of her. Daisy is very fond of her ; but, then, she is so sweet and affectionate—she loves everyone.

" Mr. Lysaght and his sister are at Paoli's Hotel. He is rather a pleasant person, with strong religious views: he has bad health, I believe. His sister is *not* a person I like ; and I shall be afraid of too much intimacy, on her account. But I need not say, as Mr. Lysaght is Mr. Beauchamp's heir, I shall be civil to him, and tolerate his sister for his sake; but she is a little inclined to be pushing."

"That will do—that will do," Mr. Beauchamp said. "It is all in one strain. I pity that poor Addy out there with her ladyship . . . And though you meant well, Mary, you made a mistake. Now read the *Times* to me, and that will be more amusing; and do tell that fellow to stop the noise of the mowing-machine. It is enough to drive one wild." Then, returning to the first part of this speech, Mr. Beauchamp said, as his wife left the room to give an order about the mowing-machine: "Poor little Addy! I am rather sorry for her. Her art studies will not be sweetened for her by my lady—poor little Addy!"

Perhaps if Mr. Beauchamp could have had a telescope which would have shown him the interior of the Accademia at Florence at that moment, his pity would have been even greater for Adelaide.

She was seated on the high stool before Andrea del Sarto's little cherubs, but she was not painting. Her own canvas only presented a blank to the passer-by. It had been turned with its face to the easel; and Adelaide sat opposite it with her palette in one hand, it is true, but the brush had fallen from the other, and lay at her feet.

Every day, for the past week, Adelaide had been in her place; every day her efforts to reproduce those little chubby cherubs had seemed more and more hopeless. Lucia had not been at her post; and day after day Adelaide had gone to the place where Savonarola hung, and found the canvas turned back, and the easel put aside in a corner.

Adelaide had been making up her mind to go and find Lucia that very morning, when she had seated herself before her picture.

"I must ask her to tell me what she thinks. It was she who advised me to put in the whole figures again, and not be content with the heads only, and now—they *may* look better, but they are not right."

These thoughts had been passing through Adelaide's mind as she mixed her colours and prepared to begin her morning's work. There were several people in the gallery, and a lady with spectacles stopped behind Adelaide and said, in an audible voice, to a gentleman with her:

"How awful! Did you ever see such a caricature?"

Adelaide turned quickly. Her dark eyes were blazing with indignation, and the lady moved away; the gentleman saying:

"Take care! She is English, and heard what you said."

Yes, she *had* heard—a caricature! Was it indeed possible—was it indeed true? With a sudden gesture of dismay, Adelaide turned the canvas, and sat, as I have described, with her palette in one hand, the brush on the ground, large tears dropping, before she was aware of it, on her lap. She brushed them hastily away, and stooped to pick up her brush, as a voice near her said:

"What is the matter?"

Turning, she saw Mr. Lysaght. Oh, the shame and misery to be caught crying by him! And more vexatious still, she could not check a short quick sob.

"Can I do anything for you? I shall be glad to help you if I can."

Adelaide recovered herself with a desperate effort, and said:

"I am going home. I am not going to paint any more to-day; perhaps, never again."

Mr. Lysaght discovered at once what had happened. There had been some rude awakening to the reality, which he had seen on one or two former visits to the Accademia was inevitable. Adelaide had power to blend colours, to make a tolerable attempt at hair and eyes, and even complexion; but she could not draw. Her figures were hopelessly at fault; and she had had no proper training or study, which can alone secure success as an artist. She had never drawn from a model in her life. Miss Castigan's notion of what was necessary had never got beyond flat copies of outlines well shaded, and then of the imitation of water-colour pictures like that of the memorable "Fisher-boy by the Stream." Only sensitive and highly organized natures can understand what this rude awakening meant to Adelaide. She always writhed under criticism inwardly, however callous she might seem outwardly: and the sweet smiling Angioletti with their scrolls displayed seemed to mock at her calamity.

The faultless painter himself would have pitied the despair which was written on Adelaide's face as she said in a voice of forced calmness to Mr. Lysaght:

"I have utterly failed. There is nothing left for me but to burn that wretched canvas, and go back to Dryborough. I——"

"May I look at the picture?" Mr. Lysaght said, as he put his hand on the canvas.

"No, oh no!" she said, springing forward to prevent him. "No! No one shall ever have the chance again of calling it a caricature. It is true, I dare say; but truth is not always pleasant."

She was wiping her brushes as she spoke, and cleaning her palette with her knife, gathering up all her little materials, and putting them into the basket where she left them every day.

"I wish you would treat me as a friend," Mr. Lysaght said, "and let me look at the right side of the canvas."

"This *is* the right side—the other is the wrong. Look!" she said bitterly; "there is my name written on it—a sign of my folly, and stupid blindness, and hideous self-conceit."

"You are very hard on yourself," Mr. Lysaght

said, "and I am so sorry for you. I expect you want to study under direction, and there are plenty of studios where, for small fees, you can do this. May I help you to find one? I shall be glad to be of use."

His kindness softened Adelaide. She went towards the easel, and seemed to hesitate whether or not to turn the canvas to the other side.

"Don't show me the picture, if you would rather not do so; but, in any case, let me be of some assistance. You know we began our acquaintance—may I say friendship?—by my being able to render you a trifling service; and——"

"Picking me up when I had fallen. This would be very much the same kind of service, only, unhappily, this time I am *not* to be picked up. I am down now, without any hope of rising again. It is not"—she said, turning her face towards him, her dark eyes still dim with the mist of tears—"it is not because these people laughed at my picture, and called it a caricature, that I am giving it up. For some time I have had misgivings about myself, and especially since I came here. I have lived with those who have loved me too well, and thought too much of me; and it is so easy to believe that good things said of you are true, and so hard to believe that bad things are nearer the mark. Do you understand?"

"Yes, perfectly. Awakening from a pleasant dream is always a painful process, the only thing is to be brave, and meet the new conditions of life with courage and perseverance."

As Mr. Lysaght had been speaking, Adelaide had slowly turned the canvas, and the copy of the cherubs stood revealed. He was silent for a few minutes, and then Adelaide said :

"Tell me the truth. I can bear it from you, however hard it may be. Tell me the truth, please."

"The figures are very much out of drawing," he said, "but the colouring is good, almost wonderfully good; but I need not tell you that colouring will not make a picture. There must be truth of outline, and, in short, the figures must live. That is the principle of all Art ; it must be true to life—for nothing can be beautiful that is not true."

"Yes," she said sorrowfully. "Do you think anyone was ever so foolish, so mistaken as I have been? Now tell me, shall I go on, or shall I give up? Is it worth my while to waste any more time in painting ?"

"I think that question is better answered by a more competent judge. Shall we find out our little Italian friend, and consult her as to the studio we ought to go to, inquire terms, and submit your work to a master?"

"Yes, if you will take the trouble, that will be best ; but it is a foregone conclusion. I know what the man will say if he is honest. What shall we do with this wretched thing?" she asked.

"Take it first to my artist, to whom I have

entrusted the copy of Savonarola, and then hear what she says as to the studio."

"Very well; I will carry the canvas under my cloak. No one can see whether it is a caricature or not if I do; let us go at once."

They set off together towards the Piazza Cavour. As they entered it, and were crossing by the fountain, they saw a procession of the black-robed "Brothers of Mercy," walking at a swift even pace under the arches which run round the Piazza on the pavement, close to the houses.

"They are going on to No. 4—that is Lucia Campbell's number!" Adelaide exclaimed. "Something must have happened."

Mr. Lysaght quickened his pace across the wide square; and he and Adelaide were at the door just as Marietta, breathless and perplexed, reached it from the other side.

"Oh, signor, signor, I could not help it; the carriage came round so quick—so very quick—round the corner by the Palazzo Strozzi, and Giovanni had just left the pavement, and then I saw him fall; but whether he tripped or was knocked down, I don't know. The 'Brothers' were passing, and lifted him, and carried him home. What will Lucia say? She has been ill for a week past; and she trusted me to take Giovanni to get some new strings for his violin. What will Lucia say?"

While Marietta was thus indulging in weak lamentations, the steady tramp of returning feet was heard down the stone stairs, and two and two the black-robed figures passed out, silently and quietly as they had come.

Marietta clasped her hands.

"Ah, signore, signore!" but the black mysterious figures passed on, and took no heed of Marietta's entreaty.

"Come upstairs at once," Mr. Lysaght said; "go first, and we will follow you."

Marietta was always a coward; and her distress was caused quite as much by the anticipation of what her mother and Lucia would say to her, as by the fear as to what her brother's injury might be.

"He left my hand a moment," she said—"just one moment! Then it was all over—all done."

They were at the head of the staircase now, and sounds of wailing and lamentation were heard from Signora Campbell, or, as she always called herself, Campobello. Giovanni had been stunned by his fall, and there was a bruise on his forehead, but he had recovered consciousness, and was murmuring "Lucia, Lucia!"

Poor Lucia, pale and wan, was supporting her blind brother's head; while his mother was wringing her hands, and pouring forth lamentations in Italian, quite forgetting her usual desire to speak only English, and to give up her native tongue.

When Marietta appeared, she changed laments into railing; and declared she was no better than a baby, and could not take care of herself, much less of her blind brother.

Lucia alone preserved her calmness, and said quietly to Mr. Lysaght:

"I do not think he is seriously hurt. Are you, caro mio? We must keep him very quiet and still. Nay, madre mia, do not be too angry with Marietta. The accidents will happen to us all. We will pray to God that no real harm may follow now."

Marietta, with a storm of angry recrimination to her mother, escaped to another room; and Adelaide, going to Lucia, said:

"Can I help you—shall I fetch a doctor?"

"No, I think not, grazie signorina;" and now Madame Campbell thrust Adelaide aside, and knelt down with a bowl of lily-leaves and vinegar, which she proceeded to lay upon the bruise in the boy's forehead, murmuring over him tender, pitiful words; the maternal love in her acting like a spell, to hush the storm of her wrath against Marietta to a calm.

Lucia left the head of the low bed, where she had been kneeling, and said:

"I have been ill, signor, and unable to work. I fear you have come to inquire about the delay in executing your commission. I have had a chill, which gave me great pain in my head and limbs, and when I tried a week ago to get to the Accademia, I was forced to return, and go to my bed. But I am better now, and shall soon be at my work again, if only you can wait."

"There is no haste. Do not think of it. I shall be at Florence all the winter," Mr. Lysaght said.

"Ah, but I must work very hard to make up for lost time, and I *love* my work," she added.

Adelaide here put down her canvas in a corner of the room, and Mr. Lysaght said:

"I am sorry Miss Millington and I arrived at such an inopportune moment. We really came to ask your advice as to a studio, where Miss Millington can have some direction in her studies."

Lucia brightened at once.

"Ah, I am so glad you came to ask this question! I knew you would want to learn more before you could really copy. Yes, there is the very place for you in the Viale Principe Amadeo. It is the studio of a great painter, but adjoining to it is another, over which two pupils of his preside. There you will learn by drawing from the casts, and afterwards from the life. I have the card. I will give it to you. I see your picture there. Is it finished?"

Adelaide sprang forward to possess herself of the canvas.

"I don't like you to see anything so miserably bad!" she said.

"Ah, well then, do not show it! I know that it is pain to show what we feel is ill done. Do you not think I have known this? I will get the card."

Lucia disappeared into a small ante-room, and soon returned with the card, stopping by Giovanni's couch to kiss his forehead, and say:

"Come sta, carissimo."

To which Madame Campbell replied:

"Non cè male. Why do those people stay? We do not want strangers now."

"They are not strangers, Mamma. One is a good friend—my patron, Signor Lysaght."

It did not escape Mr. Lysaght's notice that the little, alert, cheerful artist moved languidly and slowly, as if exertion were an effort to her.

He took the card from her, and, as he touched her hand, he noticed it was burning with feverish heat.

"We will not remain longer now; but I shall hope to come again later, and see how your brother gets on. Now," he said, turning to Adelaide, "we will go to this studio, and make arrangements for you to begin at once. Now," turning to Lucia, "Buon' giorno, addio."

She smiled faintly, and did not even ask to look at the picture which Adelaide had now replaced under her cloak, as she replied to Mr. Lysaght's "addio," with,

"We do not say 'addio' when we hope to meet again. 'Addio' is our last farewell; so I say to you, signor, 'A rivederci!' And to the signorina, also, 'A rivederci.'"

On the stairs, Mr. Lysaght and Adelaide met a

bowed figure coming up, striking his stick on every one of the stone steps. It was Andrea Maura.

He carried in his hand a few herbs and a lettuce; and as he stopped to let Adelaide and Mr. Lysaght pass, he bowed low.

"I hear there has been an accident to the blind boy. Alas, for his sister! For she is ill herself, and no one taking any care of her! And no one to think of her! Her work stopped. I know what that means; what it means to me—all but starvation! I have had the bounty of San Martino till now—*that* is stopped; and—well—I am old, and she is young and fair and clever. I should have made a fortune if God had not taken from me the use of my arm. And now I am too poor to help her; for I tell you, sir, she wants help. She starves for others' sakes. Now she is ill, she wants good food. I have brought her this little cake and a salad," he said, flourishing the little bundle in the air, and pointing to a small square cake, which lay in the middle of the bundle. "That is all I can do: I would it were more."

"The cup of cold water," Mr. Lysaght said as they passed down; and the old man continued his feeble ascent of the stone stairs, his stick tapping, as he went, an accompaniment to his murmured words: "I would it were more—I would it were more."

"That is a struggle for life," Mr. Lysaght said, "and there are many like it. That girl is absolutely in want of proper nourishment after her illness. And all her earnings go for the comfort of others—a story of self-sacrifice! We ought not to grudge her the crown which it surely wins, though the way to it looks sad and toilsome enough. I wonder what can be done to help her. If even only a bundle of salad herbs, I should be glad to offer it, like that poor old man."

"I feel as if I had no business to be so miserable about my own failure and disappointment when I think of Lucia," Adelaide said. "Let us not trouble ourselves any more about a studio to-day. Here is the turn to the Via Alfieri; and I will go home and forget this wretched attempt, and let the waters of Lethe wash it out."

"I don't see that you will help the little artist by giving up your own long-cherished scheme of studying art at Florence. Here we are at the studio: let us go in and make inquiries at least."

"Don't ask me to show this picture!"

Mr. Lysaght laughed.

"When we go to consult doctors, we let them take our temperature and feel our pulse and examine our tongues; otherwise, how can they prescribe? I think you will have to show your picture; besides, the corners of this canvas make right-angles under your cloak, and a professional eye would soon detect what you were concealing."

"There is another thing," Adelaide said. "Stop, please" (for Mr. Lysaght had his hand on the bell, which had a plate beneath, on which were the words "Studio: A. L. Guercini, G. & B. Bassano")—"stop, please; there is the question of fees. My mother and my step-father made a great effort to give me the money for my travelling expenses out to Florence. Twenty pounds means so much to them, and I could not ask them for more; so I could not pay a high fee for my lessons."

Mr. Lysaght shrugged his shoulders with half Italian emphasis.

"Surely Lady Anna would bear the expense for you!"

"I would not ask her for the world," Adelaide said; "she considers she has done me a great kindness in inviting me as a guest here. She has no intention of doing anything more. I——"

"I am sorry to hear it," Mr. Lysaght said. "If report is right, the Cowper-Smiths have an enormous income, and a cheque with three, or even four figures can hardly make the slightest difference to their finances; however, we will see what we can do here first."

As he spoke he pulled the handle, and the bell gave a querulous metallic tinkle; and a little boy with a smiling face opened the door.

"Yes, Signora Bassano was at home; but Signor Guercini, no."

Signor Bassano had been a pupil of Signor Guercini's: and had now a separate studio, where he received those pupils whom the numerous applications to his late master obliged him to reject.

He was assisted by his wife with his pupils, who in her turn had been a pupil of Guercini's; and, indeed, her husband and herself had been first brought together by studying the same models. Signora Bassano was considerably older than her husband; and she held him in the reins of a government which could not be said to be altogether silken.

But they managed between them to make a very comfortable living, and had a pretty little villa on one of the slopes which lead up towards Fiesole.

Signora Bassano had always an eye to business, and surveyed Adelaide with an inquiring—not to say inquisitive—air.

Did the signorina intend to make art a profession? No—ah—ah! The fees were on a lower scale for such. The signor, her husband, was not at home, but, with a quiet glance at the obtrusive corners of the canvas, which, as Mr. Lysaght had predicted, betrayed itself, she asked: Could she see how far the signorina was advanced? Had she a picture to show?

Once more Adelaide had to go through the ordeal which she dreaded. The unhappy canvas was brought out from under the folds of her loose cloak—which, a few years ago, used to be called "a Mother Hubbard cloak," and was beloved by those who aimed at æsthetic garments—and placed on an easel. It looked even worse here than it had done in the Accademia.

A cast of Diana seemed to be pointing the

finger of scorn at it; a Cupid, with his bow and arrow, seemed to be taking aim at it; and a large portrait of an American lady, with a broad, smiling mouth, seemed to be laughing at the poor artist from the gorgeous frame which made a setting to her amber satin gown, with its load of lace and finery, all wonderfully well painted by the signor's skilful hand—the sheen of the satin, the delicate texture of the lace, the shimmer of the emeralds, which lay upon the fat neck of the Boston lady.

Adelaide felt her to be a personality, and, shuddering, turned away, that she might not see the broad, good-natured face smiling at her poor Angioletti.

"Ah! si—si—no—it is misguided; it is not drawn in right. But does the signorina wish to be a pupil? There is colouring—which is pretty good. When will the signorina begin?"

"We must ask your terms before we decide."

The signora put her head, first on one side, then on another.

"We say five lire for each day, four hours in each day, or, for six days, twenty-five lire. The signorina must begin at the beginning. My husband would tell her this were he here. Ah, here he comes!"

And then a rapid conversation began between the husband and wife, as they stood before the picture; a conversation so largely carried on by means of signs, uplifted hands, shrugged shoulders, and sudden steps backward or in advance, that no one who was not initiated could possibly understand what was passing.

Every now and then the signor, who was clad in a loose morning coat of gray cloth, with a belt at his waist, looked round at Adelaide, and then returned to the pantomime with his wife. At last he spoke :

"Monsieur and madame, or signor and signorina, this picture is wholly bad—it is no art, it is no copy ! See!"—with a sudden dart towards the cherub—"see! this leg from the knee to the foot. I measure! *See!* it is longer than the whole body of the boy !"—then a start back, and a significant shrug, and an action of both well-formed hands, indescribable as inimitable.

"But the signorina would learn—would study? Then come here—this way," and the signor preceded them towards an inner room, where there was a picture on the easel of a girl's half-length figure, her chin resting on her hand, her eyes full of fire and intelligence.

"See! only six months' study, and this is the result; from the life ! The lady, she came here, and not one line could she draw. She could colour "—and again the peculiar action with the hands—"she could colour ! but what is that? The signorina can colour pretty well, so to say ; she can mix and blend, though the lights are wrong. Well, if she comes here—first, the model of a hand, of a finger, of a foot ; then the arm, the shoulder, the neck. At last, the full figure—all from the model. And then? Well, then from the life! and then?—a picture worth the purchase of any English nobleman."

"The signorina is not professional," the wife whispered. She was afraid her husband might name the lower fee.

Then Mr. Lysaght turned to Adelaide and said:

"Well, will you come? Will you begin at once?" In a lower voice, "Do not think of the money part; that can be managed—I feel sure it can," he added hastily. "Your friends would not wish you to lose this opportunity."

Adelaide felt she was in his hands, and made no further opposition.

"Yes," she said, "I will begin to-morrow. I will work every day, and then I shall, at least, have done my best to succeed."

So the arrangement was concluded, and Adelaide was to set her foot on the first rung of the ladder which she had attempted to scale with one bound; going back to first principles, instead of arriving at the highest place at once.

CHAPTER IX.

"LE PREMIER PAS."

"AND must you begin all over again?" Daisy said, as she nestled close to Adelaide on that same afternoon. "You, who paint such beautiful pictures? Oh! what are you doing with my portrait?" For Adelaide had suddenly started up and seized her drawing-block.

"I am going to burn it," Adelaide said, deliberately snipping it off the block, and then putting it into the low wood fire which was smouldering on the hearth.

Daisy's eyes filled with tears.

"Oh, I am so sorry," she said.

"I will take your portrait again, some day, and make it like you; that was *not* like you."

"Mrs. Gray said it was my image," Daisy murmured.

"Mrs. Gray! She knows nothing about it!" Adelaide said impetuously. "But don't be vexed, darling. When you have your photographs from Mendelssohn's I will colour one of them; that will be far better. I am *just* able to do that. But let us forget that poor portrait. Look, it is nearly frizzled up now! I can just see a bit of your hand—there! Now it is all a black mass. That is right—let the dead past bury its dead."

Adelaide laughed, and tried to treat the matter lightly, and asked Daisy if she should read to her or talk, or whether she would play the violin to her.

"I should like to do that, but I have practised an hour, and mother says I am never to do more. That is rather hard; but I promised, and I must keep my promise. I am not to ride here, and that is another hard thing. Mother is so afraid of my mounting a strange horse, and so few people ride in Florence. Percival is coming soon; then we shall all feel happier. I mean, he is so merry and nice, isn't he?"

Adelaide's reply rather disappointed Daisy.

"I hardly know your cousin," she said. "I have only seen him two or three times."

"He seems to know *you!*" Daisy exclaimed. "He was so glad that you should come to Florence, and changed his mind about Rose Smith after he had seen you."

"You told me that before," Adelaide said rather sharply.

"So I did," the child replied. "Don't you like Percy? I fancied you did."

"I like him well enough, and I shall be glad for your sake when he comes to Florence; and still more glad when your other cousin comes."

"You mean Rose Smith, and perhaps Bella. Father means to try and manage so."

"I was thinking of your cousins the Ponsonbys; you know Hester is my greatest friend."

"Oh! I forgot that. Yes, they are my 'second best' cousins, as Percy calls the Smiths at Ironstown, and he says he is my very best."

There were visitors in the drawing-room on the lower floor, and Mr. Cowper-Smith, seeing several carriages at the door on his return from Vieusseux's, made for the upper floor, where he always liked to find his little daughter. She sprang to meet him, pressed him into the luxurious chair by the fire, and seating herself on his knee, said:

"Isn't it nice to have you all to myself, Daddie? No, don't go away, Adelaide; tell her not to go, Daddie. Do stop, Adelaide."

Adelaide returned to the window, and stood looking out on the heights of Fiesole, which were becoming daily more and more visible as the leaves fell from the trees in the square.

"Adelaide is going to begin to learn drawing all over again; is not she humble to do it?"

"I am afraid there is not much humility in the case, dear," Adelaide said; "as no one thought I could draw a straight line it was time to begin to learn."

"Are you going to have a master, Miss Millington?" Mr. Smith asked.

"I am going to a studio in the Viale Principe Amadeo," Adelaide said.

"Dear me! what a mouthful! These Italian

names are as long as they are broad! I shall never learn them. Well, I hope you will succeed, Miss Millington."

"I mean to try," Adelaide said; "and I shall go on till we leave Florence, if I can afford it."

"Oh! that is easily arranged; you must let me pay the fees. Are they in advance?"

"No, I think not; Signor Bassano did not mention it; but I could not trespass on your kindness."

"Oh! that will be all right. I wonder Anna did not propose it. I always understood you were coming here expressly to study art. Anna made that a reason for inviting you rather than little Rose—didn't she, my Peggy?"

"Yes, father." But Daisy saw that Adelaide looked annoyed.

How often was she to hear that she had stood in the way of Rose Smith? It chafed her terribly, and the feeling rather increased upon her that she was, after all, *de trop*, and again and again she repented that she had ever come to Florence. How often our fairest dreams, when realized, are clouded by some mists and vapours, which, rising perhaps from trivial causes, and very often from our own fault, obscure the sun of our delight.

Adelaide left the room abruptly, and Daisy said:

"Adelaide does not like to hear about Rose Smith. I wish, dearest Dad, you could ask her to come when Percival does, or the Ponsonbys, and then Adelaide would not feel she had put her aside."

"Miss Millington is too thin-skinned, my Peggy; it is better for people in our house to be like Miss Cromwell, who, it seems, has no feelings to be hurt."

"Adelaide is very good, father; she has been telling me about an artist here, who supports her mother, and a brother who is blind, and her sister. Now she is ill herself. Oh, father, *do* you remember when you gave me all that was in your pocket for that poor woman whose husband was in prison? *Would* you give me what is in your pocket now for this artist? Her name is Lucia; and *do* give her a commission for a picture. I should so like to have a lovely Madonna del Gran Duca for my very own."

"Very well, my Peggy; yes, you may empty my pocket, but you may depend upon it your lady-artist would like a commission better than alms. You may give her both if you like, but you may find yourself in a difficulty, as I should if I offered the cash to your friend Adelaide for her studio lessons; she is not one to take favours with a smile."

Daisy relaxed her hold on her father's pocket and dropped the money back, saying:

"Yes, I dare say you are right, father, but I may give her the order to paint the Madonna del Gran Duca, mayn't I?"

"Yes, yes, and another also if you choose. And now tell me, do you like Florence better than Cannes?"

"Yes, for most things. I like being in our own house, and not meeting people on the stairs who ask me how I am; and I *am* glad not to have to sit at those long luncheons, when mother is warning me not to eat what I like best. But I miss the sea— that blue, beautiful sea, and the purple Esterelles. Father, do take me into the old part of Florence one day, please. I do get tired of only driving to the Cascine, and I want so much to go up to Fiesole. Mother is afraid I should get cold in the church, which she calls 'dampish and musty,' while Adelaide says it is ever so beautiful. Isn't it odd how different people's eyes must be? Some see beauty where others see ugliness. Mother has a reception this evening, and I am to go down. I *wish* I had not to go. My violin master is coming to play, and Mrs. Murchison will sing. And *have* you seen the flowers, father? Fielding ordered them from the florist in the Via Colonna. They are so beautiful; but it is in the spring that I shall care about the flowers, the scarlet anemones and narcissus, which cost so little. I heard Fielding say what mother has ordered for to-night cost a fortune."

Mr. Cowper-Smith sighed heavily.

"If it pleases your mother, I suppose it is all right; but I like a simpler sort of life, my Peggy. Still," Mr. Cowper-Smith said, rising and giving a prolonged sigh which ended in a yawn, "it is good for trade. The circulation of money must be of use in the long-run."

Lady Anna Cowper-Smith's reception was very much like a reception in a fashionable place anywhere. There were the usual types of those who thought themselves superior to others, and showed it; who made little cliques in certain corners of the room, the daughters calling each other by their Christian names, and planning excursions together, the mothers sitting or standing near each other, engaged in intimate conversation. Then there were those who were scarcely allowed to do more than touch the skirts of the more august circle. Of these, the mothers tried to look at ease and unconcerned and their daughters resigned to their fate, while feeling uncomfortably "out of it." There were young men, stiff and uneasy, longing to break through the ice, and inwardly thinking Lady Anna's "at homes" a bore. And then there was a sprinkling of happy people, who were not thinking of themselves at all, but were quite content to gaze from a distance at Lady Anna's diamonds and the Marchesa di Genori's topazes, and to listen to the music with real delight; one Italian lady in particular nodding her head in the fulness of her enjoyment, and proud of the feats of her own countryman on the violin.

Mrs. Murchison scarcely belonged to any particular set. She fluttered about in her very juvenile dress, apparently quite unconscious that she was in several instances making a raid on other people's domains, nor that several glasses were raised as she laughed and chattered, and that most important question was asked, " Who is she?"

Happily, in Mrs. Murchison's case the question could be answered satisfactorily. Whispers were afloat that Mr. Lysaght was heir to a fine English property, and that he and his sister were connections—*family* connections—of Lady Anna. Several Italian youths, who were less reserved than the English ones, ventured to address Mrs. Murchison without standing on the ceremony of formal introduction. They were answered in fluent Italian, with smiles which they considered enchanting, and they were charmed with an air and manner so different from the usual stiffness and reserve of the English in Florence.

The very impersonation of this reserve was to be seen at the farthest end of the brilliant drawing-room. Adelaide could not be said to shine in society; and as she sat apart in her plain ruby velvet dress, made square, with elbow sleeves turned up with some old lace of her mother's, she looked at the first glance many years older than the gay fluttering beauty who came dancing airily to her corner, saying :

"How grave you look! almost as grave as Godfrey! Don't you enjoy yourself? I do. It *is* fun to see Lady Anna doing the grand hostess. Isn't her train like the pictures in the *Ladies' Pictorial!* and how well she sweeps it across the carpet! Look at that little Italian contessa. How awestruck she is! I wonder what Lady Anna is saying to her. She does not understand it, whatever it is. Now meditate on the folly of the world. All the leaders of society in Florence come to pay their respects to the Lady Anna Cowper-Smith. If she were Mrs. Jack Smith, in a humble little *pension*, who would care to win her favour? But in this case it is such a happy union — riches fabulous, riches and rank! Godfrey is very late; but I begged him to come for me. He is on some errand of mercy. I believe he will have no rest in him till he has set up a Brotherhood of Mercy in London. We shall live to see him in a black gown and mask, with those dreadful holes for eyes, carrying a wounded man along the Strand or Piccadilly. What a lovely child that little Margaret is! and what a dress!—silvery plush high up to her throat. But how well it suits her! So few children could carry off a thick dress like that. I suppose she wears it because Lady Anna is such a fidget about her health. Here is Godfrey, and here comes Miss Cromwell. Lady Anna wants me to sing. She always deputes even a question to someone else. Poor little me! She could not come from one end of the room to the other to find me. Yes, Miss Cromwell. Do you know, I always feel inclined to call you the Protector. Do you mind? It is a feeble joke; but I *am* feeble. Yes, I will come and sing. No one will listen, that is one comfort."

Away went Mrs. Murchison, leaving Adelaide in

her corner by a statuette of that snowy Carrara marble, which has a purity about it peculiar to itself. The near contact of the white outline of the statue, with masses of yellow roses in a vase by its side, set off the dark head just below it, and the figure in the plain ruby velvet.

It was not long before Mr. Lysaght found his way to the place where Adelaide stood.

"I am very late," he said; "and I was afraid Theresa would be getting impatient, but she seems to be enjoying herself. I have been looking after our friend in the Piazza Cavour. I could not be satisfied till I had taken a doctor, under pretence of examining the boy, but really to prescribe for her. What do you think his verdict is? Miss Campbell's condition is the result of a long strain on mind and body, insufficient nourishment, and hard work. It has been hard work—incredible almost. Besides all her more important pictures, she has done designs for photograph-books and stands and fans and trivialities like that, sitting up at night to get through it, and then off in the morning to the galleries."

"It is wonderful, indeed, to think of all she has done," Adelaide said. "She makes me feel ashamed of my own complaints—terribly ashamed, just as if my own concerns were the most important in the world. I have been living in a little circle of my own, going round and round, with myself the centre. It is very humiliating to think of."

"You don't suppose you are a solitary instance of moving in your own little circle? We must all plead guilty, more or less," Mr. Lysaght said. "But it is good to know it; and better still to try to break through with a courageous effort — widen our borders, that is to say, and get rid of self."

"Mrs. Murchison is singing; we ought not to talk," Adelaide said; and Mr. Lysaght seated himself on a low cushioned seat which was placed below the statuette.

"You have been standing a long time; won't you sit down?"

As he spoke he gave a short quick cough, and said:

"The night-air in Florence does not suit me any better, or not much better, than the night-air in London."

Mrs. Murchison's song was a gay little French ditty, followed by several Neapolitan ones, which were much admired.

When she rose from the piano, Lady Anna thanked her graciously; but the little contessa took her hand in hers, and, looking up at her with tears in her dark eyes, said:

"Ah, how beautiful it is! Tante grazie, signorina, tante grazie. I cannot but weep—I do think of my youth in Naples."

"Oh, you should hear my brother sing, signora!" and Mrs. Murchison flitted down the room again, and said:

"Godfrey, I have Beethoven's 'Adelaide,' here;

come and sing it; it will be quite in harmony with your thoughts, I know."

"Do not be foolish, Theresa," Mr. Lysaght said sharply. "Besides, you are not the hostess here. I must wait till I am asked."

"Oh, I will soon settle that. Lady Anna!" Mrs. Murchison said, tripping back to the place where Lady Anna stood, slowly flapping her beautiful fan, and trying not to look hopelessly puzzled as the little contessa poured forth her admiration of the songs which had reminded her of her youth—"Lady Anna, my brother sings far better than I do. Shall I play the accompaniment for him of Beethoven's 'Adelaide'?"

Lady Anna grew her stateliest, and stopped immediately.

"We shall be very happy, I am sure; but Signor Candoletti is going to favour us with a solo on the violin."

"Oh, never mind, then; Godfrey can sing afterwards. You would like to hear 'Adelaide,' I am sure," she said, caressing Daisy's golden hair in a familiar way, which brought from her mother an instant command to ask the marchesa if there was any piece for the violin which she would prefer Signor Candoletti to play.

The marchesa—to whom Neapolitan airs, French chansons, and Wagner's "Lohengrin" were all alike—smiled and bowed pleasantly, and replied, in very pretty English:

"Ah, cara mia, it is the same to me; what the signora likes will please me much. And now sit beside me and tell me how you love our Città dei Fiori, our fair Florence."

Lady Anna, who had only asked the question in the hopes of detaching Mrs. Murchison from Daisy, heard the answer, and, just as Signor Candoletti drew the bow across the strings, was provoked to see her irrepressible guest sign to Daisy to make room for her on the lounge, where the marchesa was seated, and begin to talk to her in Italian, as if she had known her for years.

"Intolerable person!" Lady Anna inwardly exclaimed—"intolerable! And yet it is difficult to see how I can get rid of her. I must consult Percival when he comes."

Before Adelaide had been at the studio many days, she began to see her way to comparative success.

Signora Bassano led her carefully through the very earliest and easiest stages of model-drawing, and every step upwards seemed less difficult than the last. Adelaide's resolution and perseverance were now directed aright, and her progress was such as to surprise her master and mistress, and make them exchange many remarks in Italian which Adelaide did not understand, but which were to the effect that the signorina would soon show what their admirable teaching could achieve.

Perhaps they gave less credit than they should to the unflinching steadfastness of purpose, without which no talent in the pupil and no skill in the teacher can avail. But Signora Bassano at least fully appreciated the effort which Adelaide made to forget she had ever attempted to paint a picture when ignorant of the first principles of art.

There is nothing sweeter than the feeling that we are on the way at least to attain a desired end, and that by our own exertions; and there were times when Adelaide, after a long morning in the studio, where she always had her frugal luncheon, would go to watch one of the gorgeous sunsets from San Miniato or the Ponte Vecchio, feeling a spring of happiness in her which was as new as it was delightful. Hitherto her life had been, as we know, self-absorbed; and, surrounded by those who loved her with a blind love, like her mother and Hester Ponsonby, she had silenced the misgivings which would sometimes assert themselves, and believed herself to be what others believed her.

There were other influences at work which were even more salutary than those of honest and untiring study. It was impossible to be associated with Lucia Campbell without catching something that was elevating from her. By slow degrees, perhaps, but if slowly, yet surely, Adelaide began to recognise that there was some deeper spring of action in Lucia than mere desire to maintain her mother and her blind brother and sister by her efforts.

PONTE VECCHIO, FLORENCE.

That unwearied patience and forbearance which were exercised towards her mother and sister, the soft answer, the cheery words, the bright smile, even under provocation, were not, as we say, only natural to a temperament like Lucia's; for she had a high spirit that, if undisciplined, would have ill brooked control, and a keen sense of injustice which was continually ready to assert itself. Thus she saw Marietta lazy and self-satisfied, and her mother bustling, and letting all her good resolutions evaporate in words, while she was left in the forefront of the battle, where no one recognised it or bid her God-speed.

It is common now — becoming more common every day; I had almost written fashionable—to preach the doctrine that benevolence, unselfishness and earnest desire to benefit others; devotion to the poor, and giving up time and strength and gifts and worldly distinction to raise the " beggar out of the dust" and set him amongst princes, are seen in the lives of those who have no Christian principle— nay, who deny its power, because they deny Him who came to seek and to save the lost. It is common to put the elevating influences of art and music and literature in the place of the spirit which giveth life. It is common for those who do this to look down, as from a lofty vantage-ground, on those who in their ignorance, as is said, still hold to the old, old story of the love of Christ which alone constraineth us; that love which by that greatest of all motive powers can melt the heart to charity; the love of Him who died for all, that they which live should no longer live unto themselves, but unto Him who for their sakes died and rose again. In this mutable and perilous life of ours we are as ships without an anchor if we lose our grasp of that great doctrine of constraining love. We need something that is reliable in the great exigencies of life and death. As it was said not long ago by an accomplished preacher of his time, than whom none can have a keener relish for all the treasures of literature and art, nor a more refined ear and enthusiastic appreciation of music, "All these things which are His gifts to man are powerless to raise and ennoble and reform of themselves. The form of the Son of God must be recognised, and His Divine power to save and regenerate must be accepted and received with thankful hearts, or the house which is raised only on beauty, or culture, has its foundation on the sand, in the time of the stormy wind and tempest, and therefore it will be swept away."

Lucia Campbell had gone through many dark experiences in her early youth, such as Adelaide knew of only by hearsay. A father like hers, who had ruined his own health and debased his manhood, had been a pitiable spectacle even before her eyes. Her mother, who had been born and educated as a Roman Catholic, had given up her old faith and taken nothing in its place. Marietta sometimes went with her mother to kneel in one of the churches and say a few prayers with a wandering heart and careless lips; but that was all. Lucia had possessed herself of her father's Bible and English Prayer-book, and had been brought into contact with an English lady, who had given her a portrait of her dead child to enlarge, and who had taken a deep interest in the Italian girl, who had come daily to her house to execute her commission, and whom she had invited to talk to her.

She had not survived her child long, and both were buried in the old Cemetery, where so many English are resting under Italian skies. Not now in the calm and stillness of past days, for that once secluded God's acre is left like an island, where four roads meet, and the roll of the tramcar and the sound of many passing feet, as they come and go below the walls, destroy the old charm which was the atmosphere of the Cemetery when Elizabeth Barrett Browning, Arthur Clough and many another well known in the records of English poets and authors were first laid to rest there.

Lucia came to the studio in the Viale Principe Amadeo one bright December afternoon, as had been arranged, that she might return with Adelaide to the Piazza d'Azeglio, to receive an order about the painting of the Madonna del Gran Duca, which Mr. Cowper-Smith had promised to give Daisy.

Adelaide had just finished the bust of Clytie, and had won great praise for her work from Signor Bassano.

"It is wonderful," Lucia said, surveying it with a critical eye. "And after five weeks' work only! Ah, you could draw the legs of the little cherub now, so that even Andrea himself would say, 'You have worked with a will.'"

"I shall leave off for to-day," Adelaide said; "it is still early. Shall we take a turn together before we go to the Piazza d'Azeglio? But you look tired; are you tired?"

"I am always tired now," Lucia said. Then she changed her tone, and said in her usually cheerful voice, "Yes, let us go somewhere; to the Ponte Sospeso: that is near us, and we can see the sunset from there—it will be a fine one."

Then the two girls set off together, and Lucia put her hand within Adelaide's arm.

"This has been a tiring day," she said. "I have finished my Savonarola for Signor Lysaght; and I have loved the work, so that I am almost sorry it is done. The signor has been so good to us. Do you know how good? Scarcely a day has passed but he has come to read to Giovanni, and he has sung to him, and made him happy. Then he has sent me and Giovanni wine and strengthening things, and says he will take out the cost from the money for my picture. He is to pay me less, you understand: otherwise I could not have taken all the good things. And he sent me a lounge—cushioned and soft—for me to lie on when I am tired, and a large portière to keep out the draught. For our house is very cold, and the matting is worn out. Did you know all that he has done?"

"I knew he had been kind—that he always is kind," Adelaide said.

"He must be very rich," Lucia said.

"No; I think not. I mean, not very rich, like some people; but he is heir to a beautiful old place, near the town where I live, and he will be very well off one day. The gentleman who owns it has no children, and Mr. Lysaght is the next heir—the grandson of a younger brother."

"What is the gentleman named?" Lucia asked.

"Mr. Beauchamp," Adelaide replied, with the English pronunciation.

"Beecham—Beecham! How do you spell it?"

"Beau-champ," Adelaide answered.

Lucia's grasp of Adelaide's arm tightened.

"Beauchamp!—Beauchamp! Campbell—Campobello! So you make names into English?" she said. "Is Mr. Beauchamp a good man?"

"Well," Adelaide replied, "he is not able to keep his temper: he has fearful fits of gout, which give him agonies of pain, and he does not bear it well. He has a wife with an angelic temper, and she is never angry with him, and never in the least cross. He has had great sorrows, I believe, though I do not exactly know what they were. But let us talk of something else now. Tell me more about that lady you loved, and whose little girl's portrait you painted."

But Lucia seemed unable to turn her thoughts in

another direction, and was silent till they reached the Ponte Sospeso, and paying the required sous, stood midway, looking down and up the Arno. It was a glorious roseate sunset, and everything was bathed in the crimson light. Far away, beyond the long stretch of the Lung' Arno—far away, beyond the Campanile and the great Duomo, were range upon range of mountains, of that deep violet colour which must be seen to be believed. The rugged peaks of the Carrara Mountains were distinctly defined against a sky of burnished gold, in which lines of rose-coloured clouds, with beryl depths between, seemed to spring into a living glow, as the sun sank behind the heights, stretching almost to the zenith above. The Arno reflected the colours with chastened beauty on its breast, as it flowed beneath the Pont Sospeso, where the two girls stood, to the Ponte Carrara, dimly seen at the further end of Florence. As they turned to look in the opposite direction, where the upland slopes were studded with villas and campaniles of village churches, all steeped in the sunset glow, while the distant ridges of the Apennines, which shut in the valley, were white with the first snows of winter, Adelaide gave a sudden exclamation of surprise, and in another moment Percival Clyffe had greeted her with :

"So I have met you where I least expected it. I arrived by a train which took me to the Piazza d'Azeglio by eleven o'clock, and Daisy told me you were at your studio at work, and would not like to be disturbed. I have taken a siesta since then, and a very substantial luncheon ; then I came out to see something of Florence, and have seen what is more attractive to me than Duomo, Arno, or Campanile—an old friend!"

It was Percival's way to say pleasant things to everyone—but Adelaide's swift colour came to her face, and she said, in a rather stiff, shy manner:

"You will be very welcome at Florence. You have come in for one of the most beautiful sunsets.'

"Yes, I am a fortunate person this afternoon. I mean to enjoy myself in Florence, and these first few hours seem to be an earnest of what is to come."

Lucia, meantime, had relaxed her hold on Adelaide's arm, and stood a little apart, leaning on the low railing of the bridge.

The chill after sunset was creeping up, and Lucia said quickly:

"We must not stand here longer. It is full of danger—to the English especially—to be out in the cold air when the sun goes down."

"Mr. Clyffe, this is my friend, Miss Lucia Campbell," Adelaide said, looking at Percival, who answered the introduction with a bow—to which Lucia responded with a frank:

"I am glad to see you at Florence, signor."

And then they all turned towards the Piazza

d'Azeglio, under rows of newly-planted trees, bare now of leaves, and past a *caffè*, whence sounds of music and singing were heard.

Adelaide felt a strange sense of satisfaction at Percival's arrival. He put her entirely at her ease; and, before they turned into the Piazza, she was laughing and talking, as she had not done since she had parted with Hester Ponsonby.

It seemed Lucia's turn to be grave, and she did not join in the conversation. At the door of Mr. Cowper-Smith's house, she suddenly said:

"Buon' sera, Miss Millington; buon' sera, signor."

"Lucia, you are to come in, and see Mr. Cowper-Smith about the picture!"

"Not now—not to-night—grazie!"

And then Lucia's swift step was heard on the smooth pavement, and her small lithe figure vanished in the gathering twilight.

CHAPTER X.

ONLY A NAME.

THERE were some additional comforts in the two rooms in the Piazza Cavour. The thick portière hanging over the door was not the least of these, and as Lucia's hand was upon it to draw it aside, she listened for one moment to the low, deep voice which was singing to the accompaniment of Giovanni's violin.

No one heard her coming, and she stood with the curtain in her hand, drawn just wide enough to show the interior of the room, lighted by the fitful blaze of the wood fire on the low hearth, by which her mother sat with some needlework in her long olive-coloured fingers, which were loaded with rings, while bangles jingled on her thin wrists, and a heavy silver chain, with a cross attached to it, lay upon the scarlet handkerchief crossed over the breast of her gown.

Marietta was taking her ease as usual, a large cat tucked up on her lap. Pietro was one of the many stray Florentine cats, and had demanded admission a few months ago, and had been made welcome ever since.

It was not Pietro's first home, and probably would not be the last. He had been stolen from the Monastery of Certosa, where he had spent an easy, luxurious life, sunning himself on the wall below the monastery steps, with five or six other fat representatives of his race.

A chance person, who had come up to the monastery with some flour from Florence, had seized Pietro, and plunged him into the empty sack, where he had struggled and kicked in vain. His captor, however, was not sufficiently careful when he opened the sack. Pietro leaped out, shaking the dust of the flour from his large paws, and raced off, from the narrow street by the Porta Romana to the other side of the Arno. After that he picked up a scanty pittance in the Cloisters of San Lorenzo, where homeless cats are regularly fed every evening.

Such a manner of life did not suit the dignity of a cat brought up by the white-hooded Dominican who acted as lay-brother and porter at Certosa. Pietro happened to be sitting blinking disconsolately at the foot of the stone stairs, where he had taken refuge from some teasing boys, when Lucia, returning from the Uffizi, heard a pitiful mew, and stooping down, stroked Pietro's back with a gentle, caressing hand. Pietro acknowledged the compliment by rubbing against her with his tail erect, and followed

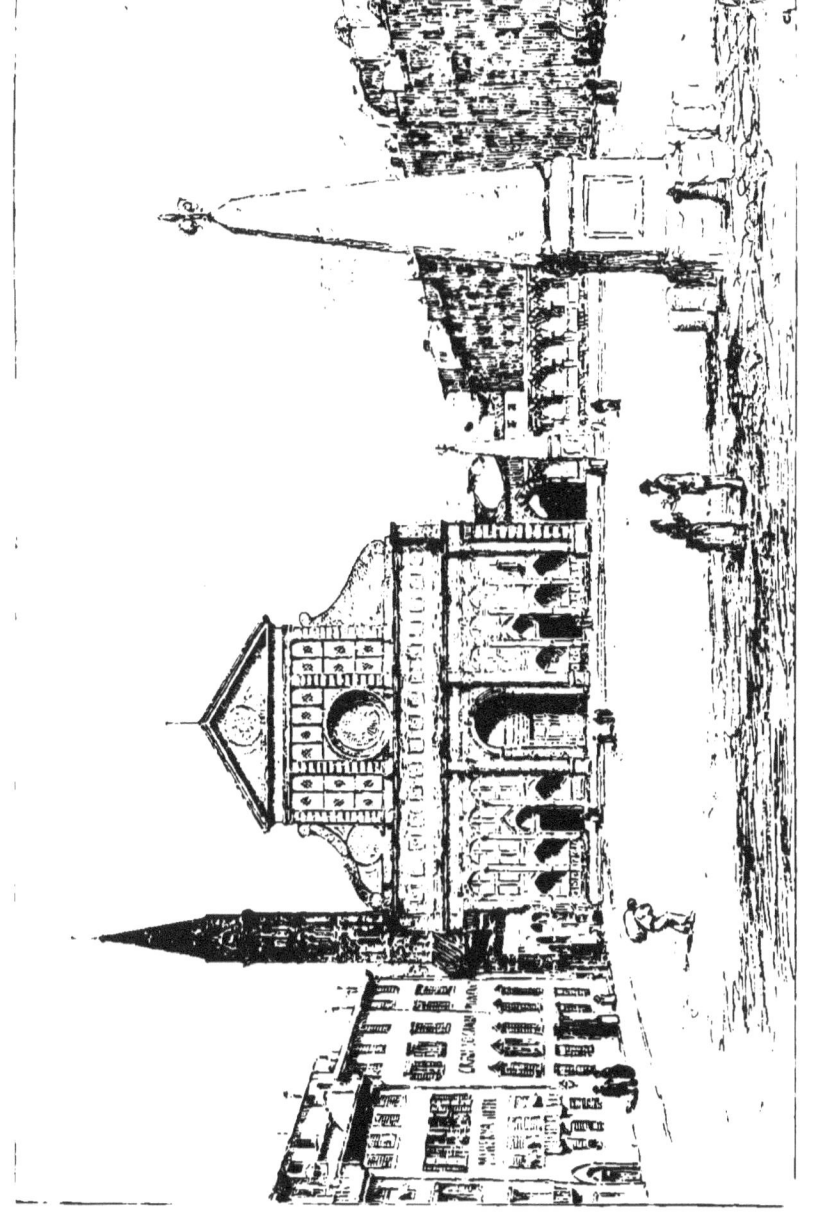

The Church of Santa Maria Novella, Florence.

her upstairs with an evident determination not to be repulsed. Marietta received him with rapture. He loved ease and comfort, and thus they had much in common; so he was not likely to be any trouble to her—for he would wash himself and need no attention—and Pietro had thus become an addition to the family, showing a marked preference for Marietta, probably from the sympathy which existed between them.

Lucia's momentary pause gave her time to take in the whole picture. Giovanni, with his pure refined face and sightless eyes, shaded by long, dark lashes, his violin held close to his cheek, and his ear drinking in the low, musical tones of Mr. Lysaght's voice as he sang Beethoven's beautiful song, which had been postponed on the evening of Lady Anna's first reception, and which he had, by repetition, taught Giovanni's quick ear to catch.

"Adelāide — Adelāide!" The name seemed to linger on his lips as if he were unwilling to part with the sound.

At a first glance there was nothing remarkable or even attractive in Mr. Lysaght's appearance. He was scarcely above the middle height, and he stooped a little, so that he looked shorter than he really was. His forehead was square and broad, and masses of dark hair, with one broad lock of gray, shadowed it. His eyes, however, when deeply moved, were like the key to the whole man. They could flash fire at a story of wrong or oppression, and they could dance with merriment when anything awoke his keen, quiet sense of humour. They could express even more than his voice, which was not as strong as it was musical—it had lost much of its old power, and, though still rich and melodious, did not ring through a room as it had done in times gone by. But his eyes, the colour of which it was hard to define, could fill with tenderness, as he looked at the blind boy's face, with its rapt, intense enjoyment of the music his fingers awoke, in soft accompaniment of Beethoven's matchless song, "Adelaide."

Our best friend—Lucia had called Mr. Lysaght "my best friend;" for had he not, by his timely help, enabled her to resume her work? And had he not done much to brighten the life of her brother, by attentions, offered with the tact and consideration which made it as much a pleasure to receive them as it was to bestow them? Madame Campbell was the first to see Lucia. She held up her finger to prevent her interrupting the music, till the last note had died away.

In those few moments Lucia found herself rehearsing, she hardly knew why, all the past two months since she had first heard Mr. Lysaght's voice in the gallery of the Uffizi, asking her if she would undertake to copy Savonarola's head for him, the beginning of an acquaintance in which Adelaide too had part; and yet on what a different level did they stand! Adelaide was an amateur, working bravely, it is true, to conquer difficulties and fit herself for higher things, but still an amateur, surrounded by the luxuries and refinements of life, while she was an artist toiling for daily bread, spending herself and her strength for those she loved, obliged to enter into the details of money, and to measure her work in the balance with so many, or so few, paper-notes and silver lire.

Perhaps Lucia had never before felt her real position press so heavily upon her as now, when the last "Adelāide" had died away; and Mr. Lysaght, turning, saw her standing with the red curtain behind her.

"I am glad you have come," he said. "I want a few minutes' conversation with you in the ante-room, please."

Then Madame Campbell spoke sharply to Lucia:

"Are you in a dream? What makes you stand there? Do you hear what the signor says? If he desires you in the next room, go at once, and I will make the coffee hot, while Marietta gets the cups."

Madame Campbell was much too far-sighted to wish to lose any chance of winning Mr. Lysaght's favour. "He is going to pay her for that picture," she was thinking; "and it is time, it is time. She talks nonsense about taking less by reason of these few comforts he has furnished for my poor blind boy. But he will not be so inclined, not if I know him.

Come, Marietta!" she said aloud; "put down that great cat and stir about."

Pietro jumped down, as if in reply, with a heavy thud upon the coarse matting which covered the floor, and began to wash his face vigorously.

Meanwhile Mr. Lysaght had held open the door which led into the little ante-room, which was scarcely more than a passage connecting the larger room with the bedrooms opening from it. It was filled with tokens of Lucia's industry in those "trivialities" which Mr. Lysaght had mentioned—screens and wooden frames, to be ornamented by Lucia's ready brush, canvases standing against the wall, and one on an easel.

Lucia did not cross the room with her usually alert step, and as she passed her brother she stooped to kiss his forehead.

"Did you hear that music, Lucia mia? Was it not divine, 'Adelāide'? Ah," Giovanni continued, "but that was the best word. As he sang it he seemed to love it. There is music in the very word."

Lucia drew back from her brother's caressing hand, and said quickly:

"He waits for me. I must go."

Mr. Lysaght had waited patiently while these words had been exchanged between the brother and sister, and now Lucia said, as she followed him into the ante-room, using the Italian word which is so expressive in its conciseness:

"Scusi, signor! I have kept you long; but I spoke to Giovanni."

"There is no haste," Mr. Lysaght said. "What a pleasure it is to see that boy's real joy in music! He must have some lessons from the master who teaches little Margaret Smith."

"I fear that cannot be," Lucia said, in a tone which struck Mr. Lysaght as unusual.

"Well, now to the business on hand. I am delighted with my picture, and have brought you my debt for it. I feel it is too little, far too little; but my purse is not inexhaustible, like Mr. Cowper-Smith's. We agreed for thirty English sovereigns; in this packet you will find that sum in Italian notes. I take it they are the most convenient for you."

Lucia took the large envelope in which the notes were put, and taking them out, said:

"It is too much, far too much, signor."

"It is our agreement. It is purely a matter of business."

"But there was the understanding, signor, that I should pay for the things which you furnished for Giovanni—the portière, the large rug for his feet, the many things you sent me to make me strong—the doctor's physic. I cannot tell what money these things cost, but I will please pay for them from this."

"Do not treat me as if I were a stranger, or take from me the pleasure of doing the slightest thing for your comfort, or for your brother's."

"Ah, signor," Lucia said, in a tone which struck Mr. Lysaght as strangely pathetic; "ah, this, as you say, is *business*. I have toiled for long years. I have taken help from none, except," with a sad smile, "now and again from poor old Andrea Maura. It would have hurt him deeply had I refused his little offerings of fruit, and herbs, and flowers."

"And do you not think it will hurt me, if you treat me less kindly than you did the poor old critic of your pictures?"

Lucia paused for a few moments.

"No, I do not," she said at last; "not in the same way. You are kind, signor, and noble, but I prefer not to be thus in your debt. If you will not tell me what is the money you spent for Giovanni and for me, then I will give you what I think it must be." And she carefully separated from the bundle of notes two for twenty lire each—a large sum it seemed to her—and laid them on the table which was between her and Mr. Lysaght. Then she replaced the other notes in the envelope, and said with a smile:

"Tante grazie, signor! tante grazie."

Mr. Lysaght took the notes and replaced them in his pocket-book. He saw that he could not press his point further, and that he must watch for other opportunities of assistance.

"And have you more commissions?"

"Yes; I am to paint the Madonna del Gran Duca for the little English lady, Margherita, as a present from her papa."

" I am delighted to hear it. I hope you will not be too modest in the fee you charge."

" I shall charge the same as before. I copied the Madonna for Signor Batista ; only I shall profit more, as he had his commission."

" Have you seen Miss Millington's work lately ?"

" Yes, to-day ; it is very good. She has pleased Signor Bassano with the Clytie."

" I saw it yesterday, and thought it surprisingly good ; but then I am no real judge, as you are."

" I went to the studio to-day," Lucia continued, " and Miss Millington and I, we walked to the Ponte Sospeso to see the sunset, and there we met the signorina's English friend—a great friend I think—Mr. Clyffe."

" Oh, so he has come," Mr. Lysaght said shortly. " I think I heard he would be here at Christmas."

" Are you his great friend ?" Lucia asked.

" A friendly acquaintance. We have been thrown together by similarity of position, and by circumstances. He is likely to be welcome in Florence. A man who can do all those things which I cannot."

" What things ?" Lucia asked.

" He can talk on any subject ; tell amusing stories of his numerous acquaintances ; dance and sing. What more is to be desired ? Moreover, he is kind-hearted and has a good temper. Now, what can I add to this character ?"

"You say he is cared for because he sings? *You* sing, signor?"

"I did sing once; but since I had that attack on my lungs, my singing is not likely to bring down an encore, as Mr. Clyffe's will."

"I could not like any voice better than yours," Lucia said simply; "it is to my ear beautiful. Then, as it pleases and delights Giovanni so much, it must delight me."

"All your thoughts seem to centre on Giovanni," Mr. Lysaght said. "What a gift it is for him to have a sister like you! You are, it seems, everything to him."

"Ah, yes! there is a double love always for those who are afflicted, if they are like Giovanni, patient and sweet under it, taking it from God as His will."

"You have learned the secret of happiness," Mr. Lysaght said; "that secret which is with them who fear Him."

"Yes," Lucia said, a strangely beautiful light in her dark eyes, as she raised them to Mr. Lysaght's— "yes, I do think I have. I do not question—I do not wonder what next. I say when much perplexed, 'It is God's will.'"

"So you hold a golden thread to guide you through the maze, and you will see light shining at last."

When Mr. Lysaght was gone, Lucia stood where he had left her for a few moments. Then, instead of following him into the room beyond, she opened a door at the further end of the ante-room, which led to the little, poorly-lighted, bare chamber, scarcely more than a closet, where she slept. The notes must be put safely away, for her mother had enough in hand for their simple requirements for the next month, and it would not do to let her have more than was necessary, or she would see it spent in some bit of finery for herself or Marietta.

Lucia kept her store in an old oak cupboard, much worm-eaten, but carved with grotesque figures, and in the centre the well-known Medici arms, balls and pointed crown above. That old cabinet or cupboard had doubtless many secrets hidden in it, and had seen many changes, since it stood, perhaps, in a chamber at the Villa Careggi, where Lorenzo turned away from the last appeal of Savonarola to repent and give freedom to Florence.

Perhaps the old cabinet had stood centuries ago in the very room where that solemn scene took place, and the dying man—who brought nothing into this world, and could carry nothing out of it—felt all his honour and greatness, his learning, and his culture, fading away in the mists of the valley of the shadow; and Lorenzo the Magnificent was to be even as the poorest monk, dying in his cell in the Convent of San Marco, ere the sun had set that day!

The door of the cupboard creaked as Lucia opened it, and took from it a little leather box, in which she placed the notes. But, instead of closing the door again, she reached up to a higher shelf, at the back of the cabinet, and brought down, covered with dust, a little wooden desk, with a brass plate on the lid, on which were engraved two letters—'J. P.'

The key was kept in the smaller box, where she had just placed the money, and Lucia felt for it, and fitting it into the lock of the desk, opened it. There lay the two letters she had placed there, now six years ago. She had been but a girl of sixteen when her father, in one of his half-lucid intervals, had made her promise that she would keep the two papers safe from every eye; the sealed one, he said, he had written years before; the open letter was to direct Lucia what to do when a certain event became known. She had read it before, but not for some time. She had been too much absorbed in the struggle for existence to think much about it, and it all seemed so vague and hard to understand; it was rambling and incoherent, but as Lucia read it her hand, generally so steady, trembled, and she said aloud:

"What shall I do? Nothing yet, nothing yet. I am not compelled to do so. It will be a sore trouble when I must do it. There can be no doubt—the name—the name! How stupid I have been! Reading the name in French, I never thought of it. I see now—I see now."

It was not Lucia's usual custom to vacillate, and to be uncertain as to what she should do. Now, however, she read and re-read the paper, put it back in the box, took it out again, and, finally, clasping her hands, she cried aloud in her trouble for guidance.

Kneeling by the old oak cupboard, her head resting on her clasped hands, she prayed silently:

"Teach me to do the thing that pleaseth Thee."

Quietness came after conflict, and then Marietta's voice was heard, complaining and irritable.

"Lucia, Lucia, Mr. Lysaght is leaving! Make haste! What *are* you doing here?"

The door, which had been locked by a rusty key, was rattled angrily, and Lucia had only time to replace her treasures, and take the little lamp she had lighted in her hand, and open the door to her sister.

"I am coming," she said gently.

"Coming, yes! You are so afraid we should get your money. You are very miserly. I know you have been locking up what Mr. Lysaght gave you for the picture. So mean!"

And this from one who owed everything to her— this from one who was a mere clog on the wheels of the household—a vain, self-indulgent girl, who was quite content to fold her hands, and reap what others had sowed.

Sometimes Lucia would give Marietta a sharp word when she was provoked beyond endurance— nay, tell her plainly that she did not intend to keep her in idleness when she was twenty-one. But now there was no angry rejoinder, as Lucia closed the door behind her, and followed her sister through the little ante-room to the larger one, where the rest of the party were assembled.

Lucia was so subdued and quiet, and moving so slowly, that Mr. Lysaght said:

"You are overtaxing your strength again. Do be careful." As he took her hand when bidding her good-bye, he felt it was as cold as ice. "Have you caught cold again?" he asked.

"No, I think not, signor. My hands are often cold." But she gave an involuntary shudder, and then, rallying, said: "A cup of coffee will warm me. Addio, signor."

Percival Clyffe's presence in the house in the Piazza d'Azeglio certainly made a great change. He put everyone into a good humour, Mrs. Gray said, and no wonder—he had always a pleasant word for everybody. Percival was decidedly a popular person, and though he might not precisely lay claim to popularity, still he never lost the chance of obtaining it. He pleased Lady Anna by telling her she had made the suite of rooms she occupied famous. Everyone in Florence said they were quite the most attractively "got up" of any of the English quarters, and that her receptions were the most brilliant. Then he told her that Daisy looked prettier than ever, that Miss Millington had worked wonders as a companion to her, and that he should write at once to his aunt Lady Mary and tell her that Adelaide was thriving and on the high road to be a distinguished artist.

Percival knew very little about art, but he made the assertion as he made many others—haphazard. He took life easily, for his own prospects were not very brilliant. The briefs never came, and he was, he said, looking out for some employment as secretary to a club or a company, or a post in the colonies. He had got his name put down on the list, through influence at headquarters, and he hoped he might succeed in obtaining a place as Judge of the Supreme Court of Judicature on the West Coast of Africa, or Cyprus—it did not matter where.

"I hope you will not succeed," Lady Anna was saying one morning, when she was at her writing-table, engaged with her voluminous correspondence, from which from time to time she turned to listen to Percival, or talk to him.

"It does matter very much where you go; fevers are so horrible on the West Coast of Africa. You had better wait and be patient."

"I am the mirror of patience, my dear aunt," he said; "and I am sure you do not hear me grumble!"

"No, indeed, you are always so cheerful; and you are welcome here as long as you choose to stay."

"Thanks, you are awfully kind; but I am afraid you do not know what you are saying. If I could choose I should prolong my present existence indefinitely."

"Very well," Lady Anna said, "let it be indefinitely. By-the-bye, Percy, what have you made out of Mr. Lysaght?"

"I knew him before I found him established here," Percival said; "he is no novelty to me."

"He will come into possession of Cruttwell, I suppose; and really I thought a few weeks ago Mr. Beauchamp was sinking. He has rallied a little, but he will not live long. Has Mr. Lysaght said anything to you about the property?'

"Not much; he is more reserved than ever I knew him."

"Is that report of living grandchildren likely to be true?"

"I have heard nothing about it here; I expect it was only report."

"Mr. Lysaght is not likely to be too eager to press his inquiries," Lady Anna said.

"You are wrong there; he is the last man to wish to wear other people's shoes. He is a very honest-hearted fellow, and besides, he has high principle. As soon as Mr. Beauchamp is gone he will advertise, and set inquiries on foot in the proper quarter; but till the old man dies, I do not know why he should move in it. The rumour reached him through an Italian in London, who lived in one of the dens in the East-end which Lysaght frequents. This man told him he had a sister who married a gentleman, whose father was furious with him, and utterly disowned him; that they had had a hand-to-hand tussle, and he threw something at his head—when he had made an attempt to see him—and was within an inch of killing him ; as it was, he was felled to the ground."

"My dear Percival, how shocking! *what* a man for poor dear Mary to be tied to for life!"

"Well, we are not sure that this furious father and Mr. Beauchamp are one and the same; though many of the particulars fitted. The place was in the south of England, the wife had been a professional singer, and the man had changed his name, and left the country with her. But as to the name, the Italian could not get very near it. It seems he had never had much to do with his sister, and he had sunk so low that he never cared to make any effort to find her. That is about all *I* know, or Lysaght knows, either."

"But, my dear Percy, this man surely can be further questioned?"

"No, he can't, for he is dead," Percival said shortly. "He was found by Lysaght in a miserable condition, and he befriended him, but he died soon after he got him into the hospital. He had earned a scanty pittance working in ornamental hair, and when Lysaght found him he was dying of inflammation of the lungs and starvation."

"How shocking! But is it not odd Mr. Lysaght never told me this history? He just hinted that he had heard a report about Mr. Beauchamp having a son, but he gave me no details."

"It is not his way to give details," Percival said, pulling himself together, and saying, as he rose out of his luxurious chair: "It is nearly one o'clock. I must go and look up Daisy; her conversation master must be gone by this time."

"Not till one precisely. Have you heard her speak Italian? It *is* so charming."

"No. I like to hear her speak English best, but for the very good reason that I do not understand Italian."

And then Percival departed, not, however, to look after Daisy, but to turn his steps towards the Via Alfieri, and thence to the studio where Adelaide worked. He had now been in Florence several weeks. Christmas was over, and the new year had dawned with sunshine and blue skies; and on the sunny side of the Arno people forgot that it was yet winter, and that cold winds would sweep down from the Apennines for many weeks to come.

It was not the first time that Percival had gone towards the studio, and had tried to persuade Adelaide to come home to luncheon, instead of eating her frugal repast in the studio. Percival had a half-formed intention of getting Adelaide to leave her work on this delightful afternoon, and go to San Miniato or Fiesole with him. He had, however, been forestalled. He had just crossed the road in front of the English Cemetery when he saw Adelaide and Mr. Lysaght turning in the opposite direction.

Mrs. Murchison had been in retirement since Percival's arrival. She had caught cold at a reception given by some English people, where she had acted in a play, and had, when over-heated, walked in the illuminated garden which filled the quadrangle of the Palazzo Bourtolin. A chill at Florence is very apt to be accompanied with fever, and Mrs. Murchison had been anything but a patient invalid.

She had got tired of the Professor; and having found herself out of her depth with him, and showed that her knowledge of Italian history was a little superficial, she had not encouraged his visits to her sitting-room, and had found the time hang heavily on her hands.

"Why doesn't that girl Adelaide come and see me? Go and fetch her to luncheon," she had said to Mr. Lysaght that morning. "Do pray make her come, for I am perishing of ennui."

Mr. Lysaght had not been at all unwilling to please his sister in this respect, and after some little hesitation Adelaide had consented to go with him to Paoli's Hotel. Suddenly, just as Percival was following them down the Via di Pinti, Adelaide turned quickly; and he saw she had forgotten something, for Mr. Lysaght left her and hastened back to the studio. Then Percival was at her side at once.

"Where are you going?" he asked, rather abruptly. "I came to take you back to luncheon. It is absurd your starving on miserable biscuits and rolls every day."

"I am going to luncheon at Paoli's with Mrs. Murchison," Adelaide replied.

"Mrs. Murchison! Who is she? Some new friend?"

"Mr. Lysaght's sister," Adelaide said. "You must have known her name."

Mr. Lysaght now rejoined them. He had Adelaide's little basket in his hand, which she had left in the studio.

"Will you come with us to Paoli's?" Mr. Lysaght said; "and then, at two o'clock, we should have time to drive up to Fiesole before the sun sets."

Percival accepted the invitation not too graciously, and the three walked on together without speaking.

"I forget whether you know my sister, Clyffe," Mr. Lysaght said.

"No, I don't," was the rather short answer. "I do not think I ever saw any of your people."

"She has been very unwell, and I find it hard to make her prudent. She has not come down to the *table d'hôte* for nearly a fortnight."

The bell was just ringing when the party turned into the salle. Mrs. Murchison was already there, wearing a very becoming fur of silver fox over a tightly-fitting black cloth dress. She received Adelaide with great warmth.

"You naughty child! not to come and see me till you were sent for! Ah! is this Mr. Clyffe?—Percival Clyffe?—I know him well by report. I am delighted to see you, or in fact to see anyone."

"That is a doubtful compliment for me, Mrs. Murchison," Percival said, laughing.

"Well, I have had a horribly dull time. Do you know, I have sketched the view from my window upstairs till I see it in my dreams, and begin to hate it. How charmed they must all be in the Piazza d'Azeglio to have your company! They are just a little dull there. I don't suit Lady Anna; I am too unconventional. Ah! Professor Scoresby, how are you?"

This was said across the table to the little Professor, who knew he had declined in favour, and yet could not quite resist the attraction of his enchantress.

"Have you settled to your satisfaction the genealogy of that fair Etruscan lady with the blue earrings in the museum? You thought you were a thousand years out in your reckoning as to her birth; but that is a small matter."

The poor Professor, being touched on a weak point, could not resist beginning a long history of the Etruscan monuments, of which absolutely nothing is really known.

Those strange Etruscan figures, shaded by their red silk curtains in the museum, always seem to gaze out from an unknown and unknowable past with a sort of stately challenge to us, who give back their stony stare with one of inquiry. "Our past is our own, and with it you pigmies of the present have nothing to do. The mystery is insoluble. Do not attempt to find the solution."

And with this even an erudite scholar like Professor Scoresby must rest content. Not that he was content; and he had at least the right to air his conjectures, and to let the result of his researches, however unsatisfactory, be known.

Long before he had got through his history Mrs. Murchison's attention had wandered, and the Professor was startled by his neighbour, a deaf man, whom most people at Paoli's rather avoided, suddenly breaking out with:

"I can't hear what you say, sir. Are you addressing me?"

The Professor, with a watery smile, shook his head, and then for the first time became conscious that his fair friend opposite was talking to Percival Clyffe, and that she much preferred the ripple of his small talk to a learned disquisition on an Etruscan lady, whose blue earrings had been supposed to assist the researches of the Professor as to the date of her birth.

Very soon, everyone at the *table d'hôte* became aware that Mrs. Murchison had found a ready listener to her flow of brilliant "nothings." As the chairs were pushed back, and the people were moving off, arranging their plans for the fine afternoon, several eye-glasses were directed towards the group of which Mrs. Murchison was the centre.

The American lady, whose husband had loudly

resented Mrs. Murchison's remarks about her eye, said in a stage whisper as she passed :

"What a flirt that woman is! She'll be taking in that young man, as she did the old one. Poor things!"

Adelaide heard the words, and she felt the colour rush to her face. She looked at Mrs. Murchison, expecting to see her show some annoyance or perhaps confusion. On the contrary, she only seemed to be laughing more merrily than ever, and Adelaide hoped that she might not have heard what was said. The next moment she was convinced to the contrary, for Mrs. Murchison said to Percival :

"Did you hear that flattering opinion of me from the Boston lady? She owes me a grudge, because I mentioned the very obvious fact that she squints. I am very incautious, but I manage to get on, nevertheless. I should not in the least wonder if, before the end of the winter, I am quite intimate with 'Mrs. Walter Fisk, junior'—for that is her style and title in the visitors' book:—'Mr. Walter Fisk, junior, Mrs. W. F., junior, Boston, U.S., North America.' I do wonder, if these are the Fisks juniors, what the Fisks seniors must be! Adelaide, how grave you look! She is always shocked at my frivolity, Mr. Clyffe—almost as much as Godfrey is shocked. Well, have you ordered the carriage for Fiesole, Godfrey?"

"It is too cold for you to drive to-day—certainly

as far as Fiesole, Theresa. You must not think of it. Your cough is not gone."

"Ah, what a dragon you are!" Mrs. Murchison said, manipulating the long ends of her fur boa, as with a graceful action she placed one end over her shoulder and the other across her slender figure. "I mean to go, all the same; so order the carriage, and let us get ready. Come with me to my room, Miss Millington, and I can lend you a fur cape. You must have another wrap."

The drive to Fiesole is one of the most beautiful in Florence. As the road winds and turns up the steep sides of the hill, on the crest of which the ancient city sits like a queen, the views of the country on every side are varied and lovely. The hills dotted with villas, the Arno winding through the plain, the blue mountains which rise towards the great rugged mass of the Carraras in the horizon, and the noble outline of the lofty range which encircle Pisa. Florence lies far below, with her Duomo and Campanile, her domes and towers. Dark masses of shade show where the cypresses are climbing up some hill-side, as custodians of the monastery or church—and here and there, their lofty spires shoot up against the blue sky, every branch distinctly traced in the translucent atmosphere, where everything is clearly defined.

It is strange to ascend from Florence, with all its old memories, where we seem to live in the past and are living, as it were, with the people of a bygone age, to Fiesole, which goes so much further back, into ages seen but imperfectly through the mists of centuries, where we can but catch here and there some clue to the life which was lived in Fiesole, on the hill, long, long before the banks of the Arno had been studded with churches or dwellings for the rich or poor, and the City of Flowers had become famous in the valley.

The carriage was left at the Piazza, and Adelaide found herself with Mr. Lysaght, while Mrs. Murchison took complete possession of Percival.

A strange pang shot through her, which she scarcely understood, as from above the little Roman amphitheatre she watched Percival Clyffe helping Mrs. Murchison as she tripped down the broken tiers of old seats to the tiny arena, where, on a block of fallen stone, she seated herself, breathless and laughing.

"Come down, you two sober people!" she exclaimed. "You stand there both looking so solemn, as if you expected the lions to come out and eat us——"

Percival sprang up, and putting out his hand to Adelaide, said:

"Come down. I will help you."

He smiled up at her with his brightest and most winning smile, but she said:

"I am quite able to jump down by myself, thanks."

And very soon she had reached the place where Mrs. Murchison was sitting.

There is something very solemn in that little amphitheatre, shut in by the encircling hills—so lonely and so quiet now—once the scene of the savage conflicts watched by excited crowds, gathered from the city above it, or flocking thither from remote towns among the mountains, to feast their eyes upon the death-struggles of condemned slaves. And it may be that the now desolate and forsaken spot once rang with the cry, "Christianios ad leones!"

Adelaide felt Mrs. Murchison's laughter and perpetual banter very much out of harmony with the place. Even when she changed her mood, and began to talk of the Etruscan walls, and show Percival how well up she was in Italian history, it was with the same self-conscious air, the same light, frivolous manner. Yet he seemed to enjoy it; and as he was, unlike the Professor, very hazy as to dates and eras, of Etruscan or Roman remains, and had never given history a serious thought, it was only likely that he should consider Mrs. Murchison as clever as she was pretty.

The shadow on Adelaide's face did not escape Percival's observation, and he left Mrs. Murchison to her brother's care, and asked Adelaide to come and show him anything else that was wonderful in the place.

"Everything is wonderful," Adelaide said, "when we think that this little city is so much older than the large one below it in the valley. The cathedral is very interesting, but you ought to see that when you have more time. Let us go up the steep path to the little Franciscan convent and church; we shall see the sunset from there. Look, it is beginning to be glorious."

"Yes—this is worth coming to see," Percival said, as they stood together on the plateau below the little church. "This is glorious! What a view it is! Tell me about it. I am very ignorant, you know. I was quite struck dumb with Mrs. Murchison's learning."

"I am not learned," Adelaide said, "and since I came to Florence I have only felt how little I really know. But after all it is not mere knowing which gives pleasure. It is better to feel a little to your very heart's depths than know a great deal which you do not feel. But," she said, "I find it is not thought 'the thing' now to express any great admiration either for people, pictures, or places. There is no one here to whom I can talk about what I like best, and why I like it, except, perhaps, Lucia Campbell and dear Daisy."

"Please talk to me," Percival said, "about all you care for; don't shut me out."

"After all," Adelaide said, "I don't want to say too much to anyone, for I have not, and never shall, have, the power of expressing myself well about things I care for most."

"You express yourself well enough to please me, anyhow," he said.

Turning to look at her face in the glow of the sunset, the night in the park when he had seen her first, with the moonlight shedding its pure radiance over her, came back to him, and he thought her now, as he thought her then, beautiful.

She was leaning against the low parapet of the walls, which are here some thirty feet in depth, and looking out over one of the fairest scenes which eye can ever look upon—with a wistful gaze.

Presently the bells of the Angelus came borne across the valley on the wind—sounding from countless campaniles—and deep and sonorous even at that distance from the great Duomo.

The bell of the little Franciscan church hard by, and the Cathedral lower down, answered with the same familiar sound, and after a silence Adelaide said:

"We ought to be going. Mrs. Murchison should not be out after sunset; and Mr. Lysaght will have the carriage closed going back. So good-bye to the view; we can come up again, and the days will be lengthening soon."

Percival echoed her words.

"Yes, we can come up again, and then you will tell me more of those things you feel."

"Perhaps," she said. "But there is Mr. Lysaght beckoning to us. I knew he would be anxious to get Mrs. Murchison away."

Mrs. Murchison was waiting rather impatiently. She had had quite enough of Fiesole, and it was getting cold. The carriage was closed in returning, and she lay back in her particular corner, muffled up in furs and Shetland shawls, and did not invite any conversation.

Only a little desultory talk was kept up between Mr. Lysaght and Percival, and it was rather a relief when the carriage drew up before Paoli's hotel, and the party separated.

Percival Clyffe and Adelaide said good-bye then, and went along the Arno, and then turned into a labyrinth of narrow streets where—in the evening glow still lingering—the Florentines were out and about, as if it were April instead of January.

These old streets of Florence have a wonderful charm, with the long narrow thoroughfares opening to right and left, where here and there light streams in, and a gable higher than its neighbours catches a sunset glory, which deepens the effect of the gloom below. Then there are the open stores, where a variety of wares are displayed—where linen and stuff goods are felt and priced by voluble housewives—where at his stall the shoemaker sits cross-legged, tapping the sole of a boot with his awl, and keeping up a conversation with some neighbour who leans in a *dolce far niente* fashion against the doorpost, and, as he puffs his pipe, uses his hands with the expressive gestures which Italians can alone understand.

It is amusing to listen to two or three Florentines in eager talk about politics, it may be, or public affairs, or domestic events. The movement of the head, and the shrug of the shoulders—the sudden start forward or step backward—all these gestures serve in the place of connected sentences, nay, even of connected words.

The sign is sufficient : and love and hate, approval or disapproval, mockery or fun, all are seen by the sign and understood by the tone of the " A—a—" or the low laugh which accompanies some sudden movement of head, arm or foot!

Emerging from the labyrinth of houses, Percival and Adelaide came out by a church, and thence into a wide, modern street—where the Jews have lately built a grand and imposing temple of stately proportions, with a dome, and rich carving, which tells of the wealth of their people in Florence, and of their devotion to their old faith—and then they turned into the Piazza d'Azeglio.

Lady Anna did not as a rule concern herself much whether Adelaide had taken her luncheon to the studio or whether she came home at one o'clock.

But that night at dinner she asked in a low repressed tone, which always made Miss Cromwell tremble and Mr. Cowper-Smith dread that he had done something amiss, and would make the bright colour mantle in little Daisy's usually pale cheeks :

"Did you take luncheon at Paoli's to-day, Miss Millington?"

"Yes," Adelaide said; "Mrs. Murchison has been ill and sent for me."

"Rather extraordinary, I think. She is a person who rather delights in setting certain acknowledged rules of good society at defiance. Perhaps, another time, Miss Millington, you will kindly let me know when you have invitations elsewhere."

"Mother, darling!" Daisy exclaimed. "Adelaide generally takes her luncheon in a basket to the studio. Mrs. Gray gets it ready for her; nothing but sandwiches and hard-boiled eggs."

"Now, Aunt Anna," Percival said, breaking in, "how *did* you find out we were at Paoli's?"

"I happened to be driving back, with Daisy, from the Cascine, and saw you and Mr. Lysaght turning out of the Via Tornabuoni with Miss Millington. It really is not of any great importance."

"Importance! no, indeed," said Mr. Cowper-Smith. "I am very glad you had a proper luncheon, my dear Miss Millington. You won't thrive in this climate if you cut your luncheons short: every doctor will tell you so."

Lady Anna leaned back in her chair in an attitude of profound indifference, and Percival said,

"Mrs. Murchison is a very amusing little woman, and wonderfully clever. She can talk like any learned professor, and she seems just as much at her ease in speaking Italian as English. She is very graceful and pretty, and the most complete contrast to her brother. They are like people dropped from different planets; both out of the common, though."

"Really!" Lady Anna said, playing with Daisy's little hand, which she had taken in hers—for Daisy always sat next her mother, that what she ate or did not eat might be watched; "it would certainly not strike me that either Mr. Lysaght or Mrs. Murchison were anything but ordinary mortals.. You are so happy, Percy, in seeing everything through rose-coloured spectacles. The world must be a delightful place to you."

"As to the rose-coloured glasses," Mr. Cowper-Smith said, laughing irreverently as he repeated his wife's words; " Mrs. Murchison is rosy enough without looking at her through pink glasses."

Percival was cracking a walnut, and appeared to be intent on peeling it. Then he said, as he helped himself to salt :

"You think some of that bright colour is laid on with a brush, as Miss Millington lays it on her pictures ?"

"I am certain of it," said Mr. Cowper-Smith; " but it really is no business of mine. I never wish to see my Peggy with any more colour in her cheeks than nature has given her ; that is all. Miss Millington does not need to use the rouge-pot to her face, in spite of starving, as I hear she does. I must say Florence air suits her."

The remark, as was natural, brought a more vivid rose-colour into Adelaide's face, and her eyes were luminous, as she said—with a desire to defend the absent, and perhaps to atone for a secret annoyance which Mrs. Murchison had caused her that day :

"I don't think people ought to be judged about colour. Some have naturally a very high colour, and

I think, perhaps, Mrs. Murchison is one, for she always looks the same."

" That I don't doubt, for a moment," Mr. Cowper-Smith said, laughing. " If she fainted dead off you would not see her grow pale."

" She may accentuate her eyebrows a little and——"

" Really!" said Lady Anna, rising, with Daisy's hand in hers—" really, it is not a subject of *any* importance to us, dearest, whether Mrs. Murchison's colour is natural or not. I do not think her a desirable acquaintance ; but there let the matter rest. Now, Percy, you must hear Daisy play that last new waltz of Chopin's ; come, darling, let Miss Cromwell play the accompaniment."

As they all went to the drawing-room, Daisy said :

" Mother, *may* the blind boy come one day and play to us? You half promised that he should. He is the brother of the artist who is to paint the Madonna for me, and the Signor says he is quite a genius. May Adelaide tell Lucia to come with him? Father said I might ask you. *Do*, mother ! I do so want to hear him."

" We will see about it, darling. I must first be sure that he comes out of a healthy home. There are so many fevers amongst the poor in Florence."

" He is not exactly poor—I mean his sister has worked so hard for them all that they live in a nice sort of house in the Piazza Cavour. Oh, I do so want to hear Giovanni—Lucia's brother, you know."

"You seem to have the whole family history by heart, darling," her mother said. "I do not think you should be told about such sad things."

"But, mother, we *ought* to know about them and think about them, that we may be thankful for all we have given us. I will tell Percy about him, and he will beg you to send for him, I know."

Little Daisy played her Chopin, and then went round to say good-night. As she kissed her cousin, she whispered something in his ear, and he returned:

"All right; I'll manage it."

And then he thought within himself that perhaps the time was over when Lady Anna would take his recommendation of what would please Daisy best.

He wondered whether Adelaide's visit had been a success. It chafed him to see her patronized and questioned, as from a superior level, as to where she had lunched, and what she had done. If only Adelaide's appearance were to be taken as a sign of contentment, that had, indeed, changed; and there was a brightness about her, and a zest which had been wanting before. She looked what, indeed, she was, —a woman who had awoke from self-absorption and self-contemplation, from accepting the loving judgment passed upon her and her work, to the conviction that she had as yet done so little worth recording, and that she had, as it were, to begin her life over again; just, as little Daisy said, she had to begin her drawing. But it was the courage and humility with which she had done this that had given an added charm to her noble countenance—a charm Percival Clyffe saw without in the least divining its cause. The obstinate adherence to huge hats and short waists and baggy sleeves and loose hair had given way also.

"Who am I to make myself conspicuous?" she had begun to say, instead of, "I like to show I am not a slave to fashion books, and am not ashamed to own it." It was an awakening in all directions; and there was another yet to come.

CHAPTER XI.

PROBLEMS HARD TO SOLVE.

"OH! to be in England now that April's there!" is a wish perhaps echoed by many who are compelled to live the greater part of their time in other countries.

Our English spring has its peculiar charm, and few hearts are so dull as to be unable to respond in some degree to the song of "the wise thrush" as he wakes at dawn, and repeats his notes with an ever-increasing joyful ring of gladness, as he tells his mate that the day is born—the spring day, which means so much to the company of birds—that happy company—which fill the air with their joyous matins and evensong at the dawn and dying of every day.

But an April morning in Florence, how beautiful it is! Then, indeed, the City of Flowers is in its glory. In lavish profusion the lilac wistaria hangs its clusters over every wall, and the Banksia roses mingle their golden blossoms with those of the Florentine hawthorn, and throw their flower-laden branches over parapet and gateway in every direction. Then how beautiful is the mass of flowers arranged on the great stone ledges of the Strozzi Palace, where they smile at every passer-by, and tempt many a centime from the purses of the English visitors! Purple and white iris, carnations, tulips and bouquets of the pale tea-rose, are offered by the flower-dealers, with bunches of lilacs and golden-brown wall-flowers, making the air fragrant with their delicious perfume.

The spring had been late even in the sunny south, and the Florentines said that the flowers were all a month behind their time. They made up for it now by an excess of beauty and a more lavish profusion than usual. After weeks of uncertain weather, with chill winds coming down from the Apennines, still in the higher ranges snow-crowned, spring, which in temperature was like an English summer, had burst forth, and Florence was in its full beauty.

It had become familiar ground to Adelaide, and no one ever entered more fully into the charm of Florence than she did. For her there might indeed be said to be sermons in the stones of palaces, convents and churches, and she would listen with wonder to some of the English who frequented Lady Anna's receptions, to whom all the memories and associations so precious to her were a blank.

Many rush through the galleries and churches in passing to Rome or Naples, and take away with them a very faint impression of what they have seen. Such people, however, let it be said, take away faint impressions from every place, whether Florence, Naples, Berlin, or London.

It really makes very little difference to many English and American tourists where they are; they have to "do" the different cities, and say they have " done them." And there is no doubt a certain enjoyment in this race from city to city; but, like many other of the races such people run, when it is over it is done with.

Of course, it is necessary to gather up a few names and pronounce them properly. It is necessary to distinguish Savonarola from Michael Angelo, and not to get "mixed" with Dante and Petrarch; to learn a few Italian phrases and expressions; to be ready with "Chi lo sa" and "Molto bello," and to pass for lovers of the "faultless painter" and Raphael. But it often amused Adelaide to hear such remarks as Mrs. Ponsonby made, who with Hester had joined the party in the Piazza d'Azeglio in February.

Mrs. Ponsonby was far more interested in retailing Dryborough gossip, and stories of Mr. Beauchamp's increased illness and irascibility, and in a novel from Vieusseux's Library, than in any visits to Santa Maria Novella, San Marco, or the Bargello. Then, though Mrs. Ponsonby drove through the Piazza of the Annunziata nearly every day, she had never seen the beautiful *bambini* in their swaddling clothes, each in his separate medallion of pale blue, each with his own expression, over the colonnade

THE CONVENT OF THE CERTOSA, FLORENCE.

before the Ospedale degli Innocenti. Then, too, the beautiful front of the old Palazzo Bourtolin was lost on her, though again and again she had stopped there to pay a visit, with Lady Anna, to some English residents in one of the spacious *piani*.

Florence was to Mrs. Ponsonby what it is to hundreds of English visitors—a very agreeable place, with old houses, and pictures, and pleasant drives. But it was necessary to avoid the narrow streets, for they were decidedly malodorous; and though Percival Clyffe insisted that she ought to see "the little poky place where Dante lived, and the funny little Church of San Martino," she was only anxious to turn away—the *odours* were so disagreeable!

It is hard to say which class of travellers and residents in foreign countries are the most objectionable—those who pretend to a deep interest in everything, who make a business of their travels, and stare at everything, whether they care for it or not, marking each point of interest or picture in their " Hare " or " Horner," and following a certain routine with slavish precision; or those who might as well be at home, and who certainly have the merit of a good-tempered, honest avowal, like Mrs. Ponsonby's, " that she didn't care for dark, narrow streets with bad smells; and that, though she liked a drive by the Arno to the Cascine, she would be quite as well pleased to be driving in Hyde Park in Lady Anna's carriage."

Certainly to neither of these classes did Adelaide

belong; and, now she had Hester for a companion, she had really much enjoyment in Florence, apart from the mornings she passed at the studio, where her progress was steady and assured.

"This is such a glorious day!" she said one morning to Hester. "I shall take a holiday, and we will go out together, lunch at Cornelio's, and have a good time. Shall we?"

"I wish I could come, too!" Daisy said. "Oh, I wish I could!"

"It would be delightful if you could, darling," Adelaide said; "but, now the weather is so beautiful, you will soon lose your cough."

Daisy shook her head.

"I never had a cough so long before." But she threw her arms round Adelaide's neck, and said: "Don't, please, say anything about my cough, because mother always says it was that day I was out after sunset with father that gave me this cold. Please remember; and will you ask whether Giovanni can come this afternoon and play to me? Marietta can bring him, can't she?"

"I will ask Lady Anna's leave. I must not do anything without consulting her."

"Oh! here is Percy. Percy will do," Daisy exclaimed.

Percy came into the room with less of his jocund light-heartedness than of old.

"Oh," he said, "I came to find out whether you two girls would come with us to Prato to-day.

Mrs. Murchison is going to sketch there. Will you come?"

"No, thanks," Adelaide said; "I have just arranged a holiday for myself and Hester. But there is nothing to prevent you from going to Prato if you prefer it, Hester."

"I would rather be with you, of course; only—won't you go to Prato?"

"No. Still, do not let me hinder you if you wish to go."

"Oh, very well," Percival said carelessly. "I must be off, anyhow; I am to meet the rest of the party at the station. Good-bye.—What is it, Daisy?"

"Percy, do please ask mother to let Giovanni come here this afternoon—do!"

"All right—why shouldn't he? I will go over to the Piazza Cavour and order him to do so."

"Not *order*, Percy; ask Marietta or Lucia to bring him. If *you* do it, mother won't mind."

Percival stooped to kiss his little cousin; then, with an indifferent whistle, was gone.

Miss Cromwell now came with orders from Lady Anna that Daisy was to go downstairs; for the doctor was there.

"Oh, dear, I do so wish mother would not have a doctor so often!" Daisy said. But she submitted to be wrapped in a large shawl, and, putting her hand into Miss Cromwell's arm, she said: "You dear old Protector! you would not wrap me up so tight if you had not to do it as your duty, would you?"

"Wait, Miss Margaret" (it was Mrs. Gray's voice); "you have not had your cod-liver oil. You *must* take it before you see her ladyship."

Daisy turned her head away.

"No, I *can't*, and I *won't* take it now! It is horrid, and I know does no good."

"You will get me into trouble if you don't take it," Mrs. Gray said; "that's all. There, that is Sam coming up, to see why you do not go downstairs."

Daisy hesitated a moment, and then opened her mouth and swallowed the contents of the wine-glass Mrs. Gray held to her lips. She shuddered at the dose, which, however disguised, has always a certain repulsiveness about it, to sensitive tastes like little Daisy's.

"That's for *your* sake, Grayling" (her pet name for her faithful nurse). "Now then, Protector, dear, let's be off. Good-bye, Hester—good-bye, Adelaide," Daisy said.

"Bless her! Is not she too good for us—too good for this world? It's just as I said—she would have been better at home. I am sure all last month the winds were sharp enough to cut anybody's head off! No wonder she got cold, dear lamb!"

"It is only a cold," Adelaide said. "We are just as likely to get colds in Florence as in England."

"Rather more likely, so it seems," said Mrs. Gray, turning away with a sigh.

"Don't you think Daisy looks very thin and

transparent?" Hester said, as she and Adelaide left the house together. "I am certain her father is anxious about her. What wonderful patience he has! I wonder how often we have heard him lectured about after-sunset chills! Cousin Anna does not spare him."

"She spares no one," Adelaide said; "but her heart is bound up in Daisy. I cannot imagine what she would do if the child were taken from her."

"It would simply kill her," Hester said.

"Grief does not kill," was Adelaide's reply; "trouble either hardens or softens us; it seldom kills us, though it may kill the joy in us for ever."

"How solemn you are all at once, Adelaide!" Hester said. "I am sure I wonder how I bear *my* troubles. I am brought out here by mother, in the hope of making me forget Hugh; it only makes me care a hundred times more for him. As soon as he has taken his degree I shall insist on having our engagement acknowledged. Cousin Mary says there could not be any objection then. I know you never liked Hugh," Hester went on; "you did not understand each other. He thought you so awfully clever, and I think he was afraid of you."

"What nonsense, Hester! pray let us talk of something pleasanter; the idea of my cleverness has, I hope, been blown away at Florence. If I have learned nothing else here, I have learned that I am a very ordinary person indeed."

"Adelaide, you don't really think so?" Hester said.

"Well, I will be honest; I think I have, perhaps, more *desire* to gain knowledge and wisdom—which is far *more* than knowledge—than many women of my age, and I think I have enough smattering of many subjects to quicken my longing for real culture. But take my conceit about my pictures as an example. It was ever so long before I could believe I was unable to copy a picture like Lucia Campbell, and—ah! you don't know what that awakening cost me. I have had other dreams too, which are fading away, and the awakening from them will hurt me more—far more!"

Hester's hand was on Adelaide's arm, and she gave it a sympathetic pressure.

"Do I know what you mean? May I guess?"

"No, don't attempt to guess—or to put into words—what I am thoroughly ashamed of. Until anyone has absolutely said they care for you, no one has a right to think it is so. It is the same thing—I mean it comes from the same root—intolerable self-conceit is the root, and bitter disappointment is the fruit."

"Oh, Adelaide!" Hester said, her round, child-like eyes filled with sympathy; "oh, Adelaide! when I first came to Florence in February I thought you looked so happy, and so *splendid*. It will all come right."

"It will all come right, because everything does,"

Adelaide said. "Now shall we turn into San Marco? It is just the right morning to think of Savonarola, sitting under the damask rose-tree in the cloister garden, discoursing, when a young man, to many of his younger brethren, who listened to him with the utmost attention. It is good to think of him here, making San Marco a school of painting in the service of religion, making himself felt as a living power, as Angelico was felt as an almost heavenly influence! And his hopes were not centred only in the narrow limits of the convent, but reached out to the City beyond. His words claimed attention — burning words, which denounced sin in a manner terrible to hear, and yet pleaded with the children with a loving and tender earnestness; and then the end—the bitter end!"

Hester listened as Adelaide spoke, her enthusiasm illuminating her face and making it beautiful. Suddenly she stopped:

"You can read it all in scores of books. Why should I tell you what you can find in Mrs. Oliphant's 'Makers of Florence,' and 'Villari' and 'Romola.' Come, let us go and look at Fra Angelico's work in the cells, and at *his* cell who is the master spirit here."

"But I like to hear you tell me everything," said Hester; "and I do like to see your face light up as you tell it. Reading is never half as good as listening."

But Adelaide had apparently changed her mood now, and the two girls walked through the long line of passages which divide the cells, on the walls of which are left the record of the life work of the Fra Angelico and his friend, the Fra Benedetto.

It is said that the lives of many a creator of beautiful things, whether poet, painter, or sculptor, are often found to be painfully out of harmony with their work. Perhaps, therefore, the great charm which seems to linger round those tender, loving Madonnas and Saints of Fra Angelico's creation, is the certainty that his life of pure, devout retirement, of gentle modesty, and meekness of disposition, was in perfect accord with the scenes which his brush has left recorded on the walls of San Marco. The man who could not paint the agony of the Cross without tears; the man who, as he worked, prayed that his work might please God; who, pure in heart, might well receive the blessing promised to such by the Lord Himself;—surely all this is shadowed forth in the ethereal beauty of his Saints, who look down on the careless passers-by, as their footfalls echo through the deserted corridors, and seems to call upon those who admire the work to give a thought to him who wrought it, as one whose highest gifts were consecrated to God's service.

Adelaide silently pointed out here and there some favourite fresco of her own, and it was not till they reached Savonarola's cell that she spoke again.

"Look, this is the prior's cell. I like to think that these two frescoes were painted by Fra Bartolommeo, when Savonarola had so stirred his soul within him that he determined never to draw anything but sacred subjects again. Can't you fancy Savonarola here in his own little cell, after he had been moving the hearts of thousands in the Duomo, coming here to pray alone? When Florence loved him and well-nigh worshipped him, how he knelt and asked for humility, and when she had turned against him and he knew it, how he prayed for patience and forbearance, and for endurance even to death? There must have been many an unseen angel here strengthening him—for he *was* faithful unto death. It is always so hard to be forsaken by those whom you trust; his great heart must have gone nigh to breaking."

"I never thought of him before in this way," Hester said.

"Yes, it is wonderful to think of him here. And in the Duomo where he preached the evangelical doctrine in all its simple beauty," Adelaide said; "for the piazza before San Marco used to be so thronged that he was allowed to preach in the Duomo, where thousands would go overnight to secure even standing room."

"Adelaide," Hester said, "I sometimes wish, don't you, that we could hear about God and His love for the first time—I mean, we hear and don't hear; nothing seems greatly to impress us. There are so few gifted people now who would give up everything for God's service. And yet all this religious fervour is thought by some old-fashioned, and that it was suited to the time, and that now we have grown beyond it—wiser and more enlightened. I really wish—I do, indeed—that I could feel more about these things—be roused, you know, by some Savonarola. Just think how we go on at Dryborough. We all go to church, and we are told to be thankful for it."

"And so we ought to be," Adelaide said. "Savonarola was a reformer, and sounded the first notes of the trumpet-call which was to break the slumber of centuries, and bring the religion of Christ to the people. It is this that the free circulation of the Bible has done; and with the word of God came freedom from the fetters which had bound the Church in misery and iron. The letter killeth, but the spirit gives life. It is that life that Savonarola tried to kindle, and so did our own Reformers. We must remember them with gratitude."

"I do not believe there is anyone now who would die for his faith," Hester said.

"There are many who *live* for it. Since I came to Florence I have known those who do this without many words and profession, without telling everyone what they feel. They show it by making their lives a beautiful picture, just as Fra Angelico made his the reflection of something above and beyond the world, and so they beautify the common life of every day as he beautified the bare walls of these cells, making them evidence at once of his power and his faith."

"Do you mean Lucia Campbell?"

"Yes; she is one, and Mr. Lysaght is another."

"Mr. Lysaght!" Hester said. "Has he ever talked to you as you have been talking to me?"

"Not often; but sometimes, and to much better purpose than I can ever hope to do."

They were out in the sunny streets again, out into the common, everyday life of the gay City of Flowers, leaving behind them the solemn mysteries of San Marco, and walking slowly towards the Duomo. The sun was very hot, and they were glad to turn into the shadow of the great church, where, by contrast with the elaborate and dazzling beauty of the exterior, the first impression is that of a vast space, bare of any ornament, and with huge pillars of a sombre hue.

Santa Maria dei Fiori seems to be an inappropriate style and title for the interior of this grave, solemn building. But when at high noonday the sun pours in from the windows of the great dome and sends floods of radiance over the space before the high altar, where priests and choristers are gathered, there is no longer a feeling of gloom, but of majestic beauty.

Within the circle, which is railed off from the nave, and into which no laymen are admitted, the great psalter and mass-books on the desks are lighted by unseen candles, which are so placed as to throw their light on the books, and thus make the words and musical notes visible, for those who stand round.

Service was going on, and presently the gates of this inner sanctuary were opened, and a long procession filed past, singing as they went round the huge nave, and not in very harmonious tones. In these processions it is always remarkable that while some of the priests seem to be really in earnest, the great proportion appear to be mere machines going through a necessary exercise, as soldiers would go through a drill, or carelessly looking about them, as if it did not much matter how the function was got through, so long as it was accomplished in the right order and at the right time.

"The letter which killeth" seems to be written on the ordinary services of the Church in Italy; and it is impossible not to see that fervent devotion seems to rest with the people, rather than the priests.

Hester wandered about, looking at the monuments and the side chapels, while Adelaide sat down and gave herself up to her own thoughts. It was easy for her imagination to fill that great church with the seething crowds, who came to listen to the fervent appeals of Savonarola, the women weeping and touched even to the giving up of all their ornaments to the burning pile, where poor Monna Brigida consigned her false tresses and the trinkets dear to her heart! Was not Hester right that no one would now die for the faith—nay, would any give up all they prized most of personal adornment, for conscience' sake? Was it, indeed, true that religion had lost the quickening power of old, and that only the scaffolding was left, and the real heart of the Church dead?

There are many intelligent and earnest minds like Adelaide's, perplexed and full of doubts as to the reality of the faith professed so glibly by us English Churchmen and women every Sunday—nay, every week day. Do we indeed believe? or is it only what has been well called "a mechanical religion," which is wound up like the large clock in the belfry tower, and strikes its appointed round of hours with unfailing regularity? And then there came to Adelaide's mind what Mr. Lysaght had said to her when, a few weeks before, she had put such thoughts into words; and she recalled his very gesture and voice as he met her doubts by several striking proofs that faith lived, and that it was shining more, rather than less brightly, than it had done centuries ago.

What was the key-note of such great benevolent institutions as Müller's Orphanage, dependent as it was on the gifts of the faithful? Mr. Lysaght had told her of ornaments and jewels thrown into that good work by the rich and the young, the noble and the wealthy; just as poor Monna Brigida had obeyed the voice of Savonarola, and, with the women of Florence, had thrown her precious things into the fire for Christ's sake. Then he went on to speak of Gordon and Hannington, of Father Damien, the friend of the lepers, living on their island with them, and many another whose watchword was "Deus vult," who gave up their lives nor counted them dear, for His sake in Whom they believed.

And when Adelaide had said there were so many good works in our own country which were carried on with zeal, and yet without any acknowledgment of God's love in Christ, he answered her in the words of a preacher of our own time, "that all the efforts made by music and painting, and beauty of form and expression, to raise the soul to higher and nobler things, to reform the masses of our crowded cities, had no stability and no constraining power, unless the form of the Son of God was recognised and His Spirit sought for, to quicken and give life."

None of these thoughts troubled Hester. She returned from her round of the church with the small edition of Hare's "Florence" in her hand, and said she really thought she had seen all she wanted —where should they go next?

"To the Bargello, if you like," and here Adelaide was interrupted by hearing her name spoken by Mr. Lysaght, the very person of whom she had been thinking.

"Miss Millington, I have been looking for you! I have come to say good-bye."

"I thought you were gone to Prato."

"No; just as we were starting, I had a telegram, which summons me to Cruttwell at once."

"To Cruttwell! Is Mr. Beauchamp dead?"

"He is dying, and wishes to see me."

"Oh, poor Lady Mary!" "Poor Cousin Mary!" came simultaneously from Hester and Adelaide.

Mr. Lysaght paused for a moment and looked round him, round and up at the great dome, through which the midday sun was still making pathways of soft radiance. His dark, expressive eyes looked full of intense earnestness, and no one, Adelaide thought, could see his face, and think that faith was

STAIRCASE IN THE PALAZZO DEL PODESTA, FLORENCE.

dead. After standing for a few moments thus, he turned and led the way silently down the cathedral to the south door. As he did so a party of English visitors were coming gaily along, laughing and talking in their ordinary voices.

" What an ugly church it is inside," one said. " Just look what Hare says : Oh ! ' Pillars washed a sombre brown.' Let us make haste ; there really is nothing here." Then, in an audible voice: "I saw that dark man at Paoli's this morning, didn't you ?"

" No ; I didn't notice him."

And then they passed out of hearing.

" It does jar one terribly to see the behaviour of our own country-people in these churches," Mr. Lysaght said, as they went out ; "the English do not appear to advantage in Italy ; less in the churches than anywhere."

They were standing on the Piazza now, under Giotto's Tower, the pigeons coming down in flocks at their feet, their white wings shining like the marble of the Facciata, or with breasts burnished with many colours of emerald and purple, in the full rays of the April sunshine.

Presently two English ladies came up, on whom Lady Anna had called, and who were always very anxious to cultivate the acquaintance.

" Now, how fortunate we are to have met you !" Mrs. Anderson exclaimed. "Come home to luncheon with us; we are quite near. Let us have the pleasure of seeing you also, Mr. Lysaght."

"Oh, do come!" echoed her daughter. "It is so frightfully hot standing here. Do come."

Mrs. Anderson and her daughter had permanent rooms in the Palazzo Bourtolin, in the Via dei Servi, and they seemed determined to take no refusal, but led the way, their scarlet parasols swaying to the right and the left, as they threaded their way through carriages and omnibuses to the Via dei Servi, on the opposite side of the Piazza.

"I wanted to speak to you particularly," Mr. Lysaght said, "before I start. Could you give me a few minutes alone? Perhaps after luncheon you would leave your friend with Mrs. Anderson, and come with me to the Piazza Cavour. I must tell the Campbells that I am leaving Florence."

"Have you seen Lady Anna?"

"Yes. I went to the Piazza d'Azeglio to find you. Percival came back after his unsuccessful attempt to persuade you to join the party to Prato."

"Is Mrs. Murchison to remain behind?"

"She cannot get ready for the journey to-day, and I think she will probably stay at Florence till I can tell her what I find at Cruttwell. I was sorry at first when Clyffe came back without you; now I am glad you refused. I was just getting into the carriage when the telegram was put into my hand. It seemed a pity to disappoint the whole party, for there are several of Theresa's friends, or rather acquaintances, from the hotel gone also. So we retired and had a short consultation, and then they drove to the station, and

I went to telegraph to Lady Mary, and then to the Piazza d'Azeglio to tell Lady Anna."

They were at the door of the Palace now, and Mrs. Anderson invited them to look into the garden, which was a perfect wilderness of flowers—kept, indeed, with more regularity than many Italian gardens; but in that wild luxuriant growth of every tree and flowering shrub, the trimness of our English gardens is scarcely ever seen or desired. The garden fills the quadrangle round which the palace is built, and was on this bright day a blaze of colour, with rhododendrons and Banksia roses, azalias and cinerarias.

The rooms occupied by Mrs. Anderson were on the third *piano*, and formed a perfect suite of sixteen rooms, which were furnished with English comfort. The luncheon was served with great taste, and Hester, who was hungry after her long morning, did it ample justice.

Mr. Anderson proposed a drive to Certosa after luncheon, and it fell to Hester to accept the invitation, as Adelaide said she had an engagement, and Mr. Lysaght and she left the room together.

"Are those two engaged?" Mrs. Anderson asked of Hester.

"Oh no, certainly not."

"I hear Mr. Lysaght has a fine property coming to him on the death of an uncle."

"Not an uncle," Hester said; "a distant cousin.'

"I should think his sister will not allow him

to marry until she has found a husband; she is evidently looking for one. I heard that that handsome young Englishman, Lady Anna's nephew, is devoted to her."

"Mother!" exclaimed Miss Anderson, seeing that Hester did not seem to like this gossip; "mother! Mrs. Murchison is devoted to everyone for a time. It means nothing."

"Then it ought to mean something, my dear. Mrs. Murchison is extremely pretty, and, really, she has such a flow of clever talk that I don't wonder people are fascinated, and that she is popular. A little fast, of course, and not likely to suit a person like Lady Anna, who stands a good deal on ceremony—more than *I* do! But Mrs. Murchison is, I hear, quite remarkably clever, and so well read and cultivated!"

Mrs. Anderson was, as may be seen, a personage who did not herself stand on much ceremony. She considered it quite legitimate to ask questions about the surroundings of Cruttwell, and Hester, always simple and frank, gratified her curiosity. Mrs. Anderson thus found herself in possession of many interesting facts, which would be served up with embellishments to some of her English cronies who were in the habit of coming in for afternoon tea on dull days, when there was nothing better to do.

Mrs. Anderson's gossip might be called harmless, if idle words and eager interest in histories of other people and their concerns can be called harmless.

But it is almost impossible for gossip to be altogether innocuous. Very often the repetition of something carelessly said of another has caused a life-long separation, and left a sting little intended.

I wonder how many of the cold bows which replace a friendly greeting—nay, even a direct cut instead of a warm hand-clasp—might not be traced in any society, whether in Florence or Cheltenham or Bath, to some foolish repetition of what might have been a very innocent remark, by one of the Mrs. Andersons of the world! And this from no direct wish or intention of deliberate mischief-making, but simply out of pure love of retailing what someone has said of somebody else! So many half-truths have thus done more real harm than a wholesale lie, and there are many who are chafed and annoyed by them, who cannot bring the offender to justice.

It has been said truly, it would be a very dull world if we might never talk of our neighbours and friends; and it is a little hard that we should be obliged to be guarded in the particular circle in which we move, if one or two people are present who will, we know, be only too likely to carry what has passed into another house, and repeat some remark, never intended for repetition. I feel sure that we all know, when we have been saying something about our neighbours' concerns, that, on thinking over those who were present, we say of some who were there that they are very unlikely to repeat our perhaps incautious remark, while a pang of fear thrills through us that one, or it may be two people are almost sure to make use of our words.

Hester Ponsonby, as she reviewed her afternoon with the Andersons, asked herself if she had too freely answered questions as to whether Lady Anna was an easy person to get on with; whether it was true that the doctors had but little hope of the delicate girl's life; whether Adelaide was always so reserved and quiet as she had been at luncheon, and whether there was really nothing between her and Mr. Lysaght.

It was no use torturing herself with vain regrets that she had not been more cautious, and, like many bright unsuspecting girls, Hester could only inwardly resolve to be more reticent in future.

When Mr. Lysaght and Adelaide reached the Piazza of the Annunziata, Mr. Lysaght said:

"I know you will befriend the Campbells when I am gone. Lucia is decidedly less able to get through work than before her illness, and there is something about her I do not understand. Poor old Signor Maura shakes his head and looks unutterable things when I meet him. That copy of the Madonna del Gran Duca is hardly up to her previous work, and she has been so long about it that I expect the funds are getting low. If the bread-winner fails what is to become of them all? If I am placed in a position to do so, I can help them, and many others more effectually than I do now—give a great deal more pleasure, and do with thousands what I could not do with hundreds. You know Cruttwell Manor well, I think?"

"Yes, I have lived at Dryborough the greater part of my life, and probably shall return there in June to spend the rest. I am beginning to long for the dull old market-place and the quiet streets—above all for my mother and the children. Since Hester came it has been better."

"What has been better?"

"I mean I have had some one to talk to of my own people, and old times. Beautiful as Florence is, I have often felt very lonely here. It was so new to me to have no one to care about my poor little doings—no one—it sounds very absurd," she said, breaking into a laugh which was not quite natural, "no one to admire my productions."

"I do not know whether this is the best place or time to choose," he said, "but I am going away; and who can tell what lies beyond any parting in this world? I have often longed to tell you—what you must, I think, know without words—that it would be my great happiness to make you happy. While Cruttwell Court was only a distant vision, and while there was the least chance of a report I heard last year being true, I could not ask you the question—which I have been often longing to ask: has another been in the field before me?"

"Please stop," Adelaide said, and Mr. Lysaght was silenced by the tone of her voice, and the pallor of her face. "Please do not say any more. You have been such a good friend to me, and taught me so much. But what you ask can never be. It is very kind of you to think of it."

"'Kind!'"—he repeated the word almost bitterly. "Very well; then I may conclude I am too late."

"I did not say so! How can I say so?" she said, in a voice so much distressed. "Oh, do not press me any more. I cannot bear it!"

Mr. Lysaght had a certain masculine obtuseness, or he might have guessed Adelaide's secret sooner. Now a light seemed breaking in upon him. Was it possible that his sister had stolen away Adelaide's happiness, by her foolish wiles? Was it possible that Percival Clyffe had deserted *her* for a woman older than himself, towards whom as a brother Mr. Lysaght felt a tender pity, but to whose vanity and folly he could not be wholly blind? He had, it is true, noticed that Percival Clyffe had been what might be called hanging about Paoli's Hotel, making many excuses for visits — to sketch, to practise a song, and so forth. He had once touched upon the subject with his sister, who only said:

"Poor boy! I am sure you cannot grudge him a little amusement. It is so deadly dull in the Piazza d'Azeglio, especially now the child is ill. Lady Anna would drive me mad in a week if I had to live with her. Poor Adelaide looks more and more like Griselda come down from her monument—she does not smile, though, but wears a solemn face of calm endurance."

Mr. Lysaght had not been satisfied, but he knew well his sister's waywardness, and that to attempt to pull her in one direction was the sure way of sending her off at a tangent in the other.

Now, however, the whole truth flashed on him. He was to lose Adelaide. He was to see her unhappy, and to be denied the power of making her happy, and all the time know that she was throwing away her affection on one who was unworthy. He knew his sister, as I have said, too well to think she had any serious views about Percival Clyffe—he was a string to her bow, and she would play upon another as soon as it suited her. She had married when very young, and her husband had been ordered out to take part in one of the "little wars" which make so many dark blots on the history of this country, and had fallen in that disastrous campaign which cost the life of the gallant young Prince Imperial of France—years ago, now—and the widow of twenty summers was still a widow—who had never led a settled life, and had really no friend or relative to whom she could turn but her brother; he had conscientiously done his best to protect her, and influence her for good.

Mrs. Murchison's faults arose chiefly from excess of vanity. She could not resist exercising her powers of fascination on anyone who came near her—old professors, learned schoolmasters, boys from college, nay, even from school; even the irate Bostonian, as she had foretold, was now reconciled, and had said to his wife:

"You bet that girl is a rare one to talk. She is that learned it's quite alarming, and so fetching, too. She told me a lot more about the grand fight we made for independence than ever I knew before. And she's a rare clever girl, talks like a book, and sings like a prairie-bird!"

This type of woman always manages to do a great deal of mischief, and the heart-aches she causes are manifold.

"I will not press you further," Mr. Lysaght said. "I beg your forgiveness for having said so much. But remember that if you want a friend you may count on me, and that I never change. It is wholly impossible for me to change!" he repeated with vehemence.

Adelaide walked on for a few paces in silence, and then she said:

"I think I had rather not go to the Campbells, but go home. Little Daisy will be expecting me, and we have come out of the way. You must turn to the left, and I can go on to the Via Alfieri, and be at home in five minutes."

"Very well," he said; "then we must say good-bye."

"Addio," Adelaide said earnestly, "addio."

"The Italians think that implies a final parting," he said, as he took her hand in his. "Surely it cannot be that? We shall meet again as friends, when this has passed?"

Tears were gathering in Adelaide's beautiful eyes, and her voice faltered as she said:

" A rivederci."

And so they parted—deep pain at both hearts—pain which neither could really express, and which Adelaide shrunk from acknowledging, though it seemed to fill her with confusion.

She had loved Percival Clyffe too well. But had she any real right to love him? She went over it all in her mind, for the hundredth time. Their first meeting that night in the Park—his coming with Lady Anna's letter in the pitiless storm—the walk up to the Court, with the rain beating upon the umbrella with which he shielded her so carefully —all his bright, winning ways—his ringing laugh— his tender care for little Daisy, when he first came to Florence—all he had said to her, as they stood looking out together on that gorgeous sunset from the wall of Fiesole, and her words: "We can come again." "Never again, never again," her heart now said. "Never again, as we then were."

That drive to Fiesole was, she now remembered, the beginning of trouble. From that day she had dated a change—the subtle change which, at first hard to define, had too soon become evident— a change she tried in vain to ignore, and cheat herself into the belief that it existed only in her own imagination—a change which many a woman has felt creeping over some dear friendship, or dearer love, and hidden in the depth of her heart the pain, which, perhaps, is made the sorer because, after all, strictly speaking, she has no right to feel it.

When Adelaide reached home she was going upstairs to what she considered her own territory when the old butler stopped her:

"Her ladyship wishes to see you, Miss Millington, before you go upstairs."

Adelaide knew she must obey the summons at once—disinclined as she felt to do so.

Lady Anna was not, as usual, seated at her writing-table, but leaning back in a chair by the fire, which was never discontinued, however bright and sunny the weather might be.

"I wanted to tell you," Lady Anna begun, "that there has been a telegram from Mr. Beauchamp's lawyer to Mr. Lysaght, requesting his immediate return. I have had one also from dear Mary. You can read it."

"The end is near now. Urge Mr. Lysaght to start at once."

"Have you seen Mr. Lysaght?" Lady Anna asked.

"Yes. He is leaving by the four o'clock train, and will go straight through to London."

"Grace Ponsonby wants to set off with him, thinkin she would be a comfort to my sister, but

I know she would rather be alone, poor darling! I could not leave my Daisy now, or I would go to her. I am miserably anxious about Daisy!"

It was the mother speaking now, out of the fulness of her heart.

"Yes, I am miserably anxious! What do you think? I know Percival tries to put anxiety aside, but her father is even more depressed than I am. She gets thinner every day, and then the cough! She never had a cough before—never—except the whooping-cough. I must really try and get a London man to come out to Florence, if there is not some improvement soon. What are a few hundred pounds to us in comparison with her health, or, I may say, her life?"

Adelaide was never quick in expressing her feelings, and yet she did long to say something to comfort Lady Anna. She felt powerless to do this, and therefore was silent. At that moment the door opened quickly, and Percival Clyffe came in.

"Back from Prato already!" Lady Anna said, gathering up something of her usual manner.

"Yes, we saw enough; it is a poor place after all; and of course Mrs. Murchison wanted to see Lysaght before he starts. I am going to the station myself to see the last of him. It is a pity you did not come, Miss Millington," he said carelessly. "Now, am I driving you away?" For Adelaide had risen, and was leaving the room. He sprang forward to open the door for her, as she said indifferently:

"You have had a lovely day for Prato!" and then she was gone.

"You used to be on very friendly terms with Adelaide Millington, Percy. You have quarrelled lately, I think."

"Quarrelled!" he said sharply; "I never quarrel with anybody; it is too much trouble; and she is the last person to have a quarrel with, because, you know, it takes two to make one."

"What do you think about Mr. Beauchamp?"

"He will die now to a certainty, and Lysaght will come in for the place."

"Unless that report is true."

"Oh, that is all over. It was mere suspicion; and, though I dare say Lysaght, with his stiff ideas of justice, will advertise, and go on trying to get at some clue, he will never find one. He is, as I told you long ago, a real good fellow, a trifle too strait-laced and superior, but he is very good all the same. Daisy does not seem very bright, Aunt Anna," Percival said, changing the subject abruptly.

"No, indeed, I am very unhappy about her. She was exposed to that sunset chill, and this is the result."

"She had a cough before that," Percival said.

For Mr. Cowper-Smith now came into the room, looking troubled and anxious.

"I have been with Peggy, my dear," he began. "She is very feverish, a spot of crimson on her cheek, and her eyes so bright."

"What is to be done?" Lady Anna exclaimed. "Shall we return to London at once."

"That will never do; the east winds are so sharp there; then there is the journey to get through," and Mr. Cowper-Smith sighed heavily.

Percival tried to say an encouraging word, but his heart failed him. He left the father and mother alone, and went up the stone stairs to the other *piano* with a quick step.

Daisy was in her low easy-chair, and Adelaide seated on a stool at her feet. The child's hand was round Adelaide's neck, as she pressed her head against her knee. Adelaide did not raise her head when Percival went in, but Daisy sighed out:

"Oh, Percy! it is such a *long* time since you came to have 'tea and talk' with me! You don't care to come and——"

"Nonsense, Daisy; I care to come very much, but I can't stop now, for I am going to the station to see Mr. Lysaght off for England."

"I wish we were going to England," Daisy said fretfully. "Oh dear, I *do* wish we were! We haven't all been happy at Florence. Adelaide isn't happy, and *you* are not exactly happy. You are always in a hurry now, and always going with 'friends' somewhere, and when you first came to Florence what nice times we had here—Adelaide making tea, and the Protector making toast, and——"

Percival stooped over the back of the chair, and kissed Daisy's hot cheeks.

"We'll have plenty more nice times," he said. "Have you a head-ache, Miss Millington?"

Poor Adelaide had kept her head buried in Daisy's lap, for she knew there were traces of tears on her face.

She sprang up now, and said:

"No, thanks. I am lazy, I think. I took a holiday to-day with Hester, and it has proved more tiring than a long morning's work at the studio."

"You had better have come to Prato, as I asked you. We had some fun out of that old Bostonian; his remarks and lectures on Art generally, and the frescoes at Prato in particular, were very instructive; it was a joke!"

"I don't think it is kind to make fun of people, Percy," Daisy said. "It might hurt their feelings, you know."

"My dear child, happily for the world, we don't allow feelings to have anything to do with our enjoyment, or interfere with it. In other words, we have to be thankful for thick skins, that are proof against barbed arrows."

"I don't understand," Daisy said. But Percival was gone.

"Adelaide," Daisy said thoughtfully, "something is wrong with Percy. What is it? He is so very different from what he used to be. I wish he did not go about so much with Mrs. Murchison. Miss Cromwell says he is running after her."

"Miss Cromwell should not gossip," Adelaide said.

"I am so tired," Daisy sighed. "I wish you would sit in the chair, and take me in your arms, like father does. Father has been here an hour, and he *does* sigh so. I can't make him laugh; and he used to tell me such funny tales of the days when he was a little boy, and lived with a cross old aunt in Ironstown."

Adelaide laid aside her hat and jacket, and then took the arm-chair, and Daisy crept into her arms. She was very quiet for a few minutes. Adelaide hoped she was asleep, for Mrs. Gray gave bad accounts of her restless nights, and broken, troubled sleep.

But presently Daisy said:

"Adelaide, do you think I am going to die?"

"I hope not, darling. We could not spare you."

"That's not an answer," she said. "I am going to tell you something. I think I *am* going to die, and—and I should like to live and get well, and be a comfort to dear father, because he thinks he made me ill that day when it was so cold, and I had not my fur cape—that day in the Cascine, you know— you remember?"

"Yes," Adelaide said; "yes, I remember."

"But if I am to die, I don't think I am afraid. I feel Someone near to help and comfort me. I don't think He will forget poor little me, when I am going, and then—oh, there will be such rest on the other side, won't there?"

Adelaide pressed the child closer; she could not trust herself to speak.

"Adelaide, I love Percy very—very much. He has been so kind to me; and I thought you liked him, and I did think he liked you. He used to talk to me about you, when he first came to Florence, and always called you, in Italian, 'Adelāide!' and he made poor Antonio play that song on the violin, and said he was jealous of Mr. Lysaght, because he could sing it—'Adelāide.' Well," Daisy went on, "I *cannot* think why lately it has been different; I can't, indeed. I should so like you and Percy to love each other, especially when I am gone away."

"Daisy darling, please do not say this to anyone but me—promise!"

"I think I shall say it to Percy," she whispered.

"No, Daisy, you must not. If you love me, you will not."

"Very well," the child replied—"very well. Things puzzle me so much; I lie and think of them at night, as I turn and twist about, and I don't get them straight. Some people so rich, like father and mother, and some so poor; and some people caring for nothing but fine things, and always laughing and making jokes, like Mrs. Murchison, and others working hard, with no time to please themselves. And then people who ought to like each other don't; oh! it is dreadfully puzzling."

"Yes, Daisy, it is puzzling, I know; but the only thing is to hold very fast to the faith that God—who is a God of love—knows best, and that He guides us all in the *best* way."

It was so seldom that Adelaide ever spoke thus, that Daisy raised her head, and said:

"I *am* glad you think like that. Do you know, people don't seem to like to speak of God and His love, and I thought *you* didn't. Now I can talk ever so much more to you—now that I know you think of Him. I think of Him so much, perhaps, because I have led a very different life from girls of my age. I have been taken such care of, and kept apart from others, so that I have had time to think: and I do believe the Lord loves me, and it *is* so nice to think *you* understand."

Adelaide felt self-reproved, as she thought how alone in her deepest feelings this child had been. Only a few months ago she could not have responded to Daisy as she did now. Her life, too, though after a very different fashion, had been self-contained and self-absorbed. She had been led by a way she knew not, and awakened from that dreamlike existence, which, whether in the pursuit of intellectual studies, or culture in art or music, has no less self for its aim and end than excessive vanity, and engrossment with dress and adornments for the person or the house; or that thirst for admiration and popularity which characterises women like Mrs. Murchison — who flutter about the world, thinking only how young they can be thought to be, or how pretty, or how fascinating; passing off as much of the "base coin" for silver in their conversation on subjects about which they really know nothing, and have thought less.

"It is very hard for me not to be selfish," Daisy went on, after a pause, "because everyone tries to make me selfish. But when I think how the Lord never, never pleased Himself, I am ashamed, and tell Him that I long to be like Him, and that, if I live to be a woman, I *will* do as much as I can for Him by helping others. And if I don't live I am going to write down in a book all I want dear father to do. I have begun it, only I don't wish anybody to know. You won't tell, will you, Adelaide?"

"No, dearest—no, I will tell no one."

"I am cross to poor mother sometimes; I was this afternoon, when she came up with patterns for a new dress, and asked me which colour I would have. I don't *want* a new dress—I've heaps; and I said so. Then she didn't look angry, as she does sometimes, but so miserable, and she went away so quickly."

Adelaide understood, now, how it was that she had found Lady Anna in such bad spirits on her return, and felt more sympathy with her than she had ever felt before. Perhaps there is nothing so hard to meet as the growing conviction, which will not be put aside, that one who is as the light of our eyes is going from us, and that all our hopes, so confidently expressed, and so fondly cherished, are fading away, and a dreary sense of coming loss taking their place.

CHAPTER XII.

DISCLOSED.

"LUCIA! LUCIA!" exclaimed Madame Campbell; "where have you been so late? The signor has been here with great news to take leave of you, and waited till he dare wait no longer. He is gone to England."

"Yes," Marietta said; "he is gone, for he was sent for to the old gentleman who is dying, so he thinks, to hear of his estate."

"Lucia!"—it was Giovanni's more gentle and musical voice—"the signor left you a message, and I was to tell you he was sorry—grieved not to see you. His voice was sad, very sad; and you are not to work too hard any more. Lucia, come nearer;" and Giovanni drew his sister's head down on a level with his lips and whispered, "The signor cares for you and for us as no one else ever did or can; and I think he is sure to come back."

"He will never come back," Lucia said; "no, it is over now. I must have time to think," she said, half to herself, half aloud—"time to think."

"What have you been doing, Lucia?" said her mother sharply. "Two rich ladies from America have been here, asking for you to paint a large screen for them, with the picture of the Ponte Vecchio on one panel, and the tower of Giotto on another. They must see you to-morrow. Their address is on this card. Now, Lucia, wake up, and be thankful; they will pay a large sum. Do you hear?"

"Yes, mother; I hear," Lucia said. "I have been with poor Signor Maura some time. I think he is failing fast. I am returning to him before night to take to him some of the jelly Giovanni did not eat."

"Poor old man!" said Madame Campbell. "You want the jelly yourself."

"Yes," said Marietta, yawning. "I do not think poor people can help poor people, and I am sure Signor Maura is a cross old creature."

"He is a true friend to me," Lucia said; and then she refused any of the coffee and rolls put aside for her, and went into her own room.

We saw her there before, and know that in the old oak cupboard were the letters which were the confirmation of her brother's claim to Mr. Beauchamp's estate entailed on male heirs. Poor blind Giovanni! How strange to contemplate the change for him and for them all! But it was not this that was the prominent thought in Lucia's mind. Their benefactor and friend, who had raised her out of the depths of despondency when her health failed, who had been like a new and bright element in her life— this was to be the return for all he had done! They were to stand between him and his inheritance, and it was left to her to disclose the fact that Mr. Beauchamp's son had left a grandson who was heir to Cruttwell Court and all it contained.

Lucia stood with the box in her hand where these important letters lay, and the thought flashed through her mind that after all she need not tell anyone of their existence. The secret had been so well kept—her father's condition when he confided these letters to her had been so pitiable—after all, half he had written might not be true. He had been scarcely responsible for his words or actions; and if it had not been for her mother's often-expressed hope that the children's future was provided for by her husband's father, Lucia might have been almost tempted to look upon the whole as a delusion. Then, as she again read the letter addressed to herself, the command seemed binding. She must at once take the necessary steps, and let Mr. Lysaght know of the existence of the letters.

The letter addressed to her, written in an irregular, straggling hand, which she had read a few weeks before, was as follows:

"I commit to the care of my daughter Lucia Beauchamp (Italian, Campobello; Anglicè, Campbell) a statement of my separation from the worst of fathers. I have towards him no feeling of kindness. When I went to him to announce my marriage to my wife Antonia, née Bellini, and asked to be forgiven, as I meant to reform, he spurned me from him, he felled me to the ground, and he cursed me with fearful curses. Had he relented to me, I might then have been saved. Too late now, too late! But I charge my good child Lucia, always trustworthy, to retain the sealed packet till she hears of the death of this old man. She will see it in the English papers, or she will hear it in some way. The old man, after twelve years, married a woman with a title. Poor soul! I pity her. There are no children; I know so much. But, as set forth in this sealed packet, there is an heir, the son of a second son of an old Beauchamp, of Cruttwell Court, whose father took a second name with a wife, who brought him money, and by that name he is called. But he holds Beauchamp, added to this name, L——"

Here a large smear had been made, and the name was illegible; but Lucia knew it too well.

What followed was a wandering, incoherent story of his wrongs and his continued poverty, with a feeble acknowledgment of Lucia's patience and kindness to him in his illness; a weak lamentation over the curse that had fallen on his boy, and that no one was to be trusted but Lucia, and that he had chosen her to act for him.

Finally, no application was to be made to the old man in his lifetime. He would rather die of starvation—see them all die—than take alms from him!

What an inheritance for children's children, even to the third and fourth generation, is left by those who hate God and persist in rebellion against Him! It is a bitter harvest indeed, to be gathered in by the innocent—a harvest which has been sown by a guilty hand! In cases like poor Lucia's and her blind brother's it may truly be said, "One soweth, and another reapeth."

Lucia had never seen her father and mother exchange any tenderness or kindness. Her mother had married her father believing he was a rich man, and that he would raise her to a position very superior to that of a public singer in second-rate concert-halls, and her disappointment had embittered her. Naturally mean and self-seeking, she never forgave the deception practised on her, and after much mutual recrimination, followed by complete estrangement, the wife went one way and the husband another. And, as we have seen, the husband became a victim in mind and body to intemperance, drinking and gambling away his mother's small fortune till he was dependent, in his half-imbecile state, on his wife's and Lucia's earnings for his very existence.

Lucia's had been a sad and troubled life, and yet how she had risen above it—how she had nobly supported her mother, Marietta, and Giovanni by continuous work, for which, it seemed, she received but little in return!

"What I do must be done at once," she said, as

she put the letters into her pocket and determined at once to go to consult Adelaide and find out Mr. Lysaght's present address, feeling that the safety of the packet was of the greatest importance.

Never, surely, were feelings more mixed than poor Lucia's as she passed through the large room again, and Antonio said, in a complaining tone:

"Marietta would not take me to play to the little signora to-day, though the English signor came for me. I know, if you had been here, you would have taken me. Marietta is so cross!"

"Indeed I am not going to the Piazza d'Azeglio to be treated like a servant!" Marietta said, roused to some energy of expression by her wounded pride. "Not I! The mother does not wish it."

"No, indeed! You are born of a noble name in England, and I have determined to go there this coming summer, and use my endeavours to find out where your grandfather is. I will make him repentant—see if I don't!"

"You don't even know grandfather's name, mother," said Marietta fretfully. "Why do you talk such folly?"

"Name! I know our name, I hope—a good English name, Campbell—in Italian, Campobello; but you know I forbid you all to say Campobello. It was only your father's foolishness. Ah me! what a poor, silly woman I was to marry him! He is dead and gone, but the saints only know what he was!"

"Mother!" Lucia exclaimed; "he was our father. Do not speak so."

She had been putting the jelly into a cup, and placing it, with some of Liebig's beef-tea, in a little basket, saying to Giovanni:

"You will like poor Signor Maura to have some of your good jelly, caro mio?"

"Yes; but do not stay long away from me, Lucia mia. And will you take me to the little signora to-morrow?"

"Yes, if you are wished for, carissimo. And now, à rivederci!"

She kissed his forehead, and was soon crossing the piazza to the Via di Pinti, where, in the topmost *piano* of a tall, dark-browed house, Signor Maura lived—a house once inhabited by people of distinction, as seen by the medallion by Luca della Robbia over the large open door, and by the faded frescoes on the walls.

Lucia mounted some eighty stone steps, till she reached the door, upon which was painted—

"ANDREA MAURA, PITTORE."

Lucia's gentle tap was recognised, and the door was opened, and she was admitted into the large, comfortless room where the poor old man lived. Everything around him told of decay and past glories of some ancient family. The proportions of the room were fine, and the ceiling was painted with a smiling company of floating Cupids with their little bows bent, taking aim with arch smiles at a recumbent Venus and attendant nymphs, who were the centrepiece of the fresco.

The tall mantelpiece was carved elaborately, and, though broken and defaced, had still some beauty left. A few dying embers of charred wood were on the wide hearth, and the old man had drawn his couch near, and was sitting crouched upon it in one corner.

There was not much else in the room. A stool and a broken carved oak chair; a chest and an old easel on which was a canvas, while several more were standing against the wall, from which some rags of ancient tapestry hung disconsolately. A cupboard (which ought to have had two doors, but had lost one, now lying on the floor), held the few articles of crockery, which, few as they were, were more than was needed.

The windows were high, and only by standing on the deep window-seat could anything be seen, and then the view was only of the roofs of houses and palaces, Giotto's tower and the Palazzo Vecchio appearing like sentinels over the irregular gabled roofs.

There was something infinitely pathetic in the resignation of the old man. He lived in his past, he believed in his past, and the picture on the easel was the last he had painted before he was disabled. No wants can be fewer than those of an Italian like Signor Maura. A hard-boiled egg after the fashion of Donatello's, a little salad, and a roll were enough for his daily needs, and he never complained.

But lately Lucia had noticed a visible decline of strength, and he had no inclination to descend those multitudinous stairs oftener than was absolutely necessary. The galleries knew him no more; and had it not been for Lucia's ministry of love, he would have been helpless indeed.

"Ah, ah! cara mia," he said, as Lucia came into the room; 'back again. Now take breath, take breath. The young should not mind a climb, only the old."

"I have brought you some beautiful jelly, signor, made for my brother. He likes you to have it."

"Very kind; but I do well without it. I am only tired and weak; that is all. But I have been saying to myself, since you left me, the time is come to tell you that when my death happens I leave you all—all my pictures. You may sell some, not all; but some will be a help. Unlike many, they are original, composed by myself. Do you hear?"

Yes; Lucia heard, and rallied herself to thank him.

"It is kind and noble of you, signor," she said.

"You have never seen them; that one on the easel—my last, my last; I keep it with its face turned to the easel. It is not for common eyes; but you may look now. Go to the easel and look. Then express to me your sentiments—freely, remember, freely. It was my last work—the portrait of one I called Madonna, Madonna, the fairest and most beautiful lady, who died at Florence in her youth—a young English signora. She lies in the old cemetery, and I will tell you her name, but to no one else. She had a little dark-eyed boy; he is in her arms. Now turn it and look."

Lucia did as he desired, and felt that his eyes were upon her as she stood before the easel.

"The first eyes that have looked on it," he murmured, "for thirty—yes, thirty years—the first. And when I die it is yours, Lucia. My possession more precious than jewels, for is not art priceless?"

Lucia's heart sank within her as she looked at the faintly shadowed figure of a woman, if young and beautiful in life, certainly neither young nor beautiful in the picture; poorly drawn, poorly painted, without any artistic merit whatsoever; the boy, with his dark eyes, the most distinctive feature of the picture, but wofully out of all proportion with his mother. What could Lucia say? Her eyes filled with tears, and she stood motionless before her poor old friend's lost ideal. It was true, then, that he never had painted; that the loss of his right arm had only perhaps saved him from bitterer pain in the constant labour which could never have been rewarded by either praise or money. For who would buy a pale, almost unintelligible, portrait like that of his dear signora and her child?

"Ah," he said from his corner by the hearth; "ah, you see now what I could do. Did you ever divine it before? You see now why I have so often bid you take care of your high lights, and that your shadows were too forcibly marked; you see now, Lucia mia; and all will be yours when I am dead and gone. I have nothing else to leave you, my brave one. This is my all, and it is yours. Turn the picture back. The time for other eyes to see it is not yet, not yet."

Lucia was thankful that the old man's meandering talk saved her from having to say anything. She turned the canvas with the face of the picture to the easel, and going back to the couch, knelt down by the old man and kissed his withered hand, saying only, "Tante grazie, tante grazie, signor mio." Then she put another faggot on the fire, placed on it the little tin saucepan, in which she had put some of Giovanni's beef-tea to heat, and putting the cup and saucer, both cracked and chipped, on a shelf by the side of the hearth, left Signor Maura with a promise of return on the morrow.

She had, perhaps, entertained some idea of laying her own story before him when she had entered the room. She had no such intention now. He was too drowsy to take in anything she said—too drowsy and too much occupied with the gift he was bestowing— the legacy he would leave her. So she left him in the dim shadows of declining day—so meet an emblem of his declining life—and bent her steps towards the Piazza d'Azeglio to find in Adelaide the sympathy for which her soul hungered.

It was getting late when she reached the door, and a carriage with some fashionably-dressed ladies had just driven up, as Mrs. Ponsonby and Hester were starting to dine with a remote connection at the Hôtel de la Grande Bretagne. Lady Anna's heart might be heavy, but that would not interfere with her receiving her English acquaintances, as she had arranged, at dinner.

"It will not be necessary, dearest," she had said to Mr. Cowper-Smith, "to let anything drop about Mr. Beauchamp's condition. He may rally—and, indeed, I think it is very probable that he will rally."

Mr. Cowper-Smith's sigh—which had brought Lady Anna's remark, as they were together in the drawing-room about seven o'clock—had not been caused by the thought of Mr. Beauchamp's approaching death. His child—his darling child—was ever in his thoughts, and he did not know how to meet the ordeal before him of a long-drawn-out dinner and longer drawn-out platitudes from the husband and wife, and their son and daughter, who were now announced by Fielding as Lord and Lady Herbert Donegal, and Mr. Edward Mosstyn, and Miss Geraldine Mosstyn.

Almost simultaneously Percival Clyffe appeared to claim kinship with his Irish cousin of the hundredth degree, and Adelaide, in her ruby-velvet, followed.

Percival had done his best to get his aunt to invite Mrs. Murchison, but he had not succeeded. How could he think of impossibilities—a little dinner-table of eight people with a ninth? What would Fielding say? And, besides, Mrs. Murchison would be offended at a short invitation. The Irish lord and lady were good-natured, free-spoken people, with a decidedly strong Irish accent, and voices pitched in a resonant key. The son and daughter had toned down their voices, and the brogue was scarcely perceptible in Miss Mosstyn, and hidden by a drawl and studious avoidance of the letter "r" by Mr. Mosstyn. He used an eye-glass with great freedom, dropping it and resuming it at intervals, and both he and his sister looked cursorily and superciliously at Adelaide, as Lady Anna introduced her.

Perhaps Lady Anna a little regretted that Mrs. Murchison had not been bidden as a guest when, just as the first course was over, and Adelaide was trying to listen to an involved statement Mr. Mosstyn was making about the first visit he had made to the Uffizi, in which he said he thought the greater part of the collection was "wubbish, and weally not worth the twouble of looking at"—Fielding, with a very grave face, bent over Adelaide, and said:

"The young artist lady whose brother plays the violin, Miss Millington, wants to see you on very particular business."

"Would you ask her to wait?" Adelaide said, unpleasantly conscious that Lady Anna's eyes were upon her.

Fielding departed, but as he handed Adelaide the first entrée, he said:

"The young lady says it is about a letter of importance for the post."

Poor Adelaide ate her entrée, and sat on thorns for another five minutes. Then she made a great effort, and looking at Mr. Cowper-Smith, next whom she sat, and who was doing his best to laugh at Lady Herbert's jokes, she said:

"Will you ask Lady Anna to excuse me? Some-one is waiting to speak to me on very important business."

"It's not the child!—it's not Peggy who is worse?" Mr. Cowper-Smith said hurriedly.

"No—oh no; it is Lucia Campbell, who is very anxious to see me. May I go?"

"Yes—yes, certainly."

And as Adelaide slipped away, Mr. Cowper-Smith said:

"My dear, Miss Millington begs you to excuse her. Someone wants to speak to her."

Lady Anna bowed, but she did not smile, and murmured, "Extraordinary!" but made no further remark.

Percival Clyffe felt strangely curious, and said audibly:

"What on earth can it be about?"

"Now, now," said Lady Herbert; "don't you be so inquisitive. Young ladies may have their secrets, I suppose. She is a very handsome person. Where did you pick her up, Lady Anna?"

"The idea of Adelaide being picked up!" Percival said, laughing. "You ought to ask, Lady Herbert, what planet she had fallen from."

"Well—well, what planet, if you like it better. The planet Venus!—now, will that suit you?"

Here Lady Anna said, in clear, distinct tones to Lord Herbert, who was very deaf, and had to encircle the ear next his hostess with his large hand:

"Miss Millington is a protégée of my dear sister, Lady Mary Beauchamp. She asked me to allow her to spend the winter with us, to study art."

"Study art. Oh—ah!—oh! She is a fine young woman; and, by-the-bye, how is your sister's husband?"

"*Not* in a very satisfactory state," Lady Anna said, with an uneasy feeling that at the very moment she was speaking a telegram might be on its way with the news of her brother-in-law's death. Not that the event itself would give her any pain, rather would she consider it a relief to all concerned, but it would not be exactly in accordance with the code of social ethics if it leaked out that on the very day of her little dinner-party she was fully aware that Mr. Beauchamp's condition was hopeless. There were certain social observances which were imperative, and Lady Anna never set them aside if she could help it.

Adelaide found Lucia in her own room, to which she had asked to be shown.

Lucia's face betrayed at once that something was affecting her deeply. She was tearless, but her large dark eyes were full of mute appeal as she fixed them on Adelaide and said simply:

"I want your advice. I am greatly troubled."

"Giovanni! is he ill? Is that why he could not come here to-day, when Daisy wanted him?"

"No, it is not of Giovanni I wish to speak; it is about these letters," and she drew from her pocket the sealed packet and the letter addressed to herself. "I would know precisely Mr. Lysaght's address. He has left Florence, as you know."

"Yes," Adelaide said—"yes. Is it help from him you want in any trouble? His address is Cruttwell Court, Dryborough, Surrey. He has gone straight there with all haste, for Mr. Beauchamp is dying, and you know Mr. Lysaght is the next heir to the estate."

Lucia was silent for a moment, and then she said sadly:

"No, he is not the next heir. Giovanni, my blind brother, is the heir, and this letter shows how it is. My father made me vow never to tell anyone of this till his father died. He said I should know it and hear of it, and then tell. The name has confused me—Beauchamp I always thought when I read it here was *Beau-champ*. My father called himself Campobello; my mother, anxious to be English, Campbell. She has ever had a notion that some day our English birth would help us; she has made us speak English—tried to *make* us English. But she really knew nothing of my father's father— no, not his very name. They married secretly, and my father having made one visit to his father, had some terrible scene, and they parted for ever. Have

you a good father? If you have, oh, be thankful!
It is hard to feel—so hard—that one's parents are
not good."

"My father died when I was a little child,"
Adelaide said; "but I know he was the best of
fathers. My mother is gentle and sweet, and she
married again my stepfather, Mr. Wardlaw."

Lucia seemed scarcely to follow all Adelaide said.
The letters were in her hand, and her eyes fixed on
them.

"It is so sorrowful for me," she said at last, "to
have to be the one to take from our best friend his
inheritance. If there were any way to prevent it, I
would take that way."

"But there is none," Adelaide said decidedly—
"*none*. If the letters are authentic, of course you
have no choice."

"I shall not open the sealed packet," Lucia said;
"I know its contents—the copy of the marriage
documents. What do you call them in England?"

"The marriage certificate."

"Ah, yes. Well, I shall post them now. I will
write a few words with them. Give me, if you
please, a pen."

"Yes; I have plenty here," Adelaide said; "paper
and stamps, and a large envelope. Here," she
repeated, making way for Lucia at her writing-table.

Lucia sat down, and, leaning her elbow on the
table, sat with the paper before her; but she did
not begin to write.

Presently Adelaide, who had turned away that she might not seem to be watching her, heard a short, quick sob.

"Lucia, what makes you so sad?"

"Ah!" she said, "cannot you know—cannot you tell? Cannot you tell what it is to my heart to be forced to take away from the one I love better than all the world, that which I would so gladly give him? You can never know what he has been to us—to me—tender, chivalrous, good—ah! what am I saying—what am I saying, that you look at me thus?"

The truth flashed on Adelaide at last. Oh, why was life so tangled and bewildering? This very day the love that Lucia craved to possess had been offered her, and she had rejected it. And for what? Only for that which was but the shadow of a love she dared not confess to herself without shame—a love unsought—a love which she had no right to cherish. It was but too plain that Percival Clyffe, if he had ever cared for her, cared for her no longer. The brilliant, if frivolous, Mrs. Murchison suited him far, far better. In her presence of late she had felt the sharp contrast between her own slowly expressed feelings and opinions, and Mrs. Murchison's sparkling repartee and apparent knowledge of every subject under the sun. Her superior in everything—so Adelaide in her humility thought—superior, certainly, in all that made her a centre of attraction wherever she went, and a magnet indeed to Percival Clyffe.

Adelaide was always self-possessed, unlike poor Lucia, who, now that she had broken the ice, poured forth her troubled heart to Adelaide, and said again and again:

"Pity me—pity me! I love Giovanni, and I love *him!* Is it wrong?—is it wicked? Do you think he will be angry?"

"Angry! Why?" Adelaide asked. "He will be sorry for you—very sorry—much more sorry than for himself. I think you need not be so unhappy. It is not as if Mr. Lysaght were a poor man; he is able to live without following any profession; he will not suffer. Do not be unhappy about the loss of the fortune to him; that is the last thing he will care about."

"This is a comfort," Lucia said; "this is a comfort to hear. I will try to take comfort. But you, who know what Mr. Lysaght is—you can feel for me?"

"Yes, I can feel for you," Adelaide said; and then to herself she added, "more deeply than you think." But she continued aloud: "You must write your letter now, and then it can be posted. You will feel happier when it is gone."

Lucia took up the pen, and wrote these few words:

"DEAR SIGNOR,

"The enclosed will tell you of what I cannot write. Antonio is heir to the fortune of his grandfather.
"Yours in sorrow to say this,
"LUCIA."

The letters were put into the envelope and sealed, when a quick step was heard in the corridor, and a sharp rap at the door, followed by :

"May I come in?"

"There is some curiosity downstairs to know why you have deserted the party," Percival said. "What is wrong?" he asked, looking from Adelaide to Lucia. "Is the poor blind boy ill?"

"No; he is well, signor," Lucia said, rallying herself with a great effort; "he is well. And I must bid you good-evening. Buon' sera, signor!"

Then, with a sudden gesture, she threw her arms round Adelaide, pressed her in a close embrace, and was gone.

"I say," Percival began, "what is the matter with that poor little girl?"

"I suppose there can be no secret in it. Giovanni is Mr. Beauchamp's heir—not Mr. Lysaght."

Percival gave vent to the usual expressions of astonishment when unexpected announcements are made.

"And why did she come and tell you?" he asked.

"Perhaps because she wanted sympathy," Adelaide said coldly.

"Sympathy! I should not want sympathy if I found myself suddenly in Giovanni's place. Sympathy!"

"There is such a thing as sympathy in joy as well as sorrow," was the reply. "Perhaps we ought to go downstairs now."

"Are you going to tell Aunt Anna the particulars with which you do not seem inclined to favour me?" Percival asked.

"They will soon be known by everyone."

"Perhaps it is all a mistake," Percival said. "I dare say it is; only there have been queer stories afloat about there being a son or grandson in Italy."

"I do not myself think there can be any doubt, from what Lucia has told me; but, of course, we shall hear more soon. Had we not better go downstairs now?" she repeated.

But Percival did not seem inclined to hasten. He stood leaning upon the back of a high chair, the very picture of a young English gentleman in his irreproachable evening dress, which has a power of making even short and ill-built figures look well, and sets off a tall and finely-proportioned one like Percival's to perfection. He had all the comeliness of face and figure which goes to make a handsome man. His eyes were of the true Irish blue under their dark lashes, and his rather wide mouth was shaded by a fair moustache. This appendage hid the form of the lips, and the slightly retreating chin was not noticeable except in profile. But any keen observer would at once have concluded that this tall and handsome young Englishman had no strength of purpose, and wanted stability and steadfastness.

There are many like him, from whom we have probably all suffered more or less in our time.

Kindliness, good nature, and desire to please, with a ready appreciation of all that is fair and good in others, have blinded many to the grave defect, which brings those who trust in these unstable folk to confess at last, in the bitterness of their soul, that the staff on which they leaned has broken, and pierced them with an exceeding sharp pain.

"Are you anxious about Daisy?" Percival asked. "You ought to be a good judge." He asked this question instead of following her to the door. "Please stay one moment, and tell me what you think."

"I think she is very much weaker than when we first came to Florence. This cough is very persistent. You can hear it now."

As she spoke Miss Cromwell, ready dressed to go down into the drawing-room, which was one of the privileges of her office in Lady Anna's establishment, came in, and as she did so the little, short, quick cough smote on Percival's ear. With all his varied moods and all his changes, he was constant in his love for his child cousin, and he had been like an elder brother to her.

"Daisy is very feverish," Miss Cromwell said, "and her cough is so troublesome. Mrs. Gray is very anxious about her."

"Old Grayling always croaks," Percival said, with the ready desire to put aside the thought of coming trouble.

"No," Miss Cromwell said; "Mrs. Gray has

always been hopeful, and that makes me think more seriously of what she says now."

"They ought to have another doctor—a man from England, or take her home at once," Percival said. "Is she gone to bed?"

"No; she is sitting in the chair by Mrs. Gray's fire. She is so restless, and does not want to go to bed yet."

Percival went through the intermediate rooms to find Daisy, and she held out her arms to him as he knelt down by her chair.

"Oh, Percy! I *am* glad you are come! Where is Adelaide?"

"She is gone down again to the company, Peggy,—a deaf old gentleman and his noisy old wife and his dull son and daughter have been dining here tonight. Are you not glad you are not in the drawing-room to see them?"

"Yes, rather," Daisy said, with a sigh. "I couldn't play my violin, and it would vex mother. Percy, perhaps I shall never play the violin again."

"Nonsense! You will play at my wedding. You know, we always settled that."

"Percy, *are* you going to be married? Grayling said she thought you were. I *hope* not to that lady with the rosy cheeks who laughs and talks so fast."

Percival gave rather an awkward laugh.

"Not that I know of, Peggy. Of course, I shall ask your leave first."

"If you did, I should tell you *who* I wished you to marry. Shall I whisper it?"

She drew his head down to her burning cheek, and said in his ear, "Adelaide!" He started up suddenly, but Daisy held him fast.

"Everyone thought you really *did* mean to marry Adelaide. The Protector was sure of it, and Grayling too. I *was* so glad. Now I hear them say that it is a lady ever, *ever* so much older than you are, who pretends to be young. Oh, *don't*, Percy; don't do that!"

He tried again to laugh carelessly, but he did not quite succeed.

"Good-night, my Peg; and tell Mrs. Gray and the rest of them to mind their own business;" and then he was gone.

CHAPTER XIII.

IN CRUTTWELL COURT AGAIN.

IT was a soft April evening, when all the loveliness of an English spring was at its height. Peace seemed to brood over Cruttwell Court, and no sound broke the stillness; for the birds had ceased their evensong, and the ring-doves had told out their tale of love for that day. Even the whisper in the dark, plumy branches of the firs, where the doves built their nests, was only faintly heard, and the village-street outside the old Norman gateway seemed more silent and quiet than ever. Mrs. Ponsonby's house was shut up and deserted, and the Rectory had few inmates, for the Easter holidays were over, and the boys had gone back to school, and the girls and Hugh were away.

As gentle Mrs. Wardlaw came out of her house and turned towards the gateway, she was conscious of her own light footfall as she passed under it— even so slight a sound made itself heard; and she trod more warily, as if afraid to waken some sleeper. Half-way up the drive she met Mr. Birley.

" Is there any change ?" she asked.

"No. He has rallied a little, but it is only the leaping up of the flame before it dies out. Ah!" said Mr. Birley, "to be brought face to face with a death-bed like that is a lesson we may well take to heart."

"Is he still so restless?"

"Yes; there is something on his mind, but I cannot get him to speak to me. He holds poor Lady Mary's hand, and clings to it. I have prayed by him, but he made no sign one way or the other. It is three days since the telegram was sent, and Mr. Lysaght will be here soon. I don't know how the Squire will take it—whether his presence will increase his restlessness."

"I do not think I shall go up to the house," Mrs. Wardlaw said; "I will turn back with you, for you have given me the latest news. I suppose Dr. Townley sleeps at the Court?"

"Yes; and the London man is coming again early to-morrow. Quite useless; but Lady Mary is so anxious, poor thing, to leave nothing undone."

"I am sorry Mrs. Ponsonby is away at this time; dear Lady Mary must feel so lonely! And Adelaide, too—she might have been a comfort to her."

"I think Lady Mary prefers being alone. She has borne so much alone for so many years, that she may well bear on to the end."

"It has been a sad life for her, and she has endured it with the patience of a saint," Mrs. Wardlaw said, her eyes filling with tears, as she parted at the gate of the Rectory with Mr. Birley.

She returned to Nina and Susie and her husband, and made his coffee, and sat down to write out some notes for him for his history.

Mr. Birley stretched himself out in his easy-chair in his study, and seemed disinclined to give his wife any more particulars than she already knew.

And so the fair spring twilight deepened, and the stars peeped out between the branches of the dark trees, and all the varied and delicious fragrance of the sgring filled the calm air with that mingling of scents, which is so subtle and so beyond any words to describe.

Marked indeed was the contrast between the peace without and the unrest within. The windows of Mr. Beauchamp's room were open, and every now and then, at a sign from Lady Mary, Preston moved a large fan backwards and forwards, and then stopped again at her bidding. No word had been spoken since Mr. Birley had left the room, and the restless tossing to and fro and low moans of the sick man were hard to see and hear unmoved.

About nine o'clock Dr. Townley came and administered a reviving draught, felt the pulse, and, in answer to Lady Mary's look, said:

" It is rather stronger." Then, in a still lower tone : " Mr. Vassall is here waiting for Mr. Lysaght's arrival. He telegraphed from Paris, and he must be here by ten o'clock."

" Don't whisper,' the Squire said; "I hate whisperers!" Then, as Dr. Townley left the room, he said, " Mary, is anyone here?"

"Preston is here, dear."

"Send Preston away; I want to be alone with you."

Preston laid down the large fan and went into the dressing-room at a sign from his mistress. Several other servants were there, and the professional nurse, whom Mr. Beauchamp would not tolerate in the room.

"Mary, you have been a good wife to me. You are well provided for. Lysaght will have what he *must*, but no more—not a penny more!"

"I shall be content—more than content. But I wish, dear, you could think of Him who has promised to forgive."

"Forgive!" and the old man's eyes shone with a strange light.

"Forgive, as you hope to be forgiven."

"I can't forgive."

"Oh, dear, do not say that; if there is anyone you should forgive, do it now."

"It's too late!"

"It is never, never too late."

"Yes; I never forgave my son. I had a son, Mary. He is dead and gone—it is too late! You knew I had a son?"

"I guessed it from things I heard you say. You never mentioned him by name."

"Forgive! he was a reprobate, he was. True, I felled him to the ground, and I left him to be picked up by others. That was the end; years before I knew you, my good, patient wife. Oh, Mary—Mary! pray—pray! I don't care to hear Birley: *you* are different."

Poor Lady Mary controlled her voice as best she could, and bending over the hand which never loosened the clasp of hers, she said in low, clear tones,

"'In all time of our tribulation, in the hour of death, and in the day of judgment, good Lord deliver us.'"

To her surprise, Mr. Beauchamp repeated the words, and said, "Go on."

And Lady Mary went back to the familiar entreaty —so familiar to us as we take it on our lips, in that mechanical, half-hearted fashion too common in our services, but fraught with deepest meaning in the face of great emergencies and suffering:

"'By the mystery of Thy holy incarnation, by Thy precious death and burial, by Thy glorious resurrection and ascension, and by the coming of the Holy Ghost, good Lord deliver us!' By His death, and by His most holy life we are forgiven; shall we not forgive for His sake?"

"It is too late—too late! but I'll try—God help me!"

Then he wandered, and talked of Johnnie as a fine little fellow, and called to his mother to come and see him sit a horse. Then he said he would thrash him for speaking ill to his mother, and rambled on in a past in which the gentle, patient woman at his side had no part. It was a relief when he almost lost consciousness again, and Preston was recalled, and Dr. Townley came again, administered another draught, and went to the window to close a shutter, as the night air was chill. As he did so, looking down the avenue, he saw a man's figure coming up in the dim, mysterious light, and that figure was Godfrey Lysaght's.

The omnibus had brought Godfrey Lysaght from the station, and set him down at the King's Head, where he left his luggage, and walked up to the Court alone.

In the gathering shadows, with the stars' faint radiance seen through the firs, the place looked dark and solemn, and Godfrey felt oppressed with the solemnity of the shadow of death which he knew lay over the house rising in a sombre mass before him.

There was a light over the door, and lights in the windows, gleaming out like beacons to beckon him onward.

Dr. Townley had seen him coming, and had told Preston to go down and let Mr. Vassall, the lawyer, know, that he might receive the new master of the Court. But Mr. Vassall had been on the alert, and was already at the door, before Preston had reached the hall.

Mr. Vassall perhaps a little overdid the warmth with which he greeted Mr. Lysaght:

"I am thankful to tell you, sir, you are in time," he said, in answer to Godfrey's question. "There has been an extraordinary rally since my last telegram, which I hope you received according to your orders, at Paris. Now, what refreshment may I offer you? We have everything at command: there is no stint in this house."

"Thanks; I am not in any need of refreshment. I dined in London, having an hour to wait for my train."

"Ah, exactly; then coffee, perhaps—— But here comes her ladyship."

The door opened, and Lady Mary herself came slowly into the room. Seen by the light of the lamps and candles, Lady Mary's face was unnaturally pale. She had been so incessantly in the darkened room upstairs that she had to shade her eyes with her hand—the light dazzled her.

"My husband," she began, "has very often expressed a wish to see you during the last few days. Will you mind coming into the room and waiting till he inquires for you? Any sudden introduction would be too much for him."

As she spoke, Lady Mary held out her hand to Godfrey, and said:

"I am glad you have got here in time, and when you are rested and have taken some refreshment, will you come upstairs?"

"I will come now," he said, "if you please."

And Lady Mary led the way at once, merely bowing her head and moving noiselessly before him up the old staircase, where, in the dim light from the corridor above, he saw the faces of Beauchamps of many generations looking down on him. At the head of the stairs the light fell full on the picture of some judge who had been a Beauchamp. The deep-set eyes, under the huge gray wig, seemed to fasten their keen glance on him, and an ironical smile played on the thin lips. Godfrey never forgot that picture, nor the feeling it gave him of the living personality of one at least of his ancestors who regarded him with little favour.

He followed Lady Mary's noiseless footsteps into the large room, with its low ceiling and old-fashioned bed, from which the curtains were drawn back, so that the figure propped up by pillows was distinctly seen.

Remembering what Lady Mary had said, Godfrey withdrew to a deep cushioned chair near the window, and did not speak.

The silence was oppressive. The doctor came in from time to time, and Preston took up his place with the fan, and no words were spoken. The clocks striking made the only sound, and so the long hours passed. So far, sending for him to see Mr. Beauchamp appeared to Godfrey to have been useless. He had relapsed into a half comatose condition, breathing heavily, and only uneasily turning his head from side to side, but retaining a firm grasp of Lady Mary's hand. About one o'clock Preston touched his shoulder.

"Her ladyship wishes to speak to you, sir."

Godfrey rose and went near her.

"Will you not retire to rest?" she said. "He

may be in this state for some hours. When he rouses again I will send for you."

"The chair is very comfortable," Mr. Lysaght said. "Had I not better remain?" And he added, "Can no one relieve you?"

She shook her head, and resumed her watch with the old hand in hers, while Godfrey returned to the seat near the window.

How strange it was, he thought, that a man by all accounts so hard and so tyrannical and unforgiving should be thus tenderly cared for by a wife to whom he had granted scant kindness! What could be the key to a mystery like this? That he, who never loved anyone with a pure, unselfish love, who had never thought of sparing those about him the bursts of ill-temper and the perversity of a stubborn will, and sometimes savage moods, should thus be ministered to by that pale, worn woman, who had been unfailing in patience and self-forgetfulness and forbearance through all the thirteen years of her married life! Such things are mysteries; but we meet them continually.

It is not the most worthy who have the most love bestowed on them; it is not the unselfish and considerate who fare best at the hands of others; it is not the child who causes the mother the least trouble who is the most fondly loved. Do we not often see the pretty, gay, frivolous, and self-indulgent and indulged wife far more ready to lift her head in her widowhood than one who has never been spared or considered in the household, and whose husband had taken all her labour for himself and the children as a matter of course?

These are the strange anomalies which often fill us with wonder and perplexity. As regards Lady Mary, Godfrey Lysaght could not read all that had been in her heart during these thirteen years. Her devotion and patience were perhaps counted, half unconsciously to herself, as of duty paid for the benefit she had accepted. She had wanted a home, and Mr. Beauchamp gave it to her. She had not stopped to consider what lay before her as his wife. She had married him for what he could give her. Her brother and her sister, Lady Anna, were loud in their congratulations, and all her "little world" said it was a blessing, indeed, that she had found a home like her sister, especially as Irish affairs grew worse every year, and "poor Lady Mary was so unfitted to make her own way in life."

But though all around tried to deceive her, she did not deceive herself. She knew well enough that to marry without love and for any worldly advancement solely is a sin. She knew well enough that a penalty must follow, and she determined to make the only atonement possible, and be a patient and forbearing wife if she could not be a loving one. But something near love, which is, indeed, akin to pity, had sprung up in Lady Mary's poor heart, and especially during the last year this feeling had gathered strength, and she earnestly longed for a word which would show that her husband had turned to God for pardon, and that he might find peace. The clinging to her, and the expressions of gratitude for what she did for him, almost, indeed, equivalent to some regret for what she had suffered —had become in the last few days a further solace; and she dreaded the time, now so near, when all her efforts for the good of that poor, irascible patient should be at an end for ever.

But into these secret workings of the human heart earthly eyes cannot penetrate, and Godfrey Lysaght knew nothing of all that passed, during the silent watches of that long night, in the breast of the lady whose delicate profile was just defined against the dark crimson of the curtains, which had been drawn back in thick folds to the head of the bed.

As day dawned, and "the earliest pipe of half awakened birds" was heard, Mr. Beauchamp came back to the partial consciousness of the evening before; and the doctor, crossing to the place where Godfrey was dreaming of Adelaide, and fancying that she was standing with him in the little chapel of San Miniato, where, instead of the sleeping Cardinal, Mr. Beauchamp lay, said:

"Go near the bed now, if you please."

"Who is it?" Mr. Beauchamp said. "Is it John —is it Johnnie?"

"It is Mr. Lysaght, dear. You wished to see him."

"Yes, yes. I've not got much to say. Be kind

to *her*," he said; "be kind to *her*. Did you ever hear I had a son, sir?" he asked, after a pause.

"Yes; I have heard it."

"And that he married a singing woman—a low, Italian creature?"

"I heard the rumour, sir. I tried to find out the truth, but failed."

"Tried! What for?"

"That I might give him, or his heirs their rights."

"Rights! rights! Who talks of rights? Wrongs —wrongs—never to be forgotten, nor forgiven!"

"Do not say so, sir," Godfrey said. "Forgive as you would be forgiven."

Something of his old angry impatience replaced the softer mood as he gasped brokenly:

"I won't be preached at by you, young man. Send him away, Mary. I want no more of him."

And then Mr. Beauchamp relapsed into drowsy unconsciousness, which was, indeed, in great measure the result of the frequent injection of morphia and the doses of ether which, by the order of the London physician, Dr. Townley had administered at intervals during the night.

It seemed useless for Godfrey to stay longer, and Lady Mary saying, "When he revives again we will call you," he left the room, Preston following him, and asking if he could get him any refreshment. But Godfrey declined anything, and when he was alone he threw himself on the bed, and slept heavily till the sun was high above the horizon.

It was a quiet, still morning, the sky veiled with thin gray clouds, and not a breath of wind stirring the branches of the firs—though, as Godfrey threw up the window and leaned out, he could hear the mysterious murmur in the topmost boughs—which is seldom quite silent, an accompaniment to the voice of the turtle-doves, in their monotone of love.

Presently, too, there was the cuckoo's call from the copse in the field below; and the low of cattle, and the caw of rooks, mellowed by distance.

Godfrey felt—as so many of us have felt in strange circumstances—unable to realize them.

He had, of course, known for some years—ever since his father's death—that the estate was entailed on the next male heir; but, as he had never had any kind of communication with Mr. Beauchamp, this inheritance of his had looked very vague and dim. The rumour of a son and a son's family had, as we know, reached his ears, and he had used every means, through his lawyer, Mr. Vassall, to investigate the truth of the poor man's story in the hospital. He had always intended, when Mr. Beauchamp died, to make fresh inquiries, and to advertise again in colonial and foreign papers. But, strange to say, now that the dim vision of Cruttwell had become a reality, and not a dream in an indefinite future, he did not think of another heir at all, nor of new efforts to find him. He was filled with the sadness of the death-bed in the room he had left at midnight, and wondered what tidings would be brought to him when he rang his bell.

It is quite true that we seldom or ever feel as we expect to feel in any supreme moment of our lives, either of joy or sorrow, to which we have looked forward; and Godfrey Lysaght was no exception to what we may call the universal law.

Here, in the soft stillness of the April morning, looking out on the close-shaven turf, and beyond the lines of sombre firs to the Surrey hills, in blue, dim beauty, over which the sun, which had forgotten Cruttwell, was pouring its early rays twenty miles away, Godfrey found himself scarcely conscious of the present. For, except in the sadness which the memory of that unhappy dying man, with his patient wife sitting by his bed, left upon him, that present did not seem to be really *his!*

His thoughts were far away with Adelaide. He was in the place now most familiar to her—the place where she had said she had been like a dreamer for so long, believing all that her loving friends had told her; and then, when the wish of her heart was granted, she went to Florence to have a rough awakening to her real self, to know what she could *not* do, and wherein she failed.

All their intercourse for the last few months was mapped out before him. He was with her again in the churches and monasteries, on the heights of San Miniato and Fiesole. Was it a year ago, or was it only three days, when, almost secure of her answer, he had told her of his love? Then the distress so plainly seen in her face, the gathering tears in her beautiful eyes, the quivering lip—what did it all mean?

Men are proverbially dense where women are concerned, and Godfrey Lysaght was not, perhaps, more dense than others of his race.

It was not from vanity, or undue appreciation of himself, that he was surprised at Adelaide's answer; it was from sheer inability to think that a woman of such depth of feeling, one who had high aims and lofty ideals, could be satisfied with a man like Percival Clyffe—a mere man of the world, handsome and agreeable, bright in conversation, and kindly and good-tempered.

Was it possible that Adelaide could care for him, and that his sister's foolish flirtation had pierced her noble heart with pain? He ought to have stopped it, he told himself—he ought to have taken Theresa away; he ought to have discouraged Percival's frequent visits, the singing together, the sketching, the perpetual round of little excitements which were necessary to his sister's existence—that butterfly existence which he had as an elder brother tried his best to modify. For in the kindness of his heart he had done all in his power for her, for the sake of his dead parents, who had committed her to his care, before her first hasty marriage. Now that she was a widow and unprotected—requiring, though she did not acknowledge it, protection—he reproached himself with leaving her too much to her own devices at Florence, and encouraging, perhaps, rather than discouraging, her perpetual hankering after what gaieties Florence society could offer. He had been far too much engrossed with his own affairs—with Adelaide.

Adelaide! He sighed the word out in the beautiful refrain of Beethoven's song—"Adelāide! Adelāide!" And never one thought in all these memories did he give to Lucia. If he were dense and his mental vision dim about Adelaide, how much more dense about the little Italian artist! Her self-denying exertions, her patience in the early days of their acquaintance, her spirit, her quick perception of anything humorous, her perseverance in copying pictures, which, after all, she felt was work which would never raise her as an artist, though it maintained her and her family as a bread-winner—all this had kindled his admiration, and one of the chief interests in his winter at Florence had been her blind brother, to whom she was so nobly devoted.

Ah, little did Godfrey Lysaght think of the pain which he had all unconsciously given Lucia, or of what it cost her to tell him that her blind brother— the fragile youth who lived in his music, and was entirely dependent on her—was to come between him and his rights!

As the clocks struck ten there was a rap at his door, and a manservant entered with a breakfast-tray.

"I was to say, sir, Mr. Beauchamp is much the same, and her ladyship hopes you will breakfast in your room. Can I give you any assistance, sir?"

"No, thanks; I shall be coming down in an hour's time, and I shall wish to see Mr. Vassall."

Godfrey had only partially undressed, thinking he might be summoned at any moment to the sick-room, and had thrown himself on his bed in his dressing-gown. He now seated himself at the table where the man had placed the tray, and Lucia's letter, which had been travelling just twelve hours behind him, caught his eye.

"Florence!" he exclaimed. "Who can this be from?"

He opened the envelope, altogether unconscious of who the writer might be, and Lucia's words first caught his eye. We know what those words were, and how and where they were written. The mystery was solved now; he was not the heir of Cruttwell Court!

Though, as we know, Godfrey Lysaght had used every means to ascertain the truth of the poor Italian's story in the hospital; though he had told himself often that he would feel far better satisfied if a grandson had been discovered, still, there was a very natural feeling of disappointment and vexation as he read the contents of that letter sealed with a large seal, unbroken for all these years.

It was as Lucia had said. There was the copy

of both the marriage registers; for it was evident that Mrs. Campbell had taken care to have their marriage duly solemnized at both the English and Roman Catholic churches. The ingenuity of the invented name struck Godfrey as a proof of the cunning of Lucia's father—Beau-champ, Campo-bello, Campbell, all bearing the same meaning in the three different languages. Never surely had a plan for secrecy been more successful, and never had a man been able to hide himself more completely.

A large part of this declaration of John Beauchamp's identity with Giovanni Campobello was bitter abuse of his father and a miserable history of his visit to Cruttwell, as he said, to try and propitiate his angry parent—an interview which ended in a hand-to-hand encounter, in which the father's hand was against the son, and the son's against the father.

While the letter addressed to Lucia was, as we know, written in a feeble and meandering style, the sealed document was vigorously expressed. It had been written before intemperance and bad habits had sapped the strength of manhood, and reduced the man of scarcely forty to the imbecility of old age.

Godfrey was not like a man without a helm let loose on a sea of doubt in this time of difficulty and disappointment, with many hopes crushed, not so much as to the possession of the estate as of the power to do a great deal more for others than he had been able to do before. He had a sure trust which did not fail him now.

It is the fashion to strike out from any history of individual trial and conflict the motive power of Christian faith. It is the fashion to say that such motive power is greatly exaggerated in its effects, and that as a rule it is better to keep silence about it, and not bring it unduly forward in pictures of life, because it so seldom exists nowadays, and that the very noblest and best men and women are *not* influenced by it—a sweeping assertion that it is very easy to make, and very difficult to prove. If, indeed, it were true that this motive power is paralysed and dead, then many hearts amongst us would faint and fail, before the great mysteries of life and death. There will ever be scoffs at a faith which the scoffer cannot grasp, and there will always be a great multitude who, not able to believe themselves, are only too ready to think others are sceptics also.

That the Christian verities yet live amongst us let the lives of thousands of men and women bear witness. Thousands are still ready, thank God! to give up all that He requires of them, to recognise His hand, and instead of setting their faces like flint to meet the storms of life, even through tears they see the rainbow of hope thrown by the bright shining of the sun of a Father's love on the cloud which overshadows them.

Lady Mary was still keeping her watch by the

bedside, when a note was put into her hand. It was from Godfrey Lysaght:

"May I speak to you alone for a few minutes?
"G. B. L."

"Mr. Lysaght is in the morning-room, your ladyship," Preston said.

Lady Mary rose slowly from her chair, taking her hand gently away from her husband's, and walked feebly across the room.

"I wish he had not troubled me with business now," she thought; "it is perhaps something about the future."

It was nothing about the future, as Lady Mary found when Godfrey advanced to meet her, saying simply:

"I thought I had better tell you at once that letters have followed me from Florence which prove beyond a doubt that Mr. Beauchamp has a grandson, who is the heir of this place."

Lady Mary put out her hand, and Godfrey took it, and placed her in a chair.

"Is it true—are you sure?" she said.

"Quite sure. Mr. Vassall has examined the statements, and though he will, of course, verify the marriage register at the London church, and at the registry office, there can be no doubt."

"Let me see the papers," Lady Mary said.

"I think not, now; it would be only painful to you to read them; but let me tell you that by what we call chance—though I prefer to give it another name—I know the family Mr. Beauchamp's son left behind him. They live at Florence, and the daughter is one of the most admirable girls you can imagine. The son is blind."

"Blind!" Lady Mary exclaimed.

"Yes; a fragile, delicate boy, who is a born musician."

"Are there any other children?"

"Yes, another daughter. The girl I have mentioned is the eldest of the three children."

"And the mother!—is there a mother?"

"The mother is an Italian, a woman of many words—well-meaning, I dare say—but a woman of no culture or education. They have been living in absolute poverty for years."

"And we in affluence," Lady Mary said. "It is too terrible! What is to be done?—help me to decide!"

"The decision is made for us," Godfrey said. "Would you like to see Mr. Vassall?"

"I don't mean that part. I mean how shall we tell him—my poor husband? Oh, I fear it will rouse in him the old feelings of bitterness, even now, even now, when he feels so little—knows so little."

"I think he ought to be told—I think he ought to know the truth; that is to say, if he recovers any real consciousness again."

"Very well," Lady Mary said, with that acquiescence which comes of long habit. It was so long since she had set up her own will or judgment, that she almost forgot how to do so.

"I must go back to him. Will you come?"

She put her hand in Godfrey's arm for support, and then she said:

"I am so sorry for *you*. Forgive me for forgetting your disappointment; and I hope you will help me in all the new arrangements, and be my friend."

Preston now suddenly entered the room.

"Come back, my lady, come back! My master is like himself—he is quite rational—he calls for you!"

Lady Mary withdrew her hand from Godfrey's arm, and went hastily towards the room where Mr. Beauchamp lay.

"Mary, Mary! come here! don't leave me! What is that about the sins of the father?—what is it?"

Lady Mary took up her old position, and said in a clear, calm voice:

"He shows mercy unto thousands, dear, in Christ, think of that."

Then, after a momentary pause, she said:

"Here is Mr. Lysaght; he has something to tell you."

"I know—I know! Well, he will come after me here, and see you are cared for!"

Godfrey went close up to the head of the bed, and, speaking slowly and distinctly, said:

"I am not your heir, sir. Your son, John Beauchamp, left a son and two daughters."

The eyes of the dying man flashed with a momentary brightness.

" A son ! you say ?—a son !"

" Yes, and he is blind."

" The sins of the fathers !—the sins of the fathers !" he moaned. " Poor boy—poor boy ! May he be a better man than his father, and than I have been ! Poor boy !"

This temporary rally was passing away, but Lady Mary, bending over him, heard him say :

" I forgive—pray that I may be forgiven. Little Johnnie was a fine fellow—poor little Johnnie ! You never saw him, Mary. I ruined him. Ask that I may be forgiven ! Pray, my dear — pray for me !"

" Try to pray yourself, dear ! God is very merciful. He will hear you," was the low reply.

Lady Mary alone caught the murmured words, and Mr. Birley, coming in just then, saw that the end drew near. In solemn silence all knelt round the bed, and as the commendatory prayer was said, a peaceful expression passed over the face that had been so often disturbed by passion, and it seemed to those who watched that, through infinite love and mercy, the last prayer had been heard, and the pardon of the penitent sealed.

But oh ! the sadness of lives like that which closed as the full beauty of the April afternoon bathed the earth with a tender radiance ! So true it is that no man liveth to himself; no action, no word but has its effect for evil or for good, directly or indirectly, upon those around us.

How widespread is the influence of a good man's life, and, alas! how widespread the influence of a life spent in forgetfulness of God, and our duty to Him and our neighbour! Surely this is a grave thought, to which we all do well to take heed, lest a bitter retribution should overtake us unawares.

CHAPTER XIV.

"VAIN IS THE HELP OF MAN."

PERCIVAL CLYFFE went early on the following morning to Paoli's Hotel, and ran up the stairs, two steps at a time, to Mrs. Murchison's room. He knocked at the door, and heard her voice bidding him come in.

Mrs. Murchison was surrounded with a motley array of dresses and hats and bonnets, sketch-books, paint-boxes, her violin, and many other possessions, all in dire confusion.

"Ah, you have caught me packing. I mean to follow Godfrey to England as soon as possible. It is rather nice to think of Cruttwell Court, isn't it? I shall wake up the old place, have heaps of people staying in the house, and have delightful garden-parties for the townspeople. You must come and see us. For"—with a little laugh—" I mean to live with Godfrey till he marries—perhaps afterwards, unless ——But how frightfully solemn you look! What can be the matter? You ought to congratulate me. I shall really like to live at Cruttwell for part of the year, though I am not going to say addio to Florence for ever. Chi lo sa! I may come back again."

It was always impossible to break the stream of Mrs. Murchison's rapid chatter. It was like a little, noisy, babbling brook in its tone, not altogether unmusical, but wearisome — sometimes provoking, too — when the listener, as was now the case, was trying to get in a word edgeways.

Percival watched all Mrs. Murchison's graceful movements, as she smoothed the ribbons of a bonnet, crimped the feather of a hat, and talked on all the time ceaselessly.

"I have no maid," she said, "but I shall have one now; Godfrey is sure to let me have one, though I am secretly afraid, do you know, he will spend a lot of money on those fads of his in London—his coffee-rooms, and reading-rooms, and recreation-rooms, where he holds forth lay-sermons to the great unwashed."

"I don't think you know what I believe will be known all over Florence very soon," Percival began. "Lysaght is not the heir to Cruttwell."

"Not the heir! What rubbish! Who said so? Who can be nearer of kin than Godfrey?"

"Well," said Percival, rather awkwardly, "there is a grandson of the old man's living in Florence. A grandson is nearer than a—great-nephew—I suppose."

"I don't believe it; it is a trumped-up story. I hope Godfrey does not believe it?"

"He does not know it, but a letter has followed him to England; so he will know soon enough. It is quite true, I assure you. I am awfully sorry, but it is true."

"Does Lady Anna know about it?"

"Yes"—and Percival sighed—"yes, but she is too much engrossed with poor little Daisy's illness to think of anything else."

"Poor little mite! is she worse? I always thought they were going the way to work to kill her with kindness." Then Mrs. Murchison began to hum snatches of songs in a provokingly careless way. "Well, so all my dreams are over, and I shall have to make the best of a London flat again. It *is* provoking! What is the use of my going to England now? Oh dear! and all this finery to put back in my drawers and boxes! Godfrey said he would telegraph for me, so I thought I had better get ready. Now I shall have to stay here for the present."

"That is a gain for some people," Percival said, feeling obliged to say something. "I am awfully glad you are not going!"

"Are you?" she asked, putting her head on one side, as she went on, with a paper-knife, crimping a long ostrich feather which had suffered from a shower when driving in the Cascine a few days before. "Are you really?"

"Of course I am: how can you ask? Think

how dreary my life here would be without you: I really could not stand it."

"Why, you would have your friend Adelaide, and your little cousin."

"I don't believe I shall have her long," he said—"dear little thing! She was too good for us."

"Now, really," Mrs. Murchison said, "it is hard to say that all the too good people die, and all the too bad ones are left. I am one of the last named. Ah, I see you think so!"

"I think nothing of the kind!" Percival said, fingering the strings of the violin which lay on the sofa by him—"I think nothing of the kind. Why do you pretend to read my thoughts?"

"My dear boy, I am very quick at thought-reading, and I believe I can read yours. You think me—well, never mind. I shall soon be gone; and there will be an end of me."

She put her head on one side, and her mouth, which was beautifully formed, with a short upper lip, displaying very white teeth, showed a little vexation.

Why did not Percival come to the point? He was a long time about it.

Sad to say, Mrs. Murchison was one of those women who have a strange delight in bringing, as it were, a fish to the bank, and then, when caught, shaking it free, sometimes with a wound in its mouth. Such anglers do not always wish to possess their prey; they like to play with it, and then, when the amusement is over, it may go! She had beguiled many an hour for Percival which would otherwise have hung heavy on his hands. Singing duets, playing duets, attending her with her sketch-book, when those bright sketches were rapidly knocked off, which were so much more attractive than Adelaide's studies of heads and figures; then that constant badinage, that sharp criticism of everyone, that brilliant superficial talk on a hundred and one subjects—all this was very amusing and delightful while it lasted; and Percival was just the preux chevalier whom Mrs. Murchison liked to show off as a captive.

Mr. Lysaght had remonstrated sometimes, but was always met with, "Poor boy! as if there were any harm in my efforts to amuse him. He would have a frightfully dull time with these Cowper-Smiths if it were not for me." Mr. Lysaght had not been satisfied, but it is always difficult to treat any matter seriously, when the persons most nearly concerned laugh it off as a jest.

To-day Mrs. Murchison was really much annoyed at the loss of her brother's fortune; and she presently assumed a pensive attitude, leaning back in her chair and gazing dreamily out of the window.

"Well," she said at last, after a silence, "what shall we do? Shall we amuse ourselves a little, if that is possible?"

"I don't feel much like amusement to-day,"

Percival said; "things are going very badly with me."

"With you! Now, that is nonsense. It is poor little me who is to be pitied—all alone here; and it is so humiliating, too, when all the people here think I am going to be 'la grande dame.' The old Professor, in the days of our friendship, got it out of me that Godfrey had great expectations. Dear me!" with an impatient tap of her foot upon the floor, "it *is* provoking—it is disgusting!"

Tears came into her beautiful eyes, but they were not allowed to fall. When cheeks are coloured, and eyes darkened below the lids, emotion must be kept in abeyance!

And now there was another tap at the door, and the opportunity Percival wished for was gone; for the old Professor came head-foremost into the room, looking vaguely with his short-sighted eyes at the heaps of various articles around him, stumbling over a violin-case, and sitting at last on one of the tallest of the hats, the crown of which went down with an ominous crack, which made Mrs. Murchison exclaim:

"Oh, you dear, awkward creature, what have you done? You must buy me a new hat—you must indeed, and choose it yourself. Could there be a greater penance?"

"Oh, I—I am very sorry! I hope no mischief is done," gasped the poor Professor.

"Mischief! Well, I should think there was—irreparable mischief!"

"I came—I ventured to come to congratulate you on what I hear was Mr. Lysaght's errand to England. A delightful place, I hear, in a part of Surrey which is interesting geologically. Some very remarkable fossils were discovered in a sand-cavern in that neighbourhood."

"Oh!" Mrs. Murchison said, "you find me in a state of mind in which life in a sand-cavern with fossils would be the most congenial to my feelings. To hide from the world—'the world forgetting, by the world forgot.' Tell him, Percival; I can't. Don't go, Percival!"

But Percival did not feel inclined to stay. "You had better tell the Professor yourself," he said; and then he took her little white hand into his for a moment, gave it a slight pressure, and was gone.

Adelaide did not go to her studio any more that week. She could not find it in her heart to leave Daisy, who clung to her more and more, and could not bear to lose sight of her.

The large fee was paid to the great London doctor, who only looked grave, talked of keeping up strength, and went through the usual formula of advice, and encouragement to persevere in his prescriptions.

But Mr. Cowper-Smith knew, as he handed him his cheque, that money was powerless to stay the ebbing current of that little life, so infinitely precious to him. Lady Anna would not give up hope, and talked of summer, and summer plans, and how they would go to some place on the southern coast of England, where the soft sea-breezes would soon work wonders. Did she *really* think that there was any earthly future for that dearly loved child? Was it the self-deception so common, when we hold fast to hope, as if hope would save what is precious to us; and fancy that, if we do not let go our grasp, we shall keep the dear one with us, whom we refuse to acknowledge as fading from before our eyes?

Daisy's condition now was more like fading than suffering. Indeed, these last few days the cough, which had broken her rest so much, and the pain in her side had almost disappeared. It seemed as if the disease had done its work, and was now stayed, because the result was sure.

The day on which the news of Mr. Beauchamp's death was telegraphed, Adelaide went early to the Piazza Cavour.

Lucia had also received the news; and the whole family were collected in the large room, discussing their future. The blind boy seemed quite unable to realize his position: he asked if they should leave Florence, and how soon.

"How soon, the dear innocent boy!—at once," his mother said. "And you will be master of a grand house, as large and grand as one of the Florence palaces—will he not, signorina?"

This was addressed to Adelaide, who came into the room while Madame Campbell was speaking.

"Ah, you, too, have had the news! Here is Lucia's telegram. I know not why *she* is chosen by Mr. Lysaght, except that she is a grand favourite! Now, signorina, about the black dresses we must wear. I have a black lace mantilla, which makes mourning; but we must have black skirts and jet ornaments. And I want Lucia to bring out the money; she is so close with the money."

"Oh, mother!" Lucia exclaimed, in a voice which had a ring of suffering in it; "do not speak so!"

"Well, it is true," Marietta said. "You do keep all your money so close, and you are very miserly."

"It is a shame to speak like that to her," said Giovanni, "and wicked too. Lucia, mia cara, *I* know what you have done for us."

Adelaide was sorry to be present at this family discussion, and she said in a low voice to Lucia:

"Can I come to your room?"

"Yes, that will be best."

"Now, do tell us of the grand place, signorina," Mrs. Campbell began. "Are there not large halls, and pictures, and a marble piazza? I know what English houses are, for I had once to sing at a duke's residence in an operetta—so grand it was, and how they applauded me! I wore a gold band in my dark hair; ah! well, an old woman is never believed when she says she was young once, and handsome."

"Cruttwell Court is a very pretty country house; some part of it is very old; it is not at all grand," Adelaide answered, moving to the door which led to the ante-room with Lucia.

"Come back soon to me, signorina," Giovanni said, "and tell me of the dear little Margherita."

"She is much the same. She wants to see you, so I will take you with me when I return."

When the two girls were alone Lucia exclaimed:

"Oh, Adelaide, Adelaide! is it not terrible? That is how they talk every hour—every minute. What will the future be? I cannot picture it. Poor mother! in the midst of English people, like Lady Anna and Mrs. Ponsonby! She will offend them, and—— Oh, I am ready to wish that this had never been known—if I had only burned the letter! It was a sore temptation. Do you think me very wicked?"

"If it was a sore temptation you resisted it, dear," Adelaide said. "But I am sorry for you, very sorry."

"No one else is," Lucia said. "No one else understands—no one else can ever be told—the hard, hard fight I have had, and shall have. Do you remember when you first saw me in the Uffizi, and heard Signor Maura finding his faults with my picture, and how gay and happy I was? I loved to work—I loved to feel I *could* work and keep them all; and now—now that the need of work is over, and I think why it is over—my heart is breaking. Oh, it is a sorrowful world!"

"It is indeed, for some of us. But, Lucia, all sorrows seem to me small when I compare them with Mr. Cowper-Smith's. His face haunts me; it is lined with grief about Margaret. Darling Daisy is going from us. Her poor father said to me when I left Hester with her, and came to fetch Giovanni: 'She is all I have to love, God help me!'"

"Yes," Lucia said, "yes, I am selfish—I am ungrateful. I will endure." Then, with the simplicity and directness of a child, she said, "Do you think it was wonderful I loved him?—coming here often, helping, cheering, when Giovanni was ill, reading and singing in his low, beautiful voice; always true, and noble, and good. Ah, the woman whom he chooses is blest indeed!"

Adelaide made no reply to this; but told Lucia that Daisy was very anxious to have Giovanni to play to her, and that Lady Anna had begged her to fetch him. "I cannot leave her long," she said; "so I must ask you to get him ready at once, please."

"Yes, I will do so; and do not think badly of me—do not forsake me!"

"Why should I? I hope we shall always be friends; and when you come to live at Cruttwell, we shall see each other every day, perhaps."

"Kiss me and love me," poor Lucia said. "I feel unworthy, but I have been helped in many a trouble;" and she added reverently, "God will not forget me now."

Hester Ponsonby met Adelaide on her return with Giovanni on the stairs.

"Daisy has been very faint: she is sitting on her father's knee now. The doctor has been here: it cannot be very long now—mother says so." Hester's voice faltered.

"Perhaps Giovanni had better not come into the room. I will go and find out, if you will wait with Giovanni here."

Adelaide threw off her hat, and went quietly into the room, where Daisy lay in her father's arms.

She looked up at Adelaide with a sweet smile.

"Giovanni—let him play to me!"

"No, darling," said Lady Anna, who was seated near, her fine features rigid with suppressed emotion—"no, darling; keep quiet."

"Music is quiet," the child said.

"Let him come—let him come," came in a low agonized tone from Mr. Cowper-Smith.

"And Percival—Percy—dear Percy! Everybody come and listen—everybody."

Very soon all were gathered together in the large room, and Daisy, looking round, said:

"I am so glad—don't cry, dear father;" for Mr. Cowper-Smith's chest was heaving with uncontrollable sobs. 'Mother, darling, you don't mind Giovanni playing to me, *do* you? If you do——'

"No, no—my sweet one, no!"

Giovanni drew the bow across the strings, and then the chords melted into the air which is so well known, and to which we all so often sing the beautiful words, which express the perfect faith and trust of a heart which leans on God in all darkness, and all distress :

"Lead, kindly Light, amid the encircling gloom,
Lead Thou me on."

"Sing, please—sing," Daisy said; and soft and low, Percival and Hester controlled their voices, and sang the words.

"And with the morn those angel faces smile," the child repeated when the last notes had died away. "I think I am tired, father, and will go to sleep now. Lay me down, dear father."

He carried her into the adjoining room, where poor Mrs. Gray stood weeping bitterly, and laid her on the bed.

"The morning will come," she said softly; "but it's very dark now."

As the dark waters of that solemn river of death touched her, there was a little shuddering and distress; but it was soon over.

"I hear lovely music," she said. "Is Giovanni playing again? And I see—I see Jesus: I do indeed. Look, father! father!"

But mortal ears heard not that music, and mortal eyes looked not on that vision. A few minutes more, and "from the hushed and silent room" the child, so dearly loved, had gone from all the wealth of an earthly inheritance, to the inheritance which fadeth not away.

It was a beautiful June day when Adelaide walked once more under the old gateway, and passed up the avenue leading to Cruttwell Court.

What a changed life was hers since, in the mists of an autumn morning, she had set out from Dryborough to join the Cowper-Smiths in London, on her way to Florence!

A changed life—rather, I should call it, an awakened life. The old aims and the old aspirations were the same, it is true; but they were definite now—not mere dreamy shadows, in which self was the only really distinct object.

She had learned a great deal more than how to draw correctly; and the battle with herself, which cost her some tears, over the distorted limbs of Andrea del Sarto's little cherubs, was not the only battle she had fought. I do not think Adelaide's experience is at all uncommon; for many girls, who have seen nothing of the world, find in the first man they meet, who has a certain amount of culture and a genial manner, the realization of an ideal.

When Adelaide first met Percival Clyffe, she was just at that point of dissatisfaction with herself which was scarcely yet acknowledged. She had been wounded by Hugh Birley's slighting remarks on her dress and her appearance, which Hester, if she did not exactly repeat to her, implied.

It had begun to strike her as possible that Hugh Birley might be right, and the Dryborough people wrong. That the "old gold" gown with the large sleeves was not so lovely or becoming as she fancied; and that large shady hats looped up at the side were not suited for a figure which was neither tall nor slender; that her studies with Mr. Wardlaw were not such as to make her a popular member of society; and that Hester, all dimples and smiles, and with a ready flow of the current coin of conversation, was far more likely to be attractive and sought after.

The two or three days spent in Percival Clyffe's society had at that very time an especial charm for her. Here, at least, was one person who knew the world, and moved in circles far wider than little Dryborough, who found her worth talking to, who expressed an interest in her, and who, she could not but feel, cared to be with her. The impression thus made was deepened when Daisy told her that it was Percy who had asked Lady Anna to take her to Florence; and then, what feeling there was, was further strengthened when, on the suspension bridge at Florence, on that bright December afternoon, Percival had greeted her with a warmth that brought the colour to her face, and made her heart beat with an undefined delight.

It was easy for Adelaide to see the very palpable conceit and "young Oxford" air of superiority which jarred her so much in Hugh Birley. Besides, she had known him from a boy in Eton jackets, and she had always disliked him for his self-assertion; and when her nearest and dearest friend, Hester Ponsonby, told her that she did not understand him, for that he was really delightful, and clever, and good, she could only pity her, and *look* incredulous.

It was not likely that Percival Clyffe should fail to attract her, and, indeed, he was very winning, and had a charm about him which many people felt. We may have our misgivings as to the depth of rippling waters. Nevertheless, shallow streams make a very pleasant music, and can reflect the sunshine and the sky as they tinkle merrily along. We do not stop to think that such shallows may soon dry up, and that in days of drought and barrenness the refreshment of such streams may fail us.

During the time of sorrow which had marked the last weeks at Florence, Percival had certainly appeared to advantage. He undertook all the necessary arrangements for the broken-hearted father; and now he had lost his child-friend, he seemed to feel that he had never known how dear she was to him.

In the face of a terrible grief like poor Lady Anna's, Percival had found Mrs. Murchison's frivolity irritating; and the little murmured expressions of sorrow, and then the immediate return to something which concerned herself, made him think as an excuse for her that a bright creature like her could not be expected to know what sorrow meant.

He forgot, perhaps, that the same bright creature had lost a gallant young husband, and *ought* to know what sorrow meant! But though he did not seek Mrs. Murchison in this trouble, he did not draw any nearer to Adelaide.

He thought her manner to him cold and unsympathetic, and talked much more freely to Hester Ponsonby and her mother about the painful preparations for taking all that was left of dear little Margaret to her own home. And now, as Adelaide passed up the fir avenue, and stood before the house, which could not choose but look bright in the summer sunshine, the memories of the moonlight night under those trees, and the walk through the driving rain, sheltered by Percival's arm, came back.

It was over—this first dream of love. Even if he were by her side then, and by his words dispelled the clouds of distrust and disappointment, it could not be the same. Mrs. Murchison was far better suited to him, she thought—" but," was the final conclusion, " I shall never be so ready to care for anyone again. I ought to be ashamed of it ; and I am. It is over now."

The door was opened by Preston. He had lost his occupation, and was glad to answer bells, or do anything which might help to pass what was a very dreary time in that silent house.

" Can I see her ladyship?" Adelaide asked.

" Yes, Miss Millington ; I think her ladyship will see you, but she is very much broken down—very much indeed. If you will step into the drawing-room, I will let her know you are here."

" Mr. Lysaght is gone, I suppose ?"

" Yes, Miss Millington. He left for London, and

then for Florence, last Monday. It is a curious business," Preston added, with the freedom of an old and trusted servant. "Foreigners are to come here, I find."

"Mr. Beauchamp's grandson!" Adelaide said; "hardly a foreigner!"

"Well, I consider it a misfortune, especially for her ladyship. The circumstances are very peculiar —very peculiar indeed. My poor master! Well, it is not for me to say anything more."

Preston had drawn up the blinds, and the long, low room became illuminated with sunshine. When he had closed the door, the profound stillness was oppressive. Adelaide felt as if she could not move, and scarcely breathe.

How beautiful was the close-shaven turf and the dark shadows of the firs lying on it; the roses climbing up by the window, almost like those she had left in Florence! The subtle charm of a real English summer-day is always felt on a return from other countries; and Adelaide felt it now. It was some minutes before Preston returned; at last the summons came for Adelaide to go to Lady Mary's morning-room.

She dreaded the meeting, but she need not have done so. Lady Mary was quite calm, though she spoke in a voice which was full of suppressed emotion.

"I am glad you have come back, my dear," she said, rising to meet Adelaide, her tall figure looking taller than ever, clothed in black. Lady Mary wore a widow's cap, with long streamers behind, which set off the refined contour of her head and shoulders. The lines on her face had deepened, but the old look of patient endurance was gone. It was replaced by an expression which is seen on the faces of those who have no longer need to bear a burden, for relief has come—no longer need to fight against the storm, for the storm is over.

The ship was in port; and though the traces of the surging sea and tempest were visible, yet there was peace underlying them—a peace won after a hard conflict.

Lady Mary received Adelaide affectionately, and, instead of referring to her own troubles, said:

"Tell me about my poor sister—my heart aches for her and her husband."

"Lady Anna is still in a most dejected state," Adelaide said. "She says very little, and seems unable to take any comfort. I think she is suffering from the feeling that all that was done was done in vain; that the life of the darling child could no more be saved by all that wealth could procure, than the life of the child of a poor man!"

"Yes, the powerlessness of money in the great exigencies of life and death!" Lady Mary said. "I can understand what she feels; poor Anna!"

"Mr. Cowper-Smith is really broken-hearted," Adelaide said. "It is so pathetic to see him studying the little book Daisy left, with 'My wishes,' written on the title-page, 'for dearest father.' He seems to take comfort in carrying them out, while Lady Anna is already studying designs from a Florentine sculptor for a recumbent figure, in pure white marble, for Willesford Church. The likeness is to be taken from a portrait Lucia Campbell—I must call her Lucia Beauchamp now—was just finishing when the dear child became too ill to sit for it."

"Ah!" Lady Mary said, "that name makes me think I must ask you about these people. From what Godfrey Lysaght says, the girl seems very good—but the mother, and the poor blind boy! Does it not seem wonderful that a man so well fitted to take his place here, with all his gifts and desire to do good in his day and generation, should be displaced by a poor afflicted boy, who seems to have no interest in the world but music—a dreamy, fragile creature, whose mother will rule here, and be of practically no use? I can submit to God's will, and I know His ways are not our ways, nor His thoughts our thoughts. But I confess while I should have hailed Mr. Lysaght as the master at the Court, I do shrink from those who have the first claim. My husband"—Lady Mary's voice faltered—"my husband died with forgiveness on his lips; and I thank God for it. He had built so many hopes on his son, and the utter destruction of them was terrible. I cannot go over that past—I had no part or lot in it. It is the present which concerns me; and I shall be glad, my dear, if you will help me to meet it. I have no daughter; and I shall be thankful to possess one in you. I have always loved you."

"Do you mean," Adelaide said, taking Lady Mary's hand in hers, and kissing it—the first time she had ever ventured on such a caress, "that I should live with you?"

"Yes. I do mean it. I must leave this place before these people come, and I have ample provision for my wants by my husband's generosity. I wish to place my personal possessions in safe keeping for a year, and travel. I thought you would like to come with me, and pursue your studies at Florence or Rome next winter."

"I must ask my mother about it," Adelaide said. "If she and my stepfather think it is right, I shall be glad to accept your offer, and be of what use I can to you."

"Your mother will consent, I think. Your sisters are growing up, and will be a comfort to her, while I —I am very desolate."

Were not such desolation and loneliness better than the daily and hourly attendance on a selfish, irascible invalid? Adelaide thought. As if Lady Mary had read that thought by intuition, she said:

"I know that many will think that I am only relieved from a heavy burden, but, my dear, I had all I deserved. I married for a home and a maintenance. What right had I to complain if the bed I had made for myself was an uneasy one? And I had my compensations; the last few weeks brought them to me; and I miss the ministry on him, which at first, and for many years, was simply the ministry of *duty*, but later became that of affection."

It is indeed true that our hermit-spirits dwell apart, and that the heart alone knows its own bitterness or its own joys, in neither of which can a stranger intermeddle.

"Adelaide," Lady Mary said after a pause, "what is Percival Clyffe doing?"

The colour rushed to Adelaide's face, and told its own tale.

"I do not know," she said. "He returned to London with the Cowper-Smiths and Mrs. Ponsonby and Hester. Miss Cromwell and I stayed behind at Florence with Fielding till the owners of the house returned."

"Some one said—I think it was Grace Ponsonby—that Percival was engaged to a young widow, Mr. Lysaght's sister. Is it so?"

"I cannot tell you," Adelaide said.

"I hope not; for, from what the Ponsonbys say, she must be very different from her brother—a very gay, frivolous person."

"She is very good-natured and very clever," Adelaide said. But her voice had a ring of bitterness in it which did not harmonize with her words.

Lady Mary put her arm round her and kissed her tenderly.

It was a silent token of understanding and sympathy, and Percival Clyffe's name was not mentioned again for many a long day.

CHAPTER XV.

UNDER A NEW MASTER.

MRS. PONSONBY was not, as we know, at all reticent, and as soon as she returned to Dryborough everyone was in possession of the history of the Beauchamps. Poor Mrs. Beauchamp—otherwise Campbell—was described in unflattering terms, and the Miss Townleys and Miss Castigan thought they really should hardly care to call upon such a person.

Mrs. Birley said it would not do to be discourteous, and if "the county" acknowledged Mrs. Beauchamp and paid its respects to the new master of the Court, of course Dryborough could not hold back. Hester's account of the Beauchamps was decidedly more favourable than her mother's, and Susie and Nina Wardlaw were looking forward to Lucia's painting and Giovanni's music, while their mother said she quite hoped these young people would compensate to her children for the loss of their sister. For Adelaide was to leave Dryborough with Lady Mary for a prolonged residence abroad.

The coming of the acknowledged heir to the Beauchamp estate, and the novelty of Italians at the Court, was a nine days' wonder. How few wonders outlive the tenth!

"The new family at the Court," as Dryborough expressed it, arrived late one Saturday evening in August. A telegram reached Preston to send the carriage to the junction, and a servant for the luggage. Preston kept his own counsel, and was determined there should be no demonstration made, or any "bell-ringing or nonsense for the arrival of a pack of foreigners."

So well was everything arranged, that the congregation in the church the next morning were for the most part taken by surprise when the party from the Court came up the aisle to the Squire's pew, where recumbent figures of the Beauchamps lay with folded hands in deep repose, which no chances or changes could disturb.

Miss Castigan felt herself strangely affected as she saw the blind master of the Court walk up the church on Mr. Lysaght's arm.

"So wonderfully forgiving of him," she said, wiping her spectacles. "It was most affecting."

"I don't see that there was any forgiveness in the case," said Miss Townley sharply. "The blind boy only claims his own."

"Ah, but what a disappointment! I call it very heroic of Mr. Lysaght—that I do!"

"Mrs. Beauchamp is the image of a gipsy woman dressed as a lady, but I suppose she must be called handsome: large eyes and coal-black hair are admired by some people, but not by me, I confess."

"I thought the blind boy very interesting, and he certainly has an aristocratic air."

"Do you think so?" Miss Townley said. "I cannot say it struck me. Now, there was a grandeur about the old Squire, for when I was a tiny child, you know, I used to watch for him coming under the archway on his fine black horse. I was a mere baby when that dreadful event happened, but I can remember it clearly."

"Oh, Miss Townley! you were at my school when the great trouble came at the Court. You were quite a big girl, and a very clever one, too," Miss Castigan added, trying to gild the pill with a little timely flattery, for Miss Townley, though generally truthful, was apt to deviate from the path of rectitude when the question of age was concerned.

The small, lithe figure which followed Mrs. Beauchamp up the aisle, with the more imposing form of Marietta, had been almost overlooked. Lucia might have passed unnoticed, but when she was leaving the church she suddenly turned to wait for Adelaide. With all the impulsiveness of her Southern nature, and quite unconscious of the eyes which were looking at her with some curiosity, Lucia kissed her, taking both her hands in hers, and saying in a low voice: "Come and see me; I am so lonely here."

Adelaide was spending her last Sunday with her

mother in the old home, and Lady Mary was staying with Mrs. Ponsonby. They were to start early the next morning for London, and all Adelaide's preparations were completed.

After the service in the church, she separated herself from her sisters, and in the dim twilight of the September evening went under the gateway towards the Court. The dark firs were murmuring their old song, and just above the topmost boughs a crescent moon was hanging its silver bow. As Adelaide drew near the house she saw lights in the hall, and heard the sound of Giovanni's violin, with a voice—a well-known voice—singing a familiar hymn of Faber's to the tune which seems to suit it so well. The wide hall door was open, and under the old stone porch Adelaide could just distinguish Lucia's figure. At the sound of footsteps Lucia started, and springing towards her, said:

"I have been waiting and watching for you so long."

"I have been to church," Adelaide said. "It is my last night here for a very long time, and I liked to be with my mother and sister for our last service together."

"Hush!" Lucia said. "Do you hear that music? Do you know the words?

"'Rest comes at last, though life be long and dreary.'

Ah, I am longing for that rest — the rest little Margherita has gained. Why am I left?"

"To do good in the world," Adelaide said. "You have so much power and so many gifts, Lucia. Do not lose heart. You have been so brave."

"I wish I were returning with you to my beautiful Florence. I would rather be working there again for my daily bread than shut up here under these dark trees; so dark and chill it is! And no one wants me."

"You forget Giovanni. How could he live without you?"

"Ah, everyone learns at last to do without the people and things they love best," Lucia said. "That is what poor Signor Maura said to me when I left him. He said he had learned the lesson of doing without his right arm, and that he should have to learn to do without me—the light of his eyes, he called me. We moved him into our old room, and made it pleasant for him, and I asked the signor to let us leave some money to keep him while he lives. The signor is going to manage our money for us. Giovanni cannot, and the madre must not—she does not know its value; and Marietta is worse. We moved all the poor signor's pictures for him. Have you heard that the lady and the little boy were signor's mother and little brother who died? Is it not wonderful? She was such a good friend to Signor Maura; and he thought he could paint her portrait. It is terrible to be self-deceived as he was. It is no portrait, no picture, only a daub—a dream, a delusion. Have we not all our dreams and delusions? You will go and visit the dear old man at Florence, for my sake?"

"Yes, I promise," Adelaide said.

"The signor said he was going to visit the Lady Mary this evening. Ah, he is coming, he is coming!" And Lucia had vanished in the dim light of the spacious hall behind her just as Mr. Lysaght came into the porch. He started, and said:

"Are you waiting for anyone? Have you rung the bell?"

"It is I—Adelaide," she answered. "I came up to see poor Lucia. She has been talking to me here."

"Will you not come in and see Giovanni?" And Mr. Lysaght turned and led the way to the familiar drawing-room, which was lighted by two lamps at the further end.

Adelaide could have fancied herself in the bare apartments in the Piazza Cavour as she heard Marietta and her mother talking in their rapid, high-pitched voices. It sounded very like wrangling, if not like quarrelling, and Adelaide's heart was full of sympathy with Lucia. As she had said, working for daily bread might almost be preferable to having no particular object in life in the stately loneliness of Cruttwell Court.

"Well, Giovanni." The blind boy started to his feet.

"Signorina! signorina! I am glad you are come! It will make Lucia happier."

"Happy—happier!" exclaimed Mrs. Beauchamp; "we are all happy now. We shall have plenty of good things. It is enraging to see Lucia mope, mope, and look like one of the blessed martyr saints. I have no patience with her!"

"We need not mind her now," said Marietta. "We can please ourselves, thank goodness! Lucia has been as sour as an unripe olive ever since our good fortune came. We need not mind her."

"But we shall mind her!" exclaimed Giovanni. "I am the master here, and I shall order all to love and reverence my Lucia. Oh, it is a shame to talk thus!"

The boy's pale face glowed with indignation; but Marietta only laughed and said:

"It is only amusing to hear you!"

"Giovanni is perfectly right," Mr. Lysaght said.

He had been standing a little apart. It was not in human nature to be insensible to the contrast between what *was* and what might have been.

This querulous girl and her garrulous mother installed at the Court, with all their little disputes and unseemly wrangles; Giovanni, who was really the master of the house, set aside!

And Lucia—did he not give one thought to Lucia? Yes, assuredly; but he looked on her as the one most likely to keep peace and to exercise an influence for good, as she had done in their humble home at Florence. He saw there was a change in her—that she was listless and silent—that her old brightness and activity seemed gone; and he thought it was the result of her changed life and of her illness in the spring.

"She is one to whom work is a necessity," he thought. "She will soon find it for herself, and the absolute rest and freedom from care will have its effect in time."

Mr. Lysaght said this as he and Adelaide walked together down the avenue under the dark fir-trees, where the night-breezes made their moan, as of waves on a distant shore.

"Lucia's brave spirit will assert itself at last," he continued. "Now all things are strange to her. It is a new and trying position."

Mr. Lysaght seemed to like to talk of Lucia, and of any subject that might put Adelaide at ease. She on her side was silent, only assenting in monosyllables to what he said.

"Lucia's kindly thought for that poor old Italian was very touching. She has left him at ease for the rest of his life. Did she tell you of the strange coincidence about my mother being his ideal—his Madonna?"

"Yes," Adelaide said; "Lucia told me about it."

"It is strange how small the world is," Mr. Lysaght went on; "everyone seems to be linked in the chain of circumstances with somebody else. The whole story is remarkable! The curious adaptation of the name; the skilful avoidance of anything which might lead to suspicion! Sad it is to think how implacable were the feelings of unnatural hatred between the father and son. The son too proud even to make himself known to the father, preferring starvation for his family to appeal to the Squire! But the father's heart softened at the last, and poor Lady Mary had her reward for years of patient continuance in well-doing."

Then after this there was a silence. They were under the old gateway now, and in a few minutes they must separate. How often it happens, as it happened that night to Mr. Lysaght and Adelaide, that the subject nearest to the heart of one is purposely avoided, while the other uses every effort to seem unconscious that it exists!

"I shall be here from time to time," Mr. Lysaght said. "I cannot resist the appeal of that poor blind boy to help and befriend him; but I shall try to make headquarters for the winter in my chambers."

Not a word of his sister, and no reference to her. Adelaide determined to ask the question, but she could scarcely summon courage to do so, or control her voice as she said:

"Will Mrs. Murchison live with you?" The words came out slowly and with hesitation.

"No; my sister's plans are uncertain. For the present she is staying with some friends near Cambridge. I shall probably be alone for the greater part of the winter, but I shall not be lonely. I have a great deal on hand in London, and I must make my pen useful now. I have enough and to spare, thank God, and I hope I shall be able to do something for those who are in need. We must say good-bye here. I hope your art studies will prosper this winter, and that we may see a picture of yours on the walls of Burlington House some day."

" That is a very distant day, I am afraid," Adelaide said ; " but, if it ever comes, I shall owe it to your encouragement and help. Do you remember finding me in despair over the little cherubs in the Accademia, and taking me to consult poor Lucia ?"

" As if I could forget !" he said. He held her hand for a moment in his, and then said : " I do not ask you that question again which I asked you at Florence. I thought then I had something to offer you ; now I have nothing but my love, which, if everything else is changed, is changeless."

So they parted. Adelaide opened the door (which had been left on the latch) noiselessly, and hastened upstairs to her own room, where so many of her dreams had been dreamed, where aspirations for a dim and undefined future had made her forget the duties of the present.

She stood for some minutes amongst all the preparations for departure, thinking over her position and trying to realize it. Why was her fate so different from Hester Ponsonby's, who had been loved and loved again, and now, in the face of all opposition, was engaged to be married in the spring to Hugh Birley ?—Mrs. Ponsonby had withdrawn an opposition in which she felt it was hopeless to persist, and was ready to welcome Hugh Birley as her son-in-law. Why would her heart turn so persistently to Percival Clyffe, while her better judgment rose up in rebellion, as it were, against herself? The bright, versatile, and popular man who had won her by sympathy when she needed it, who had first opened out to her a possible future of success, and had professed—ah, was it only profession ?—to be interested in all she did, and all she longed for, still held a sway over her. Yes, though he had fallen off from his allegiance, and had apparently given it to a gay, fascinating woman who knew the world and was versed in all the ethics of society, of which Adelaide herself knew nothing.

She did not even take into account the possibility that he might at last return to her—that he might get tired of Mrs. Murchison, and be as he had been in those first days at Dryborough, and in the first delightful fortnight at Florence. To do Adelaide justice, she did not look forward, but simply met the question as it presented itself to her then.

"Could I, feeling as I do now, care for anyone but him ? No, I could not—I dare not!"

And yet in her secret heart she felt that Mr. Lysaght stood on a vantage-ground far above Percival Clyffe. The one, earnest and full of the serious purpose of life, resolute, and, as he said, changeless; the other, with all his attractions, unstable in his plans, uncertain in his moods—one day talking of a situation in the Home Office, the next of a cattleranche in the Far West, or seeking a place at the Cape as secretary to some mining company. But all these schemes ended in nothing, and Percival Clyffe was content to be what he was—a popular member of society, whose popularity was, as in thousands of other cases, a snare to him.

Adelaide's meditations were brought to an abrupt conclusion by her sister's knock at the door.

"Adelaide, do come down; it is your last night, and supper is ready. Do come."

Yes; it was again the last night. But she was going forth with very different anticipations to those with which she had joined the Cowper-Smiths the year before. The great lessons of life had forced themselves on her, and the horizon had widened; Adelaide Millington was no longer the centre round which her little world revolved. She had learned much more since that moonlight night when she first saw Percival Clyffe's handsome face looking down on her. It had been an awakening from dreams to the realities of life—yes, and of death also. For the sweet influence of the child who had loved her, and whose dying words were so often in her ears, had come to her just when she had most needed it. Dear little Margaret, by her gentleness and unselfishness, surrounded as she was by everything most calculated to evolve a character wholly engrossed with selfish requirements, had not lived in vain. That life had left its mark; to be with her was to be with one whom the King of Love had marked for His own; and in His love had taken her gently to His arm, and shielded her from the trials which must have beset her in the long journey of life. Who could wish to recall her?

A few days later, Adelaide found herself with Lady Mary at Willesford Hall. The grief-stricken father was trying to find consolation in following out his child's last wishes. But the mother, whose hopes had been crushed, and who sat with folded hands mourning for her child, with the ever-present sense of failure in all her efforts to keep her darling with her, filled Adelaide's heart with the deepest pity as she read in Lady Anna's rigid face, marked with lines of a hard and bitter grief, the words of the prophet of old, "I do *well* to be angry." There is nothing more terrible to see than grief like Lady Anna's. The idol is taken away, and with it seems to have gone all sweetness and tenderness out of the heart which hardens itself against the loving Father who does not willingly afflict His children.

Lady Mary had felt it her duty to propose this visit to Willesford before leaving England; but it was too painful to prolong it, and it lasted but a few days.

Mr. Cowper-Smith called Adelaide to his library one evening, saying they should be free from interruptions, and that he had something to show her.

"You loved my darling; you know how I loved her!" he said; "and I am only longing to carry out the wishes she has left behind. There are difficulties; my poor wife is so resolutely set against one of them." Then he took from a drawer the little red book Adelaide had often seen in Daisy's hand, and said, in a broken voice, "You already know about this book! You can read what she has written. I know what she says there by heart; and I must obey her —but how?"

Adelaide turned the pages of the little book, on the first leaf of which was written, "*My wishes for dearest father*: I should like dear father to build a nice pretty house near the church for little sick children to come and get well out of Ironstown. Next, I should like Mrs. Gray—dear, dear Grayling—to look after them, and talk to them about me. I know what it is to be tired and to feel ill; and it is very hard to bear—how much more for poor children in dark dismal houses in Ironstown! I should like Percy, dear Percy, to have anything of mine he wishes for—my dear pony *Zoe*, and, dear father, some money; you will have no money to spend for me when I am gone away, so do let Percy have it. I love him very, very much; he was always so kind to me. Then there is Rose Smith, my cousin, dear father; I want you to have her as a little daughter instead of me. You and poor mother will be lonely at Willesford with no one. *Do* ask Cousin Barbara to give you Rose. I think she will, for she has so many little girls; and you, poor father, had only one, only me!—and God is taking me away. I am so sorry for dear father, losing his

Peggy; but God knows best. Do take Rose to be your little daughter."

No wonder this page was blotted with tears; and Adelaide's eyes were dim as she read the wishes the child's father held sacred. He broke in here:

"I would do all—all; but my poor wife will not listen to the wish about Rose. I dare not even mention it, she is so set against it. She may come round in time—poor thing, poor thing!"

Adelaide could not trust herself to speak as she read on:

"I love Adelaide very much, dear father; let her have anything of mine she likes—my dear tiny little watch, which rings the half-hours in the night. Adelaide will think how often I have touched it when I was lying tossing about at Florence.

"Then Giovanni is to have my violin, please; and you will help *him*, for he is very poor. Mr. Lysaght was so kind to him. You won't forget Giovanni, father? And Mr. Lysaght—I should like him to have my clock that sounds like the bell of the Duomo when it strikes. I love Mr. Lysaght—he is so good."

The writing grew more feeble after this, and evidently the entries had been made with increasing difficulty; but everyone was remembered. Miss Cromwell, and Fielding and Sam, all were to have keepsakes.

The last words were deeply touching:

"I leave my tender love to my dear father and mother. All I have is theirs, so I cannot leave them a keepsake; they can choose what they like best. I hope I shall be the first to meet them when they come to that lovely home where I am going—soon, now, I think. I *have* been afraid to go, but not now. I feel the Lord is quite—quite near. This is Whit Sunday—White Sunday—and I saw a pretty white dove at my window to-day, before Grayling was awake. I cannot write any more."

A few words after this were not legible.

Adelaide returned the book to Mr. Cowper-Smith, and she said:

"You are happy to have such a child, for she is yours still."

"Yes, yes; I try to feel that, and I try to realize her joys in that home she writes of; but I have many sad hours, sadder than anyone can guess. My wife, poor thing, will not take any comfort, keeps herself apart, and seems to have no interest in anything but the plans for the chapel to be built on the east end of the church, where the monument is to be placed. Have you seen the sculptor's drawing for the figure?"

Mr. Cowper-Smith drew a portfolio towards him with the design for the marble tomb.

The child's figure lying in perfect rest, her head turned upon a pillow, a smile on her lips, and the likeness—taken from Lucia's portrait—very striking.

."It will be beautiful in marble," Adelaide said; and she could no longer restrain her tears, as she read the words beneath:

"Margaret, only beloved child of John Cowper-Smith and Anna, his wife, given to them May 21st, 1874, taken from them May 15th, 1886. 'The light of mine eyes is gone from me. He takes away the desire of my eyes with a stroke. It is the Lord; let Him do what seemeth Him good.'"

"The last words ought to be what I feel," the poor father said; "and I do feel them sometimes, not always—not always! God have pity on me, and help me!"

As Mr. Cowper-Smith replaced the design in the portfolio he said:

"Can you say anything to my poor wife about little Rose? I have asked her sister to do so, but she shrinks from it."

"I am afraid I dare not," Adelaide said; "I fear to seem intrusive, and Lady Anna gives me no chance of speaking to her of Daisy."

Mr. Cowper-Smith sighed heavily.

"We must trust to time," he said, "and be patient; it is a hard blow for her, and somehow she will not let me try to soften it. But we must be patient—we must have patience!"

Yes, he had patience, and he needed it. This self-absorbed grief, which is the outcome of an undisciplined will, is infinitely sad for those who have to watch it, and feel powerless to help or comfort.

Those people who are selfish in joy and in the times of prosperity, are invariably selfish in sorrow. We see some stricken as Lady Anna was turn to the world and all it can give for consolation; but Lady Anna's love for her child had been too absorbing, and was so mixed up with herself, and her pride in her *as hers*, that she could not do this. Rather the cry of her stricken heart was, "What does it profit, all this wealth for which I craved; what do all these possessions mean? Nothing but barrenness and despair! All I could do—all that riches could do—was done, and in vain. I have lost her, and it is a cruel blow! And there is none to pity—none to care!"

So she wrapped herself up in her sorrow as in a mantle, and forgot the pain at the heart nearest her own; forgot to soothe *his* grief—forgot, indeed, everything but *herself* and her own bitter grief.

Nor was this condition of Lady Anna's out of harmony with her past life. She had lived for herself, and she was now sorrowing for herself. In such natures there is no room for the griefs or joys of others, apart from their own. Only one Hand can touch hearts like Lady Anna's, and with the touch bring repentance and healing. Only at the Cross can we learn what is the beauty of sacrifice, and the happiness which springs from all pain and weariness, when once His steps are followed, faithfully— even unto death—who pleased not Himself.

CHAPTER XVI.

AFTER ONE YEAR.

FLORENCE looked her brightest and best on the May of the following year when Lady Mary Beauchamp and Adelaide arrived there on their way from Rome, where they had spent the winter, and where Adelaide had made rapid progress in her studies. It was strange to find herself in Florence again, so full of memories of her own past, where the sound of the rippling Arno under the bridges and the great bell of the Duomo were like the voices of friends bearing messages from a vanished time.

Lady Mary had found Adelaide a congenial companion. She had the gift of silence when silence was desired, and did not think it necessary to make talk out of nothing, which manufacture is often so tiresome and destroys anything like freedom of intercourse. Lady Mary had lived in retirement at Rome, where the English have a large society, and where the faults of our modern life at home are seen perhaps more clearly in the light of the atmosphere of the Eternal City. It is the fashion to say that Rome is infinitely before and beyond Florence in interest, and there is a certain affectation in many of those who frequent it, who look down with pity on their friends and acquaintances whose travel stops short of Rome. Although Adelaide's travel had extended to Rome, she found in Florence, on her return to it, all the grace and indescribable charm which cannot be destroyed even by the intimate acquaintance of months with the grandeur of St. Peter's and the solemn memories which linger round the Forum and the Pantheon, and are borne upon the waters of the yellow Tiber. Florence holds her own, and greets those who love her with a smile as she spreads before them the wealth of her flowers, her treasures of art, and welcomes them to the dazzling beauty of the facciata of her Duomo, to her Campanile soaring heavenward, and her encircling hills, which take the deepest violet hue as the sun sinks behind the Carrara mountains, and sends an afterglow of the purest rose colour across the deep blue of the overarching sky.

"After all, there is no place like it," Adelaide said, as she went up the zigzag path to San Miniato once more, stopping at every turn to recognise all the objects which had been familiar, like the recognition of friends from whom she had been separated. The heights of Fiesole, the grand outline of Monte Morello, the bridges, the towers and domes, all in the glowing sunshine of the May afternoon, were like the realizing of a beautiful dream, and made her sing out of the fulness of her heart for very thankfulness that she saw it all again.

Adelaide's step was light, and her whole bearing very different from other times. She was now self-reliant instead of self-doubting, no longer teased with the fear of what others thought of her, no longer yielding to that self-depreciation which is in reality a form of self-love.

Lady Mary had encouraged all her tastes and sympathized in her work. They had read a great many books together, for Lady Mary had a low, clear voice, and she read while Adelaide worked at her water-colour sketches, which at last rivalled Mrs. Murchison's. She had acquired the happy art of expressing what she felt with her brush, and all the poetry of her nature came forth in her pictures of world-famed ruins, set against the sunset skies of Italy, with which her portfolio was full.

The graver studies had gone on at a studio in Rome, and one of her compositions, from the living model of a Roman peasant and her child, had won great praise for careful execution, and faithful representation of a mother and her boy. Success is always sweet; and though Adelaide in her secret heart thought less of her productions now than she had done of the "Fisher-boy," still, there was the feeling dear to most of us who labour with pen, brush, or chisel, that the power that is in us is growing, and that patient labour, and determination to conquer difficulties, irrespective of criticism or opinions, is winning its reward.

When Adelaide reached her favourite position before the church which crowns the height of San Miniato, she sat down on the steps of the Piazza and drew from her pocket some letters which had awaited her from Florence. One from a happy bride, Hester Birley, written from Lucerne, where she was finding out how delightful life was with one to share all her joys, and especially when that one was like her Hugh, so superior as he was to the average of man. Adelaide smiled a little scornfully as she read these words.

"Poor Hester! dear little Hester! She is to be envied for her faith in Hugh; but superior—will she ever find out that he is anything but that?" Then, checking herself, "How crabbed I am! and who am I to laugh at her, for being taken by the outside! Dear Hester, I must write to her to-morrow."

The other letter was from Lucia. She had grown more accustomed to her life, and Giovanni was so thoughtful and kind. He had asked the signor to find the right place at the back of the Court where to build a studio—a real artist's studio—and she was to be settled in it before long. Then she should get back to her work, and feel happier. "Happy I do not think to be, but life is very bright sometimes."

Evidently the old spirit was reviving in the little artist. And Adelaide was glad to mark it, and to feel that Lucia's heart-wound would heal, as her own had healed. But then her cure had been hastened!

Percival Clyffe, in spite of the anger of his aunt, Lady Anna, and threats of discontinuing all her favours to him, had married Mrs. Murchison.

He had done it at last, from a consciousness, perhaps, that he had given her every reason to believe he cared for her, and that in honour he could not draw back. As to Mrs. Murchison, she was well pleased; the only drawback was the want of money; but she employed her powers of fascination to such good purpose, that a slight acquaintance with one of the chiefs of the Colonial Office was worked so well that Percival Clyffe, backed by Lord Fernclyffe's influence, was appointed judge of one of the Supreme Courts of Judicature in a distant part of Her Majesty's Empire.

Thither they drifted, and Mrs. Percival Clyffe was spoken of as a sparkling, charming person, round whom a little coterie gathered, in a place where she reigned as queen, and succeeded in making many besides the learned Professor at Paoli's Hotel believe in her, as a literary queen who, by the hard-heartedness and gross stupidity of publishers, could not gain a hearing. She instantly plunged into a book to be entitled "My Life in the Tropics." And if the material at her command is worked up with a certain clearness of style and good grammar, which her previous efforts rather wanted, the book may prove what Percival foretells—a grand success.

I do not know whether Percival Clyffe casts many backward glances. Men of his type have a happy facility of effacing their past — especially if it is not altogether creditable to themselves—with a sponge. But sometimes he hears—echoing from that past in which his wife has neither part nor lot —the voice of a child, tender and musical, and he hears her say, "Percy, dear Percy," and again "*Adelaide.*" Perhaps his love for his little cousin was the deepest and purest love he had ever known, or ever will know. But he was very well satisfied with himself and his wife. His knowledge of law was certainly not very great, but he had been called to the Bar, and it was easy to persuade himself that the title of Judge was a deserved honour, which he wore with a becoming sense of his own importance!

Adelaide turned into the church to take a look at the sleeping Cardinal, and here indeed she found a well-remembered friend. The repose and perfect rest of that beautiful figure seemed to fill her soul with an answer of peace. She had gained much since she had last gazed upon the pure beauty of that marble face, and it was with a feeling of thankfulness that she remembered how sore her heart had been when she last sat there, and how wonderfully the smart of wounded pride, as much as wounded love, had been cured.

"It was all a mistake," she said to herself, as she tripped lightly down the steep hill with its tall cypresses and its wooden crosses. "It was all a mistake. I wonder how many other people have made the same. I wonder if I am very much unlike the rest of the world—rather, I ought to say, very much more foolish. Few people would have been as weak as I was; and yet I knew nothing of life, and I believed all that was said to me. Perhaps it was natural, considering how I had lived in my own little world, where everyone thought so far too highly of me. It is all over; and I hope I am better for the lesson I was so slow to learn."

She was at the foot of the hill now, and passed under the old gateway into the shadows of the old town beyond it, where across the narrow streets the westering sunshine lay in bands of glory, and burnished the higher gables of the tall roofs till they gleamed like bronze against the blue sky.

The Florentines were standing at their doors or leaning out of their windows, the Italian tongue sounding like the echo of the Arno as it rippled and tinkled under the Ponte Vecchio. Adelaide paused at the opening between the houses, and leaned over the parapet, looking towards the Carrara mountains for a few moments. Suddenly she heard her name:

"Adelaide—Miss Millington!"

She turned quickly, and stood face to face with Mr. Lysaght.

"I found Lady Mary at the Hôtel de la Grande Bretagne, being directed thither by the courteous personage at Vieusseux's Library, with whom I had many conversations last year. He told me Lady Mary Beauchamp had entered her name as a subscriber for a month."

"Yes," Adelaide said; "I went there this morning, and wrote our names in the book. When did you come?"

"A few days ago. I was in want of a little rest, and I had an errand here for Lucia Beauchamp. Her poor old friend was dying, and she wished to possess herself of his pictures. A very pathetic sight it was to see the old man to the last clinging to his old faith in himself and his productions. Of course, I had a double interest in him, for Lucia's sake and for my own. He knew my mother; and one of the crude pictures, scarcely more than a daub, represents her and my little brother, both of whom are buried in the old English cemetery."

"For Lucia's sake." Why did those three words stand out from all the rest and give Adelaide a sudden pang? Presently Mr. Lysaght said:

"What are you going to do to-morrow?"

"I shall drive in the afternoon, probably, with Lady Mary; but in the morning I shall go to the Boboli Gardens, and make a sketch there of the famous view. Last time I was here I had never learned to sketch, and now I like it better than any part of my work."

They were at the door of the hotel now, and Adelaide said, with something of her old constrained manner:

"I think I must say good-bye. Lady Mary will be expecting me."

Mr. Lysaght said: "Then good-bye till to-morrow. I hope you may have a fine day for your sketch."

"Mr. Lysaght is in Florence, my dear," Lady Mary said. "He called here this afternoon."

"Yes; I met him." And then, feeling obliged to say something, she added: "He looks very well—much stronger than he did last year."

Lady Mary went on quietly working at her embroidery, and merely said:

"Yes, I think he does. I hope your tea is not cold, my dear; if it is, call Mason, and she will get some more hot water."

"It is very nice, thank you," Adelaide said absently; and as she sat stirring the cup of sugarless tea with the spoon, Lady Mary was wondering whether or not there was really anything between her and Mr. Lysaght; but she had too much tact and kindliness to ask the question.

Adelaide seemed in a great hurry to be off the next morning, sketch-book and camp-stool in hand. She crossed the Ponte alle Grazie, and was soon at the entrance of the Boboli Gardens.

She had made up her mind where to take up her position for her sketch—the point (familiar to those who know those beautiful gardens) whence the Duomo and the tower of the Palazzo Vecchio appear between a row of cypress-trees and the walls of the Pitti Palace.

Adelaide was soon lost in her endeavours to catch the full beauty of the scene before her, and forgot everything in the earnestness with which she studied the view, making it her own, before she began to reduce it within the limits of her sketching-block.

Her dark expressive eyes were full of that wistful longing which the artist always feels when contemplating a fresh subject for a study. The fine outline of her head and brow were not now hidden by one of "the monstrous hats" on which Hugh Birley had made such uncomplimentary remarks. Adelaide wore on the dark masses of her hair a closely fitting cloth cap of the same colour as the plain gray dress of homespun, which fitted her perfectly. Her sketching-block was on her knee, and her large red sunshade fixed on its long handle behind her, shadowing her with a rosy hue.

All unperceived, Mr. Lysaght had come almost up to her, before she was conscious of his presence. When at last she turned her eyes from the view before her with an inquiring glance, still half absorbed in her work, she started, and her whole countenance lighted with a glad surprise.

It gave him courage, and he came nearer and sat down by her, watching her, as, after "Good-morning" had been exchanged between them, she began to rub the colours on her palette, having first put in a few rapid lines in pencil, to guide her brush.

Florence, from the Boboli Gardens.

Her long, delicate fingers seemed to be full of life, and swiftly but surely there dawned upon the paper before her a reflection of the scene on which so many artists' eyes have lingered lovingly, and left with a regret that, after all, such a vision of glowing beauty of sky and mountain, of dome and tower, accentuated by the tall forms of the dark cypresses, is beyond their power to reproduce.

A long silence followed, broken only by the buzz of an insect, or distant voices in another part of the gardens. Then Mr. Lysaght said:

"When can you spare a moment to look at me and listen? I have been very patient; it has been the patience of hope, Adelaide."

But still those mobile fingers moved, and still the picture grew under her hand, and she did not speak.

"Something in your face tells me that hope is to meet its reward at last. Am I wrong, or am I dreaming? and shall I, must I awake to know that that welcoming smile of yours was but as a vision which will fade?"

Again a pause.

"Adelaide, was I dreaming when I thought you were glad to see me?"

She stopped her brush now, and held it suspended in her hand. At last she raised her eyes to his.

"It is I who have been dreaming," she said. "This is my awakening."

"To what?" he asked.

The answer was in so low a tone that, bending towards her, he could hardly be sure of the words.

"To what—to what have you awakened?"

"To know that I love you," she said.

There is no need to lengthen out this old story, told in the City of Flowers in that radiant May-time, when all things around her seemed to be rejoicing with Adelaide's new-found joy. Many and many a time has the same story been rehearsed by the rippling waters of the Arno, under blue Italian skies, as well as in the colder regions of the far North.

And there is no more beautiful story than that of a love which has its foundations struck deep, though hidden, and is the union of two souls bound together by the golden band of faith—a faith which reaches far into the land where the shadows of earth pass away and the substance remains—where there is a blessed awakening in His likeness Who is the Fountain of light and life and love!

THE END.

BILLING AND SONS, PRINTERS, GUILDFORD.

WORKS BY MRS. MARSHALL.

ON THE BANKS OF THE OUSE; or, Life in Olney a Hundred Years Ago. With Illustrations. Price 5s. Third Thousand.
"No better story than this has been written by Mrs. Marshall."—*Guardian.*

IN FOUR REIGNS: Recollections of Althea Allingham from George III. to Victoria. 5s. Fourth Thousand.
"A most charming tale of bygone days. The tone of the book is eminently high and refined."—*Literary World.*

UNDER THE MENDIPS: a Tale. Fourth Thousand. 5s.
"One of Mrs. Marshall's charming stories, told with all the wonted freshness and grace which characterize her books."—*Westminster Review.*

THE TOWER ON THE CLIFF. 1s. sewed, or 1s. 6d. cloth.
"The old dead time lives once more in her pages."—*Saturday Review.*

THE MISTRESS OF TAYNE COURT. 5s.

IN THE EAST COUNTRY WITH SIR THOMAS BROWN, Kt. Fourth Thousand. 5s.
"A singularly delightful and interesting work."—*Spectator.*

MRS. WILLOUGHBY'S OCTAVE. 5s.
"We have seldom read anything more pathetic."—*Spectator.*

IN COLSTON'S DAYS. Fourth Thousand. With Illustrations, 5s., cloth.
"Extremely well written."—*Morning Post.*

CONSTANTIA CAREW: an Autobiography. 5s., cloth.
"Much superior to ordinary religious fiction."—*Spectator.*

TWO SWORDS: a Tale of Old Bristol. Price 1s. sewed, or 1s. 6d. cloth.
"The lesson of the book is excellent, and the story is gracefully told."—*Literary World.*

CHRISTABEL KINGSCOTE. Fifth Thousand. Crown 8vo., Frontispiece, 5s., cloth.
"As fascinating a tale, and as prettily told, as the reader can wish for. We remember no book which we have more pleasure in recommending."—*Athenæum.*

BRISTOL DIAMONDS; or, The Hotwells in the year 1773. Eighth Thousand. Price 1s. sewed, or 1s. 6d. cloth.
"Mrs. Marshall's stories are always first-rate."—*Church Bells.*

SEELEY AND CO., ESSEX STREET, STRAND.

BY THE SAME AUTHOR.

BENVENUTA; or, Rainbow Colours. 5s., cloth.
"A pleasant story of family life."—*Athenæum.*

DOROTHY'S DAUGHTERS: a Tale. Fourth Thousand. 5s., cloth.
"This interesting and well-written volume."—*Record.*

DAME ALICIA CHAMBERLAYNE: of Ravenshome, Gloucestershire. Fourth Thousand. 5s.
"Most pleasant reading."—*Academy.*

THE ROCHEMONTS: a Story of Three Homes. Third Thousand. 5s., cloth.
"A pleasant and wholesome story."—*Scotsman.*

HELEN'S DIARY; or, Thirty Years Ago. Seventh Thousand. Frontispiece, 2s. 6d., cloth.

MILLICENT LEGH: a Tale. Fifth Thousand. In crown 8vo., with Frontispiece, 5s., cloth.

BROOK SILVERTONE, and THE LOST LILIES: Two Stories for Children. Third Thousand. Illustrated, price 2s. 6d., cloth, gilt edges.
"We can heartily recommend this attractive little volume. The stories are genuine, life-like, and entertaining. The lessons are skilfully interwoven with the narrative."—*Record.*

VIOLET DOUGLAS; or, The Problems of Life. Seventh Thousand. Crown 8vo., with Frontispiece, 5s., cloth.
"A pleasant, healthy story of English life, full of sound religious teaching."—*Standard.*

THE OLD GATEWAY; or, The Story of Agatha. Seventh Thousand. Crown 8vo., with Frontispiece, 5s., cloth.
"It is pleasant and gracefully written, and Roland Bruce is a character of no ordinary beauty."—*Guardian.*

EDWARD'S WIFE; or, Hard Judgments. A Tale. Fifth Thousand. Crown 8vo., Frontispiece, 5s., cloth.
"This is a very charming story, fresh, natural, and touching."—*Christian Advocate.*

SEELEY AND CO., ESSEX STREET, STRAND.

BY THE SAME AUTHOR.

JOB SINGLETON'S HEIR, and other Stories. Fifth Thousand. Crown 8vo., Frontispiece, 5s., cloth.

LADY ALICE; or, Two Sides of a Picture. Crown 8vo., Frontispiece, 5s., cloth.

JOANNA'S INHERITANCE: a Story of Young Lives. Fifth Thousand. Crown 8vo., Frontispiece, 5s., cloth.

LIFE'S AFTERMATH: a Story of a Quiet People. Price 5s., cloth. Ninth Thousand.

"The story is admirably told, and the interest well sustained throughout. The descriptions of English scenery are in many instances beautiful."—*Christian Observer.*

A HISTORY OF FRANCE: Adapted from the French, for the use of English Children. Crown 8vo., Twenty-six Engravings, 5s., cloth.

NOW-A-DAYS; or, King's Daughters. A Tale. Fifth Thousand. Crown 8vo., 5s., cloth.

"We have seldom met with a more pleasing specimen of what a wholesome work of light literature should be."—*Record.*

A LILY AMONG THORNS. Fifth Thousand. 5s., cloth.

"This volume is clever, and very naturally written. It is a book to read and to recommend."—*Watchman.*

MRS. MAINWARING'S JOURNAL. Eighth Thousand. Crown 8vo., Frontispiece, 5s., cloth.

"Rarely have we come across a more touching volume. It appeals to everyone who has the least feeling."—*John Bull.*

HEIGHTS AND VALLEYS: a Tale. Fifth Thousand. In crown 8vo., with Frontispiece, 5s., cloth.

BROTHERS AND SISTERS; or, True of Heart. Sixth Edition, with Frontispiece, 5s.

"The hopes and fears of a large family in a cathedral city are drawn with much spirit. The dialogue is easy, and the tale above the average."—*Guardian.*

SEELEY AND CO., ESSEX STREET, STRAND.

TALES BY MISS WINCHESTER.

PEARL OF THE SEA. Price 5s., cloth.

'A charming conception.'—*Saturday Review.*

A CRIPPLED ROBIN. *Second Edition.* Price 5s., cloth.

'A pretty story, and there is fun as well as feeling in many of the chapters.'—*Times.*

A CITY VIOLET. *Third Edition.* Price 5s., cloth.

'Miss Winchester, whose power of delineating character is giving her an honourable place among the writers of serious fiction, has never done anything better than this.'—*Spectator.*

A NEST OF SPARROWS. *Fifth Edition.* Price 5s., cloth.

'Miss Winchester not only writes with skill, but writes from the heart, and with full knowledge of her subject. Her story is most genuine, pathetic, without being sad.'—*Pall Mall Gazette.*

UNDER THE SHIELD. A Tale. *Fourth Edition.* Price 5s., cloth.

'We wish all religious stories were written in the same simple and natural way. We can conceive no more healthy reading for children.'—*Academy.*

'We welcome with real pleasure another book by the author of "A Nest of Sparrows." "Under the Shield" is to be noted for its purity of tone and high aspirations. . . . There is true fun in the book, too.'—*Athenæum.*

THE CABIN ON THE BEACH. A Tale. *Third Thousand.* Price 5s., cloth.

'This tender story cannot fail to charm and delight the young.'—*Guardian.*

THE WAYSIDE SNOWDROP. A Tale. *Second Edition.* Price 3s. 6d., cloth.

'A bright flower indeed. With all her tenderness and grace Miss Winchester narrates one of those pathetic stories of a poor London waif that at once arouse the loving sympathy of children.'—*Guardian.*

CHIRPS FOR THE CHICKS. With Thirty-one Illustrations. Price 2s. 6d., cloth.

'The book is worthy to be a nursery favourite.'—*Guardian.*

'The merriest, most amusing, and infinitely the most rhythmical book of poetry for young people produced this season. . . . Others besides children may read the "Chirps" with pleasure and amusement. The illustrations are very happy.'—*Standard.*

SEELEY & CO., ESSEX STREET, STRAND.

RECENTLY PUBLISHED.

FOREST OUTLAWS; or, St. Hugh and the King. By the Rev. E. GILLIAT. With Sixteen Illustrations. Price 6s., cloth.
"Distinctly one of the very best books of the season."—*Standard.*

BELT AND SPUR: Stories of the Knights of Old. With Coloured Illustrations. Price 5s.
"A very high-class gift-book of the spirit-stirring kind."—*Spectator.*
"A sort of boy Froissart with admirable illustrations."—*Pall Mall Gazette.*

THE CITY IN THE SEA: Stories of the Old Venetians. With Coloured Illustrations. Price 5s.
"Very stirring are the tales of the long struggle between Genoa and Venice . . . boys will read with keen interest the desperate battles between the rival fleets of galleys."—*Standard.*

STORIES OF THE ITALIAN ARTISTS: from Vasari. With Coloured Illustrations. Price 5s.
"The book is full of delightful reading, carefully chosen from a rich treasury of curiosities."—*Spectator.*
"Another very charming volume."—*Saturday Review.*

BORDER LANCES: a Romance of the Northern Marches. By the Author of "Belt and Spur." With Coloured Illustrations. Price 5s., cloth.
"The book is a good one . . . the illustrations are excellent."—*Spectator.*

FATHER ALDUR: the Story of a River. By A. GIBERNE. With Sixteen Tinted Illustrations. Price 5s., cloth.
"The nature of tides, the formation of clouds, the sources of water, and other kindred subjects are discussed with much freshness and charm."—*Saturday Review.*

SUN, MOON, AND STARS: a Book on Astronomy for Beginners. By A. GIBERNE. With Coloured Illustrations. Twelfth Thousand. Price 5s., cloth.
"Ought to have a place in village libraries and mechanics' institutions; would also be welcome as a prize-book."—*Pall Mall Gazette.*

AMONG THE STARS; Or, Wonderful Things in the Sky. By A. GIBERNE. With Illustrations. Third Thousand. Price 5s.
"We may safely predict that if it does not find the reader with a taste for astronomy, it will leave him with one."—*Knowledge.*

THE WORLD'S FOUNDATIONS: Geology for Beginners. By A. GIBERNE. With Illustrations. Third Thousand. Price 5s., cloth.
"The exposition is clear, the style simple and attractive."—*Spectator.*

SEELEY AND CO., ESSEX STREET, STRAND.

RECENTLY PUBLISHED.

SUE; OR, WOUNDED IN SPORT. By E. VINCENT BRITON, Author of 'Amyot Brough.' Price 1s. sewed; 1s. 6d. cloth.

'We do not know when we have been so charmed as we are by this modest volume. . . . . Over and over again one is reminded of some of George Eliot's best scenes in English country life; and though it may seem exaggeration to say so, there are some points in which Mr. Briton has surpassed George Eliot.'
Guardian.

AMYOT BROUGH. By E. VINCENT BRITON. With Illustrations. Price 5s. cloth.

'With national pride we dwell on a beautiful English historical novel. . . . this sweet unpretending story, with its pretty engravings.'—*Academy.*

FATHER ALDUR: The Story of a River. By A. GIBERNE. With Sixteen Tinted Illustrations. Price 5s. cloth.

AMONG THE STARS; OR, WONDERFUL THINGS IN THE SKY. By A. GIBERNE. With Illustrations. *Third Thousand.* Price 5s.

SUN, MOON, AND STARS. A Book on Astronomy for Beginners. By A. GIBERNE. With Coloured Illustrations. *Twelfth Thousand.* Cloth, price 5s.

'Ought to have a place in village libraries and mechanics' institutions; would also be welcome as a prize-book.'—*Pall Mall Gazette.*

THE WORLD'S FOUNDATIONS. Geology for Beginners. By A. GIBERNE. With Illustrations. *Third Thousand.* Cloth, price 5s.

'The exposition is clear, the style simple and attractive.'—*Spectator.*

A CANTERBURY PILGRIMAGE. Ridden, Written, and Illustrated by JOSEPH and ELIZABETH PENNELL. Price 1s.; cloth, gilt edges, 2s. 6d.

'The most wonderful shillingsworth that modern literature has to offer.'
Daily News.

AN ITALIAN PILGRIMAGE. By MRS. PENNELL. With many Illustrations by J. PENNELL. Price 6s. cloth.

'This charming book.'—*Academy.*

EARLY FLEMISH ARTISTS, AND THEIR PREDECESSORS ON THE LOWER RHINE. By W. M. CONWAY. With Twenty-nine Illustrations. Price 7s. 6d. cloth.

'An altogether admirable book.'—*Graphic.*

THE ARTISTIC DEVELOPMENT OF REYNOLDS AND GAINSBOROUGH. By W. M. CONWAY. With Sixteen Illustrations. Price 5s. cloth, gilt edges.

'A contribution to the subject which no student can afford to miss.'
Saturday Review.

SEELEY & CO., ESSEX STREET, STRAND.

www.ingramcontent.com/pod-product-compliance
Lightning Source LLC
Chambersburg PA
CBHW020546300426
44111CB00008B/808